# The Struggle
# against Mourning

# The Struggle
# against Mourning

ILANY KOGAN

JASON ARONSON
Lanham • Boulder • New York • Toronto • Plymouth, UK

To
Noam and Tal
Once beloved children, now themselves beloved parents

Published in the United States of America
by Jason Aronson
An imprint of Rowman & Littlefield Publishers, Inc.

A wholly owned subsidary of
The Rowman & Littlefield Publishing Group, Inc.
4501 Forbes Boulevard, Suite 200, Lanham, Maryland 20706
www.rowmanlittlefield.com

Estover Road
Plymouth PL6 7PY
United Kingdom

British Library Cataloguing in Publication Information Available

**Library of Congress Cataloging-in-Publication Data**

Kogan, Ilany.
    The struggle against mourning / Ilany Kogan.
        p. ; cm.
    Includes bibliographical references and index.
    ISBN-13: 978-0-7657-0508-2 (cloth : alk. paper)
    ISBN-10: 0-7657-0508-7 (cloth : alk. paper)
    ISBN-13: 978-0-7657-0507-5 (pbk. : alk. paper)
    ISBN-10: 0-7657-0507-9 (pbk. : alk. paper)
    1. Defense mechanisms (Psychology)  2. Grief therapy.  3. Holocaust
survivors—Mental health.  4. Children of Holocaust survivors—Mental health.
I. Title.
    [DNLM:  1. Defense Mechanisms—Case Reports.  2. Grief—Case Reports.
3. Psychoanalytic Therapy—methods—Case Reports.  4. Psychotherapeutic
Processes—Case Reports.  5. Stress Disorders, Traumatic—Case  Reports. WM
193 K78s 2007]
    RC455.4.D43K64   2007
    616.89'14—dc22                                              2007010274

Printed in the United States of America

♾ ™ The paper used in this publication meets the minimum requirements of
American National Standard for Information Sciences—Permanence of Paper for
Printed Library Materials, ANSI/NISO Z39.48-1992.

# Contents

# Acknowledgments

This book has grown out of my own struggle against mourning, on the professional as well as on the personal level. It illustrates the pathway from absence of mourning to an emotional awareness of pain and loss, including the therapeutic dilemmas involved in such a journey.

The book is the result of many invitations to lecture on this topic, for which I am grateful to my friends and colleagues abroad. I wish to thank my friends from the United States: Salman Akhtar, Ira Brenner, Dori Laub, Henri Parens, Warren Poland, and Vamik Volkan for their encouragement and appreciation. To my German colleagues—Marianne Leuzinger-Bohleber, Werner Bohleber, Peter Brundl, Manfred Endres, Peter Riedesser, and Hediaty Utari-Witt—I am grateful for the creative opportunities they sent in my direction.

I am also deeply thankful to my friends and colleagues on the Israeli scene—Alice Buras, Anna Gertler, Dahlia Lapidot, Cila Smolarsky, and Gisele Vered—who have been a source of knowledge and support, especially in difficult moments in therapy.

At Rowman & Littlefield, I want to thank Art Pomponio who, from the very beginning, gave me the support and appreciation needed for completing this project. I am also grateful to Mary Catharine La Mar and Karen Ackermann for their industriousness and involvement with this book.

I wish to express my appreciation for the outstanding skill and devotion of Ms. Chava Cassel, my English editor, whose help was invaluable to me all along the way.

To my family members, husband, and children, who gave me the strength to realize this book, I am greatly indebted.

Finally, I am grateful to my patients who allowed me to accompany them on their analytic journey.

The following chapters have appeared elsewhere, as noted, and are reprinted with permission.

*Chapter 2.* Presented at the Thirty-eighth Congress of the IPA, Amsterdam, August 1993. Published under the title: "Termination and the problem of analytic goals: Patient and analyst, different perspectives," *International Journal of Psychoanalysis* 77 (1996): 1013–29. Copyright © Institute of Psychoanalysis, London, UK. Reprinted by permission.

*Chapter 3.* Presented at the Fortieth Congress of the IPA, Santiago de Chile, August 1997. Published (shorter version) in *The Edge of Experience* (2001), ed. Grigoris Vaslamatzis and Andreas Rabavilas, London and New York: Karnac Books, pp. 67–89. Also in *Idantitat und Differenz—Zur Psychoanalyse des Geschlechterverhaltnisses in der Spatmoderne* (2000), ed. Hildegard Lahme-Gronostaj and Mariane Leuzinger-Bohleber. Published (full version) in *Psychoanalytic Psychology* 20, no. 1 (2003): 117–30, under the title "When words are used to touch." Copyright © 2003 by the Educational Publishing Foundation (American Psychological Association). Reprinted by permission.

*Chapter 4.* Presented at the Conference on Migration, Bressanone, Italy, July 1997; at the Conference of the Arztliche Akademie, Hamburg, Germany, March 1999. Published (shorter version) under the title "Psychoanalytishe Behandlung einer Migrantin" in *Zeitschrift fur Politische Psychologie*, ed. Freihart Regner and Elise Bittenbinder, Jahrgang 4 2000: 523–33. Published (full version) in *Mind and Human Interaction* 2, no. 12 (2001): 95–107 under the title "Romania and its unresolved mourning—Those who emigrated and those who stayed behind." Published (full version) under the title "Rumanien und seine umbewaltigte Trauer: die Emigranten und die Zuruckgebliebenen" in *Zwischen den Welten—Psychosoziale Folgen kommunistischer Herrschaft in Ostmitteleuropa*, ed. Petra Morawe, Baden–Baden: Nomos Verlagsgesellschaft (2004), pp.121–31. Also in *Kindheit jenseits von Trauma und Fremdheit—Psychoanalytische Erkundungen von Migrationschicksale im Kindes und Jugendalter*, ed. Peter Brundl and Ilany Kogan, Frankfurt: Brandes & Apsel (2005), pp. 274–87.

*Chapter 5.* Presented at the Conference on Remembering, Acting and Enacting, Gottingen, 1999. Published (shorter version) in *Errinern, Agieren
und Inszenieren: Enactments und szenische Darstellungen im therapeu-
tischen Prozess,* ed. Ulrich Streeck, Gottingen: Vanderhoeck & Ruprecht,
2000, pp. 127–43. Published (full version) as "Enactment in the lives and
treatment of Holocaust survivors' offspring" in *The Psychoanalytic Quarterly* 71 (2002): 251–73. Copyright © The Psychoanalytic Quarterly, 2002.
Reprinted by permission.

*Chapter 6.* Presented at the IPA Congress, Rio, 2005. Published (shorter
version) in *Adoleszenz-Bindung-Destruktivitat* (2004), ed. Annette Streeck-
Fischer, Stuttgart: Klett-Cotta, pp. 343–64. Published (full version) in
*Representationen des Holocaust im Gedachtnis der Generationen* (2004),
ed. Margrit Frolich, Yariv Lapid, and Christian Schneider, Frankfurt:
Brandes & Apsel, pp. 90–112. Also in *Trauma Der Psychoanalyse? Die Ver-
treibung Der Psychoanalyse Aus Wien 1938 Und Die Folgen* (2005), ed. Wie-
ner Psychoanalytischen Vereinigung, Wien: Mille Tre Verlag Robert
Schachter, pp. 199–219.

*Chapter 7.* Presented at the German Psychoanalytic Society (DPG), Berlin,
October 1999; at the Munchner Arbeitskreise fur Psychoanalyse, Munich,
1999. Published in *The Psychoanalytic Quarterly* 72, no. 3 (2003): 727–67.
Copyright © The Psychoanalytic Quarterly, 2003. Reprinted by permission.

*Chapter 8.* Presented at the Conference on Trauma and Youth Culture,
Bressanone, Italy, 2005; at the APsA, winter meeting, New York, January
2006.

*Chapter 9.* Presented at the EPF New Style Conference, Sorrento, 2003.
This article was originally published in the *Journal of American Psychoana-
lytic Association* 52 (2004): 735–59. Copyright © 2004 by the American
Psychoanalytic Association. All rights reserved. Reprinted by permission.

*Chapter 10.* Presented at the IPA Congress, New Orleans, March 2004, in
the panel on "Working with psychotic and non-psychotic patients in situations of terror and military dictatorships." Reported (shorter version) in

*International Journal of Psychoanalysis* (2004) under the title "Working with psychotic and non-psychotic patients in situations of terror and military dictatorships." Report of panel held at the Forty-third Congress of the IPA, New Orleans, 85: 1247–49. Copyright © Institute of Psychoanalysis, London, UK. Reprinted by permission.

# Introduction

*Give sorrow words: the grief that does not appear*
*Whispers the o'er-fraught heart and bids its break*
— William Shakespeare, *Macbeth*, Act 4, Scene 3, Lines: 209–210

"We all mourn: *C'est la condition humane*," eloquently states the psycho-analyst Henri Parens (2001). It is impossible to shield our lives from the impact of the inevitable, be it loss of familiar surroundings, bereavement, aging, or death. But, in fact, we are not always able to mourn, because we often distort reality or deny our losses.

What is mourning? In brief, and in the context of this book, mourning is the conglomerate of favorable processes that develop in the face of loss. It includes acceptance of reality and readaptation to it. Mourning means acceptance of one's perpetual vulnerability to loss and betrayal, as well as to one's own limitations and to the finality of life. The pain incurred in having to acknowledge these reactions to loss sometimes make us unable to go through the mourning process. Often, this pain is warded off by means of various defense mechanisms.

Mourning is necessary because it permits us to relinquish attachments and attitudes that have lost their realistic usefulness, thus facilitating growth and development. Freud defined the outcome of mourning as fol-lows: "The task of mourning is to detach the survivor's memories and hopes from the dead" (1913, p. 65). Anna Freud refined this definition by stating, "mourning, taken in the analytical sense, is the individual's effort to accept a fact in the external world (the loss of the cathected object), and to effect corresponding changes in the inner world (withdrawal from the lost object)" (1960, p. 58). Bowlby (1960) saw mourning as the psycholog-ical process set in motion by the loss of the loved object, and suggested that it commonly leads to the relinquishment of the object.

The elaboration of mourning eventually leads to a better differentiation between self and object, past and present, reality and fantasy. It also leads to a reorganization of the ego, and a smoother interaction between the inner and outer world. The mourning process facilitates the integration of dissociated parts of the self and the consolidation of the sense of identity (Grinberg 1992).

In this book I deal with obstacles on the road to mourning. I use case studies to help provide an understanding of the impediments to the work of mourning in specific situations, and to describe the therapeutic tools that were employed to achieve a healthier outcome. The book focuses on various defenses, their function and importance, and the difficulty of relinquishing them. It also highlights my own dilemmas in these contexts.

I have found that I convey my thinking most effectively by means of case illustrations. Thus, using detailed descriptions taken from analyses, I explore the long and anxiety-provoking journey to mourning of patients who have employed an array of defenses in order to avoid facing the painful feelings inherent in mourning. Often, the cases are illustrated with verbatim exchanges from the sessions. The reader is invited to be "present" and follow the intimate patient-therapist dialogue from a close perspective, learning about the problems and dilemmas of both patient and therapist when confronted with loss.

A remark made about my first book, *The Cry of Mute Children* (1995), which struck a responsive chord in me, served as one of the triggers for writing this book. "All of the cases described in your book end in success," was the comment. Reflecting upon this, I wondered how much we analysts determine the patients' final choices in analysis as well as in life. Poland (2006) makes a beautiful observation in this regard: "The analyst is a translator, and the translator has no right to determine how the patient-author unfolds that story, not even what ending the author chooses. The analyst's responsibility to question never diminishes the patient's full right to unique personal answers." And, indeed, in many of the cases that I treated, the successful result was in great part the patient's choice. However, in my former book, I nevertheless chose to mostly present cases with successful results. This apparently was an expression of my omnipotent fantasies about what therapy can achieve. This realization led me to also include here cases that were less successful and, subsequently, to work through my therapeutic narcissism, redefine my analytic goals, and mourn the limitations of therapy.

Schafer described the powerful, personal way that therapists are affected by the limitations of therapy. "Through them, he must recognize that his effectiveness as a healer is quite limited, which means that important narcissistic ideas about himself and ideals for himself are forcefully contradicted by experience. The roots of these ideas and ideals lie in infantile fantasies of omnipotence, which no one ever renounced completely" (1973, p.138).

The present book includes cases that brought me face to face with the limitations of my ability as a therapist, cases with varying degrees of success in achieving the analytic goals. The issue of defining the analytic goals and the different meanings of "successful" therapy from the respective viewpoints of therapist and patient are discussed in some of the chapters.

The first section of the book explores the theme of manic defenses and denial. It is illustrated with cases studies of patients whose manic defenses had survival value and were used by them to prevent fragmentation and psychic death. This section also describes my doubts and dilemmas as an analyst with regard to the price patients may pay for relinquishing these defenses, and my deliberations about leading them on their difficult journey to mourning.

Going beyond the individual, the second section of the book is an attempt to describe the impact of unresolved mourning on large groups. Specifically, it focuses on issues of mourning in Romania, my country of birth, based on my supervisory work there, and on the transmission of the Holocaust trauma from one generation to another in Israel. The first chapter of this section integrates my psychoanalytic understanding of the patient's unresolved mourning due to the loss of primary objects and familiar surroundings with my analysis of Romanian society's unresolved mourning. The other chapters deal with the impact of the transmission of the trauma of the Holocaust, with its accompanying traumatic fantasies, to an entire generation. The integration of perpetrator and victim self-representations, which had an impact also on those not directly affected by the Holocaust (Moses 1993; Volkan 1998; Volkan et al. 2002; Brenner 2002a), left its mark on a major portion of Israeli society. This too is discussed in this section. The clinical material illustrates the means employed by Holocaust survivors' offspring to deal with the pain and mourning transmitted to them by their parents. The mechanisms of "enactment," as well as reparative defenses such as creativity, are explored.

While the second section of the book deals with the impact of unresolved mourning of Holocaust survivor parents on their offspring under normative life situations, the last section deals with the inability to mourn in life-threatening situations and the problems of conducting psychoanalysis in the shadow of terror. The first chapter in this section differs from the others in that it presents a psychoanalytic review of the movie *Europa, Europa*, which deals with the absence of mourning following loss and its impact on the hero's identity. The last two chapters deal with the topic of psychoanalysis in the shadow of terror and with the intrusion of external traumatic reality into the treatment. The last chapter in this section demonstrates how external traumatic reality may become interwoven with internal reality, and thus intensify manic defenses, particularly among offspring of Holocaust survivors, who are often haunted by the traumatic past of their parents.

Although I discuss the intrusion of external traumatic reality into the treatment from the perspective of my clinical experience in situations of chronic crises in Israel, I believe it is an issue of universal relevance. The events of September 11, 2001, in the United States, and the bombings in Madrid and London, which maimed and killed their victims, caused massive suffering and destruction, and left in their wake both individual and collective traumatization. Working as an analyst during such times presents enormous problems: "I am not sure that one could ever be prepared or 'trained' enough to know what to say or do at such times," states Brenner (2002b). In my experience, conducting analysis in the shadow of terror necessitates that the analyst deal with certain treatment-related issues: the impact of traumatic reality on the defenses of both partners of the analytic couple and a rethinking of the role of the analyst in a shared life-threatening situation, which includes the recognition and acknowledgment of the analyst's own reactions to external reality.

The main questions that I wish to raise in this book are: How does the analyst help the patient be in touch with pain and mourning? Is the relinquishment of defenses always desirable? And what is the analyst's role in these cases? Should the analyst struggle to help patients relinquish these defenses, which they may experience as vital to their precarious psychic survival? Or should s/he accompany them on their way to self-discovery, which may or may not result in the patients' letting go of their defenses when faced with the pain and mourning inherent in trauma? The utilization of various defenses and the resulting unresolved mourning reflect the magnitude of the anxiety and pain that is found on the road to mourning. The ability to mourn and the capacity to bear some helplessness while still finding life meaningful are the objectives of the analytic work in this book.

The clinical chapters in the book illustrate the journey to pain and mourning, and ultimately to a more intact self.

A brief description of the clinical chapters of the book follows.

*Chapter 2—Forever Young.* This chapter describes the patient's journey from manic defense to mourning, as viewed from the perspective of the termination phase of analysis. The termination phase confronts both patient and analyst with the limits of omnipotent ideas about life, as well as about psychoanalysis. This theme is illustrated by a case study of a forty-year-old woman striving for everlasting youth and immortality through compulsive attempts to bring a third child into the world. The birth of her child was an omnipotent enactment that served to deny and replace internal as well as external reality. The discussion highlights the impact of the fear of growth and aging on both partners of the analytic couple, and describes the analyst's temptation to collude with the patient in avoiding the depressive anxiety aroused by aging and death.

*Chapter 3—Lust for Love.* This chapter examines the case of a patient who attempts to deal with her inner emotional deadness and self-destructive fantasies by means of various forms of eroticism—such as homosexual love affairs and working in a sex therapy clinic—for infusing herself with a sense of life. In analysis, this took the form of demanding to touch and be touched by the analyst, which threatened the continuation of analysis. The chapter illustrates the analyst's predicament in dealing with a patient who threatens to act out violently and dangerously if the analyst does not acquiesce to her demands in some way. It also shows how a verbal interaction with the analyst, which was experienced by the patient as a physical touch, enabled the continuation of the analytic work and the working through of the patient's manic defenses.

*Chapter 4—Romania and Its Unresolved Mourning.* The problem of unresolved mourning is illustrated in this chapter. The working through of the traumatic elements of migration with a patient of the same national origin as the therapist is interwoven with the therapist's own unfinished mourning for her country of origin. The chapter illustrates how Romanian society is trapped, to this very day, in its unresolved mourning.

*Chapter 5—From Enactment to Mental Representation.* The chapter deals with the impact of the traumatic past of Holocaust survivor parents on their offspring. These damaged parents, who suffered from a state of unresolved mourning, often transmitted feelings of aggression and pain to their offspring, who carried these feelings for them; this affected an entire generation and had an impact on society as a whole. The chapter explores an attempt of Holocaust survivors' offspring to avoid the mourning transmitted to them by their parents by means of a mechanism called *enactment*. The chapter uses case material to illustrate the process of transforming enactment into mental representations, which then allowed the work of mourning to begin.

*Chapter 6—Trauma, Resilience, and Creative Activity.* The link between trauma, resilience, and creative activity is explored in the analysis of a Holocaust survivor's offspring. In this case, resilience is defined as the offspring's ability to acknowledge and work through the pain, guilt, and mourning deposited in her by her mother. Creative activity is one of the pivotal factors in resilience to trauma and hardship. It serves as a tool to facilitate acknowledgment and working through of the painful feelings transmitted by the offspring's traumatized parent.

*Chapter 7—On Being a Dead, Beloved Child.* The chapter presents a long, detailed analysis of a patient who was a replacement child for parents, each of whom had lost a child during the Holocaust. At the core of this analysis is the bereaved mother's omnipotent fantasy of resurrecting her dead, beloved child by means of the living child, the way this fantasy shaped the mother-child relationship, and the impact it had upon the character structure of the child. In addition, the discussion of the case study highlights the countertransference difficulties of the therapist, who belongs to the same traumatized large group as the patient.

*Chapter 8—Who Am I? Trauma and Identity.* This chapter presents a psychoanalytic review of the movie *Europa, Europa*. It deals with a young adolescent who, during the Holocaust, flees from one country to another and from one culture to another in order to save his life. He spends several years in an elite Nazi school for Hitler Youth, where he passes as an Aryan. The chapter reveals the survival value of the absence of mourning in life-threatening situations and the emotional price paid for survival.

*Chapters 9 and 10.* These two chapters involve cases in which manic defenses are reinforced as a result of the encounter with external traumatic reality, and in which analysis becomes difficult under the shadow of terror. Both chapters describe how the perception of external threatening reality activates the Holocaust trauma in the unconscious of individuals who have been directly or indirectly affected by the Holocaust, thus having an impact on a major portion of Israeli society.

*Chapter 9—The Role of the Analyst in the Analytic Cure during Times of Chronic Crises.* This chapter deals with the problem of the analyst's role during times of chronic crises and the impact of a shared life-threatening situation on the defenses of both members of the analytic couple.

*Chapter 10—Working with Sons and Daughters of Holocaust Survivors in the Shadow of Terror.* The focus of this chapter is the impact of external traumatic stimuli on the perception of reality and on the defenses of Holocaust survivors' offspring.

# Revisiting Defenses against Pain and Mourning

Mourning is a concept that originally appeared in papers dealing with depression and melancholia. It has been defined in many different ways, beginning with the work of Freud (1917) and Abraham (1924). One of the most complex aspects of mourning, and one that has not yet been completely elucidated, is the distinction between normal and pathological mourning (Volkan 1981). Referring to this subject, Grinberg (1992) contends that the psychoanalysts who have written about these two forms of mourning have not been able to state precisely which were the specific factors conditioning the two pictures. Even the use of the terms describing them has given rise to controversy. There are authors who insist that *mourning* should be restricted to the pathological state, reserving the term *grief* for the reaction that is considered normal. Others use the term *mourning* for the healthy processes of dealing with loss and *bereavement* for a more desolate and pathological reaction. Bowlby (1961) emphasizes that the word *grief* denotes only the sequence of subjective states that follow loss and accompany mourning. In his view, mourning includes the entire psychopathological process caused by object-loss.

In this book mourning includes overcoming pathological defenses and shedding the regressive elements that block the way to the establishment of the adult aspects of the personality when one is confronted with loss and bereavement, aging and death, stress and trauma. Mourning involves the various functions of the ego, including the attitudes and defenses of the individual.

I will first examine the more diffuse concept of psychic pain, which is inherent in mourning, and then explore various defense configurations employed to avoid pain and mourning. The journey along the road to mental health includes working through these defenses. In the absence of mourning, we remain attached to early internal objects, which are frustrating and often defensively idealized. These unmourned fragments of the psyche, which include internal objects and parts of the self that are connected to them, are usually repressed. The individual is thus depleted and his knowledge of self is impoverished.

I will review the following clusters of defenses illustrated by the clinical material in this book basing myself on early and contemporary literature: (1) manic defense; (2) enactment; (3) denial; and (4) reparative defense. The objective of this book is not to present a comprehensive review of defenses but rather to show how the various case studies described here add to a deeper understanding of these defenses.

## PSYCHIC PAIN

The early literature dealing with psychic pain is meager. Freud (1926) introduced the concept into the psychoanalytic literature under the rubric of *Seelenschmerz* (pain of the soul). His reference was to a child crying for his mother, and he viewed it as analogous to bodily injury and loss of body parts.

Freud regarded psychic pain as a phenomenon parallel to physical pain. In "Project for scientific psychology," he suggested that this kind of pain resulted from a marked increase in the quantity of stimuli impinging upon the mind, thus causing "a breach in the continuity" (1950, p. 307) of the protective shield. In "Mourning and melancholia," Freud related pain to object-loss and compared melancholia to "an open wound" (1917, p. 253). Later on, in "Inhibitions, symptoms and anxiety" (1926, pp. 169–72), Freud linked his economic explanations to his object-related hypothesis regarding the origins of mental pain. He suggested that the libidinal energy (cathexis) invested in the longing that is concentrated upon the lost object, and which causes anxiety, is similar to the libidinal energy invested in the injured part of the body, which leads to pain. The prolonged nature of the above psychic process, and the impossibility of halting it, produces a state of mental helplessness which is similar to the helplessness induced by overwhelming pain, thus, the painful character of object-loss (Freud 1926, addendum C).

Weiss continued this line of thinking. "Love objects become, as we know, libidinally bound to the ego, as if they were parts of it. If they are torn away from it, the ego reacts as though it had sustained mutilation" (1934, p. 12).

Grinberg (1964) also referred to the connection between physical and psychic pain, but from the perspective of object-relations theory. He believed that if pain appears in any mourning situation resulting from object-loss, it is because object-loss is experienced by the unconscious fantasy as an attack upon the body-ego; this attack provokes physical pain, which in turn is experienced as psychic pain.

Joffee and Sandler (1965) pointed out a further aspect of psychic pain connected to object-loss. They regarded psychic pain as the discrepancy between the actual state of the self and the ideal state of well-being. When a love object is lost, we not only lose the actual object, but also lose the aspect of our own self that is the complement in us of that object, as well as the well-being that is intimately bound up with it.

Pontalis also connected psychic pain with object loss. Pain stems from the fact that the object is irrevocably lost but eternally retained: "Where there is pain, it is the absent lost object that is present; it is the actual, present object that is absent" (1981, p. 90).

Basing himself on the writings of Kahn (1979), Joseph (1981), and Kogan (1990) on this subject, Akhtar summarized the concept of psychic pain as consisting of "a wordless sense of self-rupture, longing and psychic helplessness that is vague and difficult to convey to others. It usually follows the loss of a significant object or its abrupt refusal to meet one's anaclitic needs" (2000, p. 229).

## DEFENSES AGAINST PAIN AND MOURNING

Schafer (1968, 1976) claimed that defenses have meaningful content, including wishes and fantasies concerning the self and objects. Defenses are unconsciously intentional, complex actions with the aim of warding off some unpleasurable affect.

There are many defenses aimed at avoiding or controlling pain and mourning. These defenses can lead to either healthy or pathological results, especially on a temporary basis and depending upon the individual's overall psychic economy and external environment. Joffee and Sandler (1965) included indignation, de-idealization, and enhanced individuation among the healthy responses to pain, and an attitude of hopelessness and helplessness among the pathological responses to it.

Defense configurations explored in the different chapters of the book include manic defense, enactment, denial, and reparative defense.

## Manic Defense

Manic defense is the common thread that binds the various chapters of the book. I will present a brief review of this concept.

Freud (1917) described manic defense as a retreat from depression, but it was Klein (1935) who detailed the underpinnings of this defense, and Winnicott (1935) who broadened the understanding of it. A large part of the psychiatric and psychoanalytic community evinced little interest in this concept, and although there are many references to it in contemporary literature, only a few authors (Ogden 1986; Burch 1989; Grinberg 1992; Akhtar 2001) have explored it comprehensively.

Freud (1917) pointed out that the most singular peculiarity of melancholia is its tendency to turn into mania. In such a case the ego apparently supposes that it has dominated the object-loss and is free from the suffering it has had to bear. It then tries to exert omnipotent fantasies in order to both control and dominate objects that have become dangerous and persecutory and also to try to save and repair the objects that it feels it has damaged.

Klein (1935) defined manic defense as a set of mental mechanisms aimed at protecting the ego from depressive as well as paranoid anxieties. She delineated many forms of manic defense and often used the term in the plural. She described manic defense essentially as the individual's attempt to evade the exquisite pain of guilt in the early depressive position. The defense is really a collection of defenses involving a denial of psychic reality and therefore of the importance of the objects that are loved and taken in, a denigrating contempt for the objects that are loved so that their loss will not be experienced as important, and a triumphant and omnipotent form of putting everything right. Thus, the ego "endeavors ceaselessly to master and control all its objects" (1935, p. 277), escaping dependency and potential loss.

In Klein's view, the constituents of manic defense are omnipotence, denial, and idealization.

*Omnipotence* is the main characteristic of mania. It is utilized to control and master objects, so that a sense of separateness and envy are avoided. Omnipotent defenses may create confusion between self and object, and this confusion is expressed through omnipotent narcissistic object-relations (Rosenfeld 1987) leading to an enduring state of narcissism (Segal 1983). The illusion of omnipotence, which makes the manic defense effective, derives from omnipotent fantasies that are an essential aspect of the infant's inner world. The destruction of the object in fantasy provides the infant with a mechanism for handling negative experiences and tolerating aggressive impulses. Klein pointed out that by means of the manic defense the subject may destroy his internal objects, but because he is omnipotent, he can immediately resuscitate them (a mechanism called "suspended animation"). The child's feelings of omnipotence also make marginal reparation possible in fantasy after aggressiveness has run its course. Klein regards the disparagement of the objects' importance and the contempt for them as a specific characteristic of manic defense. As a result, the ego effects a partial detachment from the objects while at the same time a longing for them.

*Denial* refers specifically to the denial of psychic reality. It serves to mitigate the individual's awareness of his dependence upon others and also his dread of what may be a persecutory experience as a consequence of this dependence. (I will explore this defense more in depth later in this chapter).

*Idealization* is a mechanism that helps avoid the pain inherent in ambivalence by a paranoid retreat into separating the good feelings from the bad. This is achieved by splitting the good from the bad aspects of the object to create an ideal object and a persecutory one. Idealization tenaciously retains a view of a world and oneself that is "all good." This, in turn, defends against the individual's guilty recognition of having injured others, whether in fact or in fantasy.

The previous three mechanisms are interrelated. According to Rosenfeld, "It is typical to find an idealization of the good object so that it can be kept as far away as possible from the persecuting bad object, and thus avoid confusion with it. This defensive process is combined with the mechanism of denial that in its turn is backed up by omnipotence: it is omnipotent denial that can completely deny the existence of bad objects. In the unconscious this process is equivalent to the annihilation of the whole disturbing object-relationship, so that it is clear that it involves the denial not only of the bad object, but of an important part of the ego, which is in a relationship with the object" (1983, p. 262).

Winnicott broadened the understanding of manic defense, emphasizing that it is intended to "deny the depressive anxiety that is inherent in emotional development, anxiety that belongs to the capacity of the individual to feel guilt, and also to acknowledge responsibility for instinctual experiences, and for the aggression in the fantasy that goes with individual experiences" (1935, pp. 143–44). Winnicott's important contribution was that he ascribed to manic defense the individual's inability to give full significance to inner reality. It is an attempt to fly away from internal reality, especially if this reality includes depressive anxiety or mourning. In a situation where manic defense is used, mourning cannot be experienced.

Winnicott outlined four components of manic defenses: denial of inner reality; flight from inner reality to external reality; suspended animation; and denial of sensations of depression through the reversal of depressive feelings.

*Denial of inner reality* involves a repudiation of internalized bad objects, which by becoming generalized can include the rejection of good inner objects. "Many who live normal and valuable lives do not feel they are responsible for the best that is in them" (p. 133).

*Flight from inner reality to external reality* involves omnipotent fantasies that are not so much the result of the inner reality itself as a defense against the acceptance of it. Fantasy thus fulfills an intermediary role between internal and external reality. The flight to external reality in order to avoid a painful internal reality may also take the form of exaggerated fear of death and exploitation of sexuality (as I illustrate in chapters 2 and 3 of this book).

*Suspended animation*, which refers to omnipotent control of bad internal objects, may also destroy good relationships. As a result, the individual may feel dead inside and the world may appear to be an emotional desert.

*The reversal of depressive feelings* and the use of exalted opposites for reassurance are important elements of manic defense.

In his comprehensive exploration of the subject of mourning and guilt, Grinberg (1992) maintained that the manic defense is used especially when depressive anxiety is very intense. Grinberg added splitting to the cluster of mechanisms of manic defense (denial, omnipotence, idealization). In his opinion, manic defense includes all the defenses that belong to the paranoid-schizoid position, and that form a powerful, integrated system directed against psychic reality and depressive experience. Hate, guilt, despair, the need for reparation, ambivalence, and so on, are all denied by means of the manic defense.

A different view of manic defense in contemporary psychoanalysis is that of Ogden. Ogden regarded manic defense as a normal part of development, because the conflict between the pain of dependence and the need for objects is always present to some degree. He described manic defense as an "in-between phenomenon, incorporating elements of the psychic organization of both the paranoid-schizoid and the depressive positions" (1986, p. 84). He contended that everyone relies on this defense to varying degrees in times of difficulty. When dependency needs are an unacceptable part of reality, this defense is mobilized. It returns to the ego the illusion of omnipotence or self-sufficiency. Intensely negative interpersonal experiences that preclude trust render dependency both excruciatingly painful and ultimately unsafe. This impossible situation may be tolerated only through ongoing reliance on the manic defense, in which dependency is abruptly denied.

### Enactment

In this book, I explore the mechanism of enactment as it relates to intergenerational transmission of the trauma of the Holocaust, another subject examined in the book. Enactment is typically employed by Holocaust survivors' offspring in dealing with the burden of pain and guilt transmitted to them by their parents (see chapters 5, 6, 7, 9, and 10).

Enactment, which has the purpose of externalizing conflict, is based on projection that is acted out (Hinshelwood 1991). Freud (1916) used the term *projection* when he described delinquent acts performed by criminals who, in his view, act out because of an unconscious sense of guilt. Projection was defined by Klein as a mechanism that "helps the ego to overcome anxiety by ridding it of danger and badness" (1946, p. 6). She found this mechanism important in the externalization of internal conflicts played out with external objects.

In the more recent literature, Renik (1990) viewed the enactment of wishful fantasies as an unconscious, persistent effort to attain unobtainable goals by magical means, thus defending against the depressive affect. Arguing with Dorpat (1977), who suggested that the depressive affect elicits relinquishment of unobtainable goals with eventual formulation of new, obtainable ones, Renik claimed that the depressive affect creates many maladaptive responses; the goals, even if realistically unobtainable, are not relinquished. Renik believes that through the enactment of fantasies, the individual fights his feelings of helplessness in relation to unobtainable goals.

I wish to distinguish between *enactment in reality* and *enactment in fantasy*, as it relates to the offspring of Holocaust survivors.

*Enactment in reality* (termed *concretization* by Bergmann [1982]) is defined by her as the compulsion of Holocaust survivors' offspring to recreate their parents' experiences in their own lives through concrete acts. It refers to the externalization of traumatic themes from the past and functions as a "substitute-for-mourning" mechanism. In chapter 5, I review the concept of enactment as it pertains to the Holocaust, and I define it as a general term that includes the attributes of both *acting in* and *acting out*.

*Enactment in fantasy* occurs when the offspring, in his endless effort to understand the parents and thus help them, recreates the traumatic experience and its accompanying effects in fantasy (Auerhahn and Prelinger 1983; Laub and Auerhahn 1993). Thus the offspring becomes "the protagonist in scenes from the parents' unconscious fantasies—fantasies that are almost always a sadistic distortion of narcissistic struggles for survival with objects from the parents' past" (Metcalf 1977, p. 259). The shared fantasy between parents and offspring helps the parents survive psychically and prevents the parents' collapse under the burden of pain and mourning connected to their own traumatic past.

At the core of the compulsion to enact the parents' traumatic experiences in reality or in fantasy we find another mechanism that hinders the work of mourning. This mechanism—*primitive identification* (Freyberg 1980; Grubrich-Simitis 1984; Kogan 1995, 1998)—is a unique form of identification whereby the offspring completely identifies with the parent and assumes the parent's traumatization. Completely absorbed in his parent's feelings, the offspring often unknowingly becomes the bearer of the parent's burden of mourning and guilt in his own life; this may lead to a loss of the offspring's separate sense of self and to the inability to differentiate between his self and the damaged parent. This phenomenon is similar to the identification that takes place in pathological mourning. Freud (1917) described this identification as a process whereby the person in mourning avoids working through the loss by maintaining a fantasy that he or she is the lost loved one, or will become the lost loved one, thus magically reversing a calamity that has occurred (Abend and Porder 1986).

## Denial

Denial is one of the main defenses employed when an individual is confronted with aging and death, loss and bereavement, stress and trauma. This defense weaves its way in various forms through all of the chapters in this book. In its psychoanalytic application, denial is defined as a defense against painful or unpleasurable ideas, effects, and perceptions.

Denial has always been a complex concept that has acquired many meanings and connotations, depending on the context. In addition to its dictionary definition—"the act of saying no"—the term *denial* and its synonyms *disavowal* and *self-deception* refer to the reality-repudiating aspect of defensive activities and not to a discrete defense mechanism (Dorpat 1987; Fingarette 1969; Hilgard 1949; Weisman 1972).

Freud (1923) was the first to describe the denial defense. Using data accrued in psychoanalytic treatment, he hypothesized that some young boys, seeing the absence of a penis in girls, reject the evidence of their senses and imagine that they did see the girl's penis after all. He termed this defensive activity "denial" (or "disavowal").

Early psychoanalytic accounts of denial by Sigmund Freud (1940) and Anna Freud (1936) limited the scope of denial to the perception of external reality. Many have disagreed with this restricted view of denial. Klein (1935) viewed denial specifically as one of the important components of manic defense, particularly the denial of the reality of some part of the mind, or of psychic reality. In the same vein, Hartmann (1964), Jacobson (1959), Lewin (1950), and Waelder (1951) discussed the denial of various affects such as anxiety, guilt, and anger, claiming that internal reality may also be denied. From a different viewpoint, Dorpat (1979) argued that denial is the crucial defensive activity involved in the formation of contradictory attitudes.

Denial also has adaptive value (Klein and Kogan 1989). It was utilized by Holocaust survivors during times of massive trauma (see chapter 8), and may also be employed in times of chronic crises (see chapters 9 and 10).

The elaboration of this defense, as illustrated in the various chapters, enables the patient to get in touch with and work through pain and mourning, leading to an eventual readaptation of the ego to both external and internal reality.

### Reparative Defense

Klein (1920) viewed "reparation" as the strongest of the constructive and creative urges. She believed that reparation is the fantasy of putting right the effects of the aggressive component, and is intended to mobilize creative activity (Klein 1929). This process is different from sublimation, a term coined by Freud (1908), which is the conversion of sexual impulses into sophisticated, creative skills.

Creativity can be a defense against pain and mourning. Ella Freeman-Sharpe, in her article "Pure art and pure science" (1935), expresses the idea that creation leads to a fundamentally good experience, psychically and physically linked to harmony and rhythm, at the same time that it represents a triumph over aggressiveness and anguish.

The creative act may have direct access to the deepest layers of the psyche, which is where psychic pain usually originates and resides. Creativity speaks from the unconscious and facilitates the mentalization of the non-verbal substrate of the psyche. Creative activity involves a certain amount of self-holding, illusory though omnipotent manipulation of objects, and a certain mastery of pain through "self-dosed" (Cooper 1988, p.125) suffering and surviving of that suffering. The relationship between object-loss, a frequent precipitant of mental pain, and creativity has drawn considerable attention (Pollock 1975, 1977; Hamilton 1969, 1976, 1979). Poetry, as an expression of creativity, may occupy a special place in the ego's efforts to manage, mourn, and master mental pain (Akhtar 2001).

In this book I deal with the function of creativity from two perspectives:

(1) Creativity as an attempt to repair both the object and the self. Klein (above) maintained that the offspring, believing that his hate and hostility has damaged the loved object, must now repair it. Basing himself on this premise, Grinberg viewed creativity as "the re-creation of a loved object that has been felt as being in ruins . . . it is the re-creation of an internal world and an ego in ruins" (1992, p. 233). Chasseguet-Smirgel (1984) expressed a different view of creativity. She argued that

there are two categories of reparation, which are expressed through two radically opposed creative acts: one, which enriches and fills up the ego (and which can generate guilt), and the other, which indeed repairs the object. In this book, I use a case illustration to show a different viewpoint from that of Chasseguet-Smirgel. In my view, reparation of the damaged object and reparation of the self actually operate together (chapter 7).

(2) Creativity in search of an internal source of anguish. In therapy, this form of creative act helps convey information about the patient's inner world, thus enhancing empathy with the self and facilitating mourning (see chapter 6).

**I**

# OBSTACLES TO
# INDIVIDUAL MOURNING

# Forever Young

*[I]n the unconscious everyone is convinced of his own immortality.*

—Freud 1915, p. 289

In this chapter I will explore and illustrate the difficult journey from manic defense to mourning undertaken by both members of the analytic couple, as viewed during the termination period of analysis and after it. I will examine it from the different perspectives by which patient and analyst viewed the termination of analysis and the "analytic goals."[1] Analysis consisted of a struggle with the patient's manic defenses—her denial of inner reality and her omnipotent attempt to replace it with delusional fantasies that she felt compelled to enact.

The case study is that of a thirty-eight-year-old woman who, in analysis, revealed bisexual longings, which culminated in parthenogenesis—the wish to have a baby without a man (Deutsch 1933; Fast 1979). During the treatment, this became a psychotic obsession that she felt compelled to realize, in spite of the tremendous obstacle of being unable to achieve a successful pregnancy for years and give birth to a live baby.

Much psychic work was needed to enable the patient to overcome feelings of hatred and destruction, as well as to moderate her fear of death. The emotional experience in analysis enabled her to work through her maternal internal representation and her identification with an angry and destructive introject. After a long and painful analytic journey, she was able to experience something life-giving in herself and was able to identify with a procreative mother. This identification was a psychic factor that facilitated pregnancy and birth.

Reflecting on the apparently positive outcome of this analysis, I sometimes asked myself whether our difficult struggle with the fear of death and with psychic pain had truly been crowned with success in the birth of a child. Was this result, as we—both patient and analyst—assumed, an affirmation of life-giving forces within the patient? Or was this immaculate conception—having a baby without a man—a "manic defense" (Klein 1935; Winnicott 1935; Aktar 2001) that helped her avoid the mourning and pain inside herself? Was psychic change in this case a reality or an illusion?

## THE CASE

### The Omnipotent Needy Child

Before quoting a few fragments from the patient's analysis to illustrate the previously mentioned theme, I would like to introduce her and provide a glimpse into our first meeting. Dina, a scientist, married for the second time, and mother of two, sought help because of recent crippling panic and near-delusional experiences of being watched and intruded upon. She described the scenario of her panic with ease. Someone, a man of course, was peeping through the window and planning to break in, rape, and murder her. The first anxiety attack occurred as she roamed about her kitchen, naked, in the middle of the night, after intercourse with her husband. Subsequently, she could no longer stay alone at home in the evenings or drive alone after dark, because of the recurring attacks, and this greatly restricted her independence. Dina sought help in order to "exorcise the devils."

At our first meeting Dina's vivacity seemed to fill my office. She was in her mid-thirties, big, blond, and pretty, though not sophisticated in her dress. She gave me a firm handshake, a big, warm smile, and addressed me in a loud, booming voice. I was aware that I immediately felt drawn to her witty remarks and warmth.

Dina related her history without much difficulty. She was the third child in a single-parent family. Her mother had been abandoned by her second husband (Dina's father) when Dina was around two years old. The mother struggled to raise her three children, a son from her first marriage, Dina, and Dina's younger brother from her last marriage. Dina's father, a distinguished writer, lived in the big city surrounded by authors and famous actors. He visited his family frequently, but mostly when he was sick and needed care. Dina remembered the lovely vacations she would spend with her father in the city; he introduced her to the magical world of the theater and to his interesting friends, and treated her to ice creams topped with whipped cream in theater cafés.

Dina's first marriage was unsuccessful from the start. Her husband's first wife had walked out on him, leaving him with a one-and-half-year-old son. While she admired his fine qualities as a father and his intellectual prowess, he reminded her of her own father, who was physically repulsive to her. From the start of her marriage, Dina was unhappy and obsessed with suicidal wishes. She sought help and was referred to analysis, which she left after nine months. Dina and her husband went abroad for a period of two years. While overseas, Dina became pregnant. In her fifth month she left her husband and returned to her mother to give birth to her son. Dina's second husband was an old family acquaintance. He was twenty-two years her senior and twice divorced, with a son around Dina's age from his first marriage.

In the initial interview I realized that on a nonverbal level, mainly through her smiles and appreciative glances, Dina was intent on seducing me into liking her. She addressed me in a way that was flattering to us both. I must be very good since she had been referred to me. She admired young, successful, professional women like herself. She definitely wanted a female analyst, since she believed that only a woman possessed the wisdom and sensitivity necessary to understand her. Men are mostly small boys at heart, and they achieve high positions in this world because of social prejudices. "There is a weak sex and an inferior one," Dina concluded her speech with a smile. Our session drawing to a close, Dina decided that she felt comfortable enough to disclose her biggest secret. Her second child, a daughter, had been conceived by artificial insemination, as her present husband was sterile.

Impressed by her verbal ability, the richness of her associations, and her complex life story, I recommended analysis to Dina (four times a week) as the treatment of choice. She readily accepted my suggestion and appeared eager to begin treatment. Little did I know of the tremendous obstacles that would lie ahead of us on our analytic journey.

The first problem was the use of the couch, which was difficult for Dina because of losing eye contact with me. She felt that not seeing my facial expressions spoiled our togetherness. At the same time, I became aware that Dina was making fewer attempts to charm me. Only later in analysis did I realize that by losing my "face" Dina could reveal her own "face," and be in touch with her angry and destructive feelings toward me.

An episode at the conclusion of her long analysis confirmed this. At the end of our last session, when she got up off the couch, Dina looked at me and said: "You look much nicer than the person I saw in my mind's eye throughout these years." We both smiled. I knew then that using the couch had been the right way for Dina to find the hate, as well as the love, in herself.

## Phase I: Struggling with Denial of Death and Separation

In the first phase of treatment, we struggled with Dina's manic defenses—her need to avoid separating from her mother and, as a result, to avoid mourning her.

Dina had been very attached to her mother, whom she had loved and admired greatly. Her mother had been a courageous woman who, while often bitter and dissatisfied, had coped admirably with the unfortunate lot that had befallen her. Dina portrayed her father as weak and incapable of dealing with family responsibilities. Dina felt that her mother regarded her, her only daughter, as a partner with whom to share her life. From early childhood, Dina strove to make her mother happy. Dina claimed that she never got angry at her mother and never rebelled against her. She believed she looked so much like her mother that when she looked in the mirror, she would see her mother's image rather than her own. Later in life, funny incidents, such as meeting men who had courted her mother and who mistook Dina for her, only reinforced this belief.

Listening to Dina, I was struck by her use of the present tense in describing her relationship with her mother who had been dead for over eight years. When I remarked about this, Dina confirmed my silent hypothesis that she had never really accepted her mother's death and never mourned her. After the funeral, Dina had enlarged photographs of her mother, framed them, and hung them throughout the house. In times of need she would talk to these photos, and she also taught her children to communicate in that way with Grandmother. For a long period of time, Dina had many dreams about bringing Mother back from the dead.

Several months after Dina left her first husband and returned to her mother's home to have her baby, her mother suffered a stroke and was hospitalized in critical condition. The stroke occurred the day after the two had had a violent quarrel. Dina remembered it as one of the few quarrels she had ever had with her mother. She left, slamming the door behind her, not knowing that that was the last time she would ever communicate with her mother. Dina was in labor in another hospital on the night her mother died. She related with wonder that at the time her mother was dying, she dreamed that her mother was falling out of her arms and calling to Dina for help, which she was unable to give. Dina delivered her first child, a son, the next day, and several hours later was informed of her mother's death. Thus, giving life and losing a beloved object became inseparably linked for her.

Much psychic work was devoted to the first treatment goal of overcoming Dina's manic defenses—her denial of the loss of her mother and inability to separate from her. Through her unconscious fantasies and dreams, Dina conveyed to me how terrified she was that I might take her mother away from her. In one of her dreams, while her garden was unattended for a short period of time, a man came by and uprooted her trees. Her associations revolved around me in the role of a new mother, uprooting her own mother (the old trees): "Maybe you are the best mother in the world, but who wants to give up one's own mother?"

With the strengthening of the therapeutic bond, Dina was able to work through her ambivalent attachment, the mixture of love, guilt, and unconscious, destructive wishes toward the internal maternal object. I will illustrate this with some fragments from analysis:

Dina claimed that lately she had been feeling uncomfortable around her eight-year-old son because he liked to touch her breasts when he came near her. She decided to forbid it, and subsequently her son drew the following pictures:

Her son explained the meaning of his drawings as follows: The first drawing is of a child standing facing a breast. Between the two is a heart pierced by an arrow (the symbol of love). The second is of a child facing a bitten breast. The child, who has taken a bite out of it, says "tasty." The third drawing shows a child calling to a snail, "Mummy, Mummy, do come out."

I realized from the boy's drawings that Dina was conveying a message to me from the little girl inside herself. Since the child was calling to a mother who was hidden in a shell, covered by a protective shield, I won-

child   breast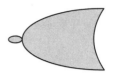

child 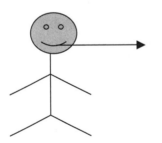 tasty

bitten
breast

child 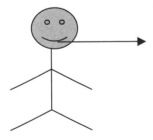 Mummy,
Mummy,
Do come out

snail

dered whether Dina might have experienced my reactions to her in analysis as insensitive and unempathic.

Examining my countertransference feelings made me realize that I sometimes felt overwhelmed by the flood of associations and fantasies that Dina directed toward me in treatment. I noticed that they made me recoil into a kind of silence to protect myself from the flood. Perhaps Dina experienced my silence as a protective shield against her neediness, and she was crying out to me through her son's drawings.

I suggested to Dina that perhaps she was feeling frustrated by me in analysis, as I understood from the drawings that the little girl inside herself was asking me not to barricade myself in, which she herself had recently done when confronted with her son's passionate love.

Dina reacted to my interpretation by relating a dream. In the dream, she took her children to a live show, where a naked woman danced in front of them. The woman, who somewhat resembled her mother, had a body that was far from perfect, not a body that should be exhibited in public. The woman moved in a way that revealed an enormous vagina, the size of almost half her body. Dina said that she was afraid of the influence that this show might have on her children. She continued by bringing up a childhood memory. The memory dealt with an episode that had occurred when she was three years old. She was left at home with her brother and desperately wanted to go to the toilet, but the door to it was locked. She then defecated in her pants and her mother found her curled up in the drawer under her bed, feces smeared all over her.

Relating Dina's childhood memory to her dream, I realized that her unconscious longing, as well as her fear, was to become a meconium-covered fetus in my womb. I suggested to Dina that perhaps she was frightened by the longed-for closeness she experienced in analysis, and that she assumed it was also frightening for me. But, I added, I felt she wanted me to be a strong mother who, by taking her out of her "drawer" and cleaning up her "shit," would help her give birth to her new and separate self, purged of her angry and depressive feelings.

Dina accepted my interpretations gratefully. Though aware of the long and difficult road ahead of us, I realized that, in spite of her initial fear, she could now give up some of her manic defenses and work through the mourning connected to the separation from her mother. The treatment goal of this phase suited her own life goal of individuation.

## Phase II: Accepting Her Monosexual Destiny

Another manic defense of Dina's—her inability to mourn and resign herself to the fact that she is "only" a woman, and that she does not possess the qualities and attributes of both sexes (her monosexual destiny)—is shown through her bisexual tendencies. First, I will describe the homosexual tendency of Dina's libidinal desires, her experiencing herself as a man, and her lesbian attraction to women.

Dina claimed that she loathed older women who "make passes" at her, yet she sometimes shared her husband's attraction to younger women. She vividly described an incident in which a female friend from a local theater group in which she was a member took a shower in her house. She helped the woman into the shower, noticing her "firm breasts, flat belly and beautiful triangle with black curls." In analysis Dina expressed her interest in having a lesbian experience. In my countertransference feelings, I became aware of Dina's incestuous wishes toward me, as well as of her attempts to seduce me.

The difficult obstacles posed by an eroticized transference were not immediately obvious to me. Dina's associations seemed so rich and she was so enthusiastic about treatment that I was mostly aware of the positive aspect of our relationship. Only later were we able to discover and work through the hatred lurking beneath it (as will be seen in vignettes from the fourth and fifth years of analysis).

Dina recalled memories of her mother roaming around the house nearly naked or showering in front of her. She remembered feeling repulsed by her mother's body, and often found it difficult to undress in front of other women because they might be harsh in judging the flaws in her own body. She always felt naked from head to toe under her mother's scrutinizing gaze. In analysis, Dina felt "naked" when lying in front of me on the couch.

Throughout the first year of analysis, Dina projected upon me the image of a close girl-friend of hers, whom she greatly loved and had lived with for several years after divorcing her first husband. Her friend had been with her at the birth of her baby and had handed her the baby to be breastfed. Dina believed that this was "their" baby.

During this period, Dina expressed the wish to have another child, if possible, without the humiliating procedure of artificial insemination that she had undergone to become pregnant the second time. In this phase of analysis, I still believed that Dina, in the transference, was expressing her unconscious wish to have a baby with me.

Dina had always involved her mother in her sexual exploits. At the age of eighteen, deciding to put into practice the liberal sex education she had received from childhood, she "used" a man in order to lose her virginity. She felt it important to inform her mother about it, placing a note on her bed, and thus making her a partner to the deflowering. In the transference, I was assigned a similar role: Dina informed me that while making love with her husband she fantasized about me. She revealed feelings of resentment toward me that this aroused in her, similar to those she felt toward her mother when she turned her into a partner to her first sexual experience. Dina continued, comparing analysis to lovemaking. She felt that in treatment, as in intercourse, she "undressed" and bestowed upon me her most secret inner place. Dina claimed that in contrast to sex, which she seldom initiated or particularly enjoyed, she came to treatment of her own free will and was devoted to it. Analysis was, in her words, "a situation of constant hunger, an infinite stimulation without orgasm." In the transference, Dina bluntly expressed her libidinal wishes toward me: "Why is it that there is no touching in treatment? There is something irrational here, not that I am conscious of my longing to make love to you. You don't see only me, you are supposed to help me, you are supposed to remain aloof. This also means not sleeping with me. I feel an emotional and physical closeness with women. That's why I sought out a female analyst."

My inquiry into the unconscious anger and guilt underlying her incestuous wishes met with a wall of manic defenses. "I like women," Dina said, "and I am proud of it. Nobody can really explain to me why I can't make love to my mother or my daughter; they are the closest to me."

I began to wonder if Dina could really be treated, as she defended her perverse tendencies and her incestuous wishes with such force. Gradually, I realized that Dina was attempting to live out her florid fantasies in the transference to avoid the disintegration that was threatening her psychic life. We were able to understand this threat only much later in analysis. Sensing her underlying vulnerability, I refrained from touching upon the feelings of depression and destructiveness, which were hiding beneath her manic defenses.

It became clear to me that Dina was rejecting the treatment goal of resigning herself to her monosexual destiny. Since her life goal was to avoid feeling the limitations to power resulting from having the attributes of only one gender, the treatment goal of accepting that she was "only" a woman was experienced by her as threatening and dangerous.

### Phase III: Discovering a Part of the Denied Inner Reality

In this phase of treatment, we struggled with Dina's manic defenses that she used to deny her inner reality. The understanding of her symptoms, achieved by the elaboration of her relationship with her father and her "full" brother, was a step toward reaching this goal.

Dina's father was old and senile when he died in a nursing home. Dina would visit him occasionally, resenting the fact that he had outlived her mother. Life and death collided with each other once again when Dina's father died several days after the birth of her daughter. Dina's feelings of guilt over her being absent during her father's last moments were reinforced by her fantasy that her giving life had caused her father's death.

I do not intend to describe the whole course of analysis here. However, I would like to describe a dream from this period, in which Dina saw her father and brother as two blind men, a murderer and a robber, standing trial.

Dina described her brother as possessing antisocial tendencies in childhood. He would steal animals and then kill them in a very cruel way. Dina vividly described how he repeatedly beat her. Unable to control his violent outbursts, during which he beat and hurt Dina as well as other children, her mother placed him in an institution for emotionally disturbed children when he was thirteen years old. Dina felt that analysis helped her "see" things her brother will always be "blind to": "I am aware of the physical attraction between myself and my brother, a thing he has never seen."

In the transference, I was aware of the pleasure Dina appeared to derive from her vivid descriptions of her brother's cruelty. I then realized that Dina wanted me to "see" the kind of behavior that turned her on. Here, I refrained from making a transference interpretation, but instead pointed to the dominant affect accompanying her stories of her brother's cruelty, namely, that this kind of behavior seemed to excite her. Is it possible then, I commented, that she herself might have written the script of her phobic attacks? Dina was angry and perplexed by the possibility that she herself had invented the cause of her torment: She despised violent behavior of any kind; she considered rape the greatest crime in the world, even loathing films that dealt with the subject. How could I then claim that in fantasy she was bringing rapists upon herself? Was this why she always carried pepper spray in her handbag, to ward off any attacker? At this point, Dina vehemently complained about analysis, the cruel method that destroyed her defenses, with no promise of the happiness she longed for. It became clear that Dina's life goal, which she called "happiness," was not compatible with the pain incurred in understanding her symptoms and in taking responsibility for them.

Now Dina continued to talk about her cruel father who, though consciously repulsive to her, was an object of attraction for many years. In the transference, I felt like the violent, exciting father-analyst whom she resented, but toward whom she also felt a forbidden attraction. Working through some aspects of her panic attacks, I connected her fear of the "peeping Tom" with the anxiety she felt in her relationship with Father. She remembered that Father used to kiss her on the eyes, wet, sexy kisses that she liked.

Working through her relationship with Father facilitated Dina's recounting of a family romance in which her husband, who for many years had been a friend of her parents, had had an affair with her mother. Dina claimed he had always denied it. I reminded Dina of her first phobic attack, which had occurred when she roamed about naked in the kitchen, after intercourse with her husband. I pointed out to her that even if this story were only the creation of her own fantasy, she might have invented the rapist-killer so as to bring upon herself the punishment she unconsciously felt she deserved for breaking the taboo of incest. We had to invest many months of analytical work in working through this interpretation before Dina could accept that she herself had written the anxiety-arousing script, and that the figure of the rapist-killer was also a personal creation.

In spite of her initial defensive reaction, in the end Dina was able to recognize the value of understanding her symptoms. Since one of her life goals was to free herself of her symptoms and to restore her independence, she was ready to discover this part of her inner reality and to stop denying it.

### Phase IV: Accepting the Limitations of Age and Gender

In order to illustrate Dina's manic defenses against the limitations of age and gender, I will describe her inability to give up childhood omnipotence and bisexuality, which were expressed through her wish for parthenogenesis. During this stage of the treatment, Dina experienced this manic defense as vital to her psychic survival.

From the earliest stages of analysis, Dina toyed with the idea of having a third child. She was not deterred by the fact that she was over forty, that her husband was sixty-three and sterile, and that he did not want any more children.

Thus, she underwent artificial insemination. After prolonged unsuccessful monthly artificial inseminations, she underwent gynecological tests, followed by complex abdominal surgery to ascertain the cause of her infertility. Pregnancy became an enormous challenge for her, a way of overcoming the limitations of age, and a means for conquering death. Her entire discourse in analysis at this point, her dreams and fantasies, revolved around her wish to become pregnant. Her daily routine was entirely taken up with checking her temperature each morning, taking urine tests, undergoing artificial inseminations, and awaiting results. Dina denied any anxiety over not knowing the identity of the donor of the sperm or its quality. She convinced herself that the donors were probably medical students who needed the money but who were highly intelligent and talented individuals.

Dina seemed to be living for one single goal—to become pregnant. After each insemination she was convinced she had conceived and would come to analysis in an elated mood. With the appearance of her period, Dina felt that she had lost a baby and went into a state of mourning and depression: "Each time I miscarry a dream," she said.

In the transference, for the first two years I believed that Dina wanted to have this baby with me, as I represented her mother (Pines 1993). I was the partner with whom she shared all of her exhausting efforts to become pregnant. But, at the same time, I felt like a helpless, castrated partner, as she did not accept any intervention from me. Even my meek reference to the tremendous efforts that she was willing to undergo to reach her goal was experienced by her as lacking in empathy. I felt as if I were a "dead" partner, not yet realizing that Dina's partner was not actually dead but nonexistent.

After two-and-a-half years of attempts and frustration, Dina decided that if she did not conceive within the next three months she would abandon the idea. This period was then extended to five months, at which time Dina became pregnant. After a short while, she decided to leave analysis.

I felt the powerful aggressive nature of the blow that Dina directed against me by her decision. I felt frustrated, used, and discarded. It was clear to me that Dina had placed me in the role of her first husband, whom she left five months after becoming pregnant. Dina had never loved her husband, but had always praised his "high quality sperm."

Gradually, it dawned upon me that Dina herself must have been through such experiences of being held and discarded during her childhood. Only later in analysis were we able to link this episode to her complex and painful relationship with her mother. My attempts to make her aware of her hate, of using me as a provider of sperm (penis) or milk (breast), and then discarding me after "having her fill" were pointless. Dina declared her love for me and explained her decision to leave analysis as her fight against her "addiction to treatment." Over the next few months we tried to understand Dina's wish to stop analysis at this stage. It then became clear that not only was she fighting her powerful dependency needs, but she also regarded me as a dangerous agent who was forcing her to be in touch with her own feelings of impotence and mourning in the face of aging and death. "Analysis makes one both wiser and sadder," said Dina. "I don't want that; being mature is not my goal. I came here pursuing happiness. Now that I am pregnant, I can leave." Further attempts to point out to Dina that she was using her pregnancy to ward off depressive feelings fell on deaf ears. On parting, I stressed that I would be here for her should she need me. Dina left analysis in her fifth month of pregnancy.

A month later Dina's husband phoned to inform me that Dina had miscarried the previous night. She asked him to call and inform me that she had been through a terrible experience, and also to possibly arrange a session at the hospital. I went to see Dina in the hospital the next day. She was overwhelmed emotionally, and spoke incessantly of the trauma. Apparently the fetus had died some time ago and she had to undergo an induced delivery. The problem was that despite running a high fever for days, Dina had refused to cooperate with the doctors. Only after being told that her life was in danger did she agree to the induction, feeling sure that she was destroying a live baby and hoping all the time that someone would halt the murder. Nor was this the end of her plight: After she was persuaded to push and deliver the dead fetus, she was told that some of it had remained in her womb and must be surgically removed. Dina surprised her doctors by asking them the sex of the fetus. She was told that it was female. The physical pain of the delivery was small compared to the pain of her aching psyche.

I listened to Dina very quietly, feeling overwhelmed by feelings of loss and impotence. "What can I do for her?" I thought to myself. This baby had been an investment of her entire life and future, and now it was lost. Gradually I realized that these must also have been partly Dina's feelings, which she was projecting upon me and with which I was identifying. Dina was now relying on my promise to be there for her in case of need. Before I left the hospital, Dina said smilingly that she was grateful I had agreed to see her under such unusual circumstances.

Two weeks after leaving the hospital, Dina came to me in a state of anxiety that masked her depression. She couldn't keep still for a moment, couldn't sleep, and had developed all sorts of compulsive rituals. She asked for help, to which I immediately agreed. Clearly, we still had a long and painful road ahead of us.

A short while after resuming treatment, it became evident that Dina was unable to accept her feelings of loss and mourning. In spite of my efforts to ease her suffering by being an empathic listener, Dina denied her feelings by attempting artificial insemination again. Thus, the monthly cycle of hope and depression was renewed; so was the wall of manic defenses. This time, however, I felt that I was struggling with a psychotic obsession, which had the function to defend against unbearable psychic pain as well as against the danger of disintegration.

During this period, I was first cast in the role of the ineffective gynecologist who had performed an unsuccessful "plumbing job." Like him, I was obviously impotent, since I could not impregnate her through analysis and thus fulfill her wishes. Later on, there was a shift in her feelings in the transference, and she began to view me as the murderer of her babies. The following dream, which she dreamed during this period, illustrates this: "I dreamt I came to the hospital; before I had time to get into a bed I delivered a baby, but the baby wasn't coming out of the amniotic sac. I shouted to the midwife 'Open the sac quickly, he can't breathe.' She slapped him halfheartedly and he still couldn't breathe. She said there was nothing she could do, that the baby was dead. I was angry with her, she did nothing to save him." In the transference, I referred to Dina's feelings of being my aborted fetus whom I was unable to save.

Dina confirmed this interpretation through her recurring dreams. A bus almost ran over Dina and her little daughter, or she found herself on a ship that was steered into a typhoon by its incompetent captain. In both cases, she felt that she had to leave analysis, to run for her life.

Dina bestowed upon me the power of the rapist-killer, the murderer of her most pressing wishes: "If this baby is going to be born, it will happen in spite of you and not because of you. I feel that to give up becoming pregnant is to give up life; for you it is probably a beginning, for me it's the end." It became clear to me that Dina's struggle against the acceptance of the limitations of aging and death, our present treatment goal, was vital for her psychic survival.

It eventually occurred to me that throughout this period, in which I was cast in different roles with regard to her pregnancy, I had been un-aware of Dina's fantasies of having a baby without a partner. I slowly real-ized that Dina was denying the need for a partner (me in the transference) for purposes of conceiving. When I pointed this out to her, she accepted it without any resistance. This was indeed what she felt; she wished to create this baby with herself.

The negative feelings in the transference now became increasingly stronger. Resuming the process of artificial insemination that she had abandoned for a short while, Dina was haunted by nightmares of recur-ring miscarriage as a result of her doctor's incompetence. In her dreams, she saw a fetus with a smashed head, severed limbs, and a squashed abdo-men with its guts hanging out.

In the countertransference, I began to feel guilty for my detrimental impact on Dina's life through analysis. I would emerge from the analytic session with her booming voice and powerful arguments pursuing me everywhere: If she couldn't have a child, was getting old, with death just around the corner, what was the meaning of life? And what about the void she would feel in her life if I were unable to fill it with meaning? Dina claimed that she came to analysis to find meaning, but somehow, through the same process, she had come to the conclusion that she had to give up what was most meaningful to her—having another child. I felt lost, impo-tent to answer her questions and overcome by depression. I now realized that we had switched roles, and felt that Dina has almost demolished my analytic prowess. Being cast into the role of the victim, I dreaded Dina's attempt to shatter my belief in myself and my analytic role. In this difficult phase in analysis, I understood that I, myself, had been drawn to believe the worthiness of Dina's goals, that I was almost persuaded that her goals were commendable. This realization helped me reassume my analytic role.

It then occurred to me that the transference-countertransference problems we encountered were a reflection of her complex relationship with her mother. I consequently pointed out to her my belief that beneath her anger and aggression toward me was a great need for love and support. I also added that she was probably unconsciously trying to make me feel the painful experience she herself had undergone in childhood.

For the first time in a long while Dina listened to my interpretation without immediately rejecting it. The following session she brought me a gift, a cloth on which she had painstakingly embroidered the following words: "Ambivalence is the basic condition of the human mind." This was a breakthrough in her hate and a turning point in the transference relationship toward me.

Working through the therapeutic relationship, Dina elaborated upon the difficult relationship with the maternal representation. Dina could now remember that, throughout her life, Mother had suffered from an affective disorder of the manic-depressive kind. She had never been institutionalized, but was treated with lithium. Dina remembered Mother's mood swings, and when they would change for the worse, she would feel let down and discarded. Mother would lie in bed for days, bitter and angry with everyone. She would complain about her unfortunate lot in life, about being abandoned by Father, about the fate of women. During those times, Mother was irritable, dissatisfied with whatever she did. Dina had a painful memory of Mother being angry and slapping Dina's face, which made Dina feel ashamed and humiliated. Dina did everything to appease Mother's wrath, imagining that through her good deeds she could restore her loving mother, yet at the same time feeling impotent and frustrated.

Reviewing the different phases of the analysis, I understood that through the transference relationship Dina was playing the roles of herself and her unstable mother, placing me in the complementary roles. In the first phase, Dina was my adoring and idolizing little girl who wanted to merge with me narcissistically, while harboring the murderous wish of swallowing me up and destroying me. This fantasy made her afraid of my retaliation, of being devoured and lost inside me. This phase gave way to the more powerful feeling of being my "victim," transforming me into a dangerous and aggressive mother who not only neglected her babies but actually murdered them. We connected her feeling of being my victim to the female aspect of the rapist-killer that was projected upon me. Alternately, Dina bestowed on me the role of the girl whose psychic existence was threatened by a ferocious and aggressive woman, embodied by herself. My countertransference feelings of impotence caused by not being able to help her, and my being threatened by her engulfing wrath, must have been exactly what Dina had experienced for many years from her mother.

The long and painful working through of Dina's relationship with her mother resulted in greater understanding and forgiveness, her hate of her mother to a certain extent mitigated by her love for her. As a result, Dina's feelings of guilt and persecution diminished. This became apparent through the disappearance of her phobia. Since the fantasy of the rapist-killer was now no longer threatening her, the pressing need to counteract her murderous wishes by producing life decreased greatly. Dina still occasionally underwent artificial insemination, but now felt better able to accept the fact that she might never realize her wish of having another child. She no longer felt that I was the killer of her babies, and I was again aware of her attachment to me and the diminishing of her hate.

It was during this period that Dina became pregnant. Dina believed that she succeeded in becoming pregnant because the pressure that she had felt to vanquish death had diminished. She expressed doubts about whether this baby would ever be able to fill the "void" that she felt in her soul, but "a concrete solution," said Dina, "just postpones dealing with aging and death. I will still need analysis for that." In contrast to her previous pregnancy, Dina felt no urge to run away from analysis. Her pregnancy, however, was regarded as high-risk. Dina asked the doctors to sew up her womb so that she would not miscarry. In the transference, we understood on a symbolic level that she was asking me to sew up the analytic womb so that the new aspect of her personality, which had just budded in her, would not miscarry.

Dina delivered a baby girl and remained in analysis until her daughter was almost two years old. The relationship with her child brought a new dimension into the transference relationship, through which we were able to continue the elaboration of her own infantile experiences with her mother. This, in turn, increased her capacity to love her child, as well as to better accept herself as a woman. "I found the bluebird of happiness in my very own kitchen," she said.

We were both aware that through a lengthy process of growth, in which she struggled with so much pain, mourning, and the fear of death, Dina was finally able to "give birth" to some good parts in her own self.

## DISCUSSION

I wish to discuss what this case can teach us about the movement from manic defenses to mourning in light of the following:

(1) The extent to which fear of psychic pain aroused manic defenses against change and growth in both members of the analytic couple.
(2) The extent to which manic defenses were given up in order to be in touch with mourning and work it through.

### Fear of Psychic Pain

In his brilliant paper "Termination of psychoanalysis: treatment goals, life goals," Ticho states: "The analyst should know what he considers a mature human being to be" (1972, p. 318). This statement, which demands of the analyst secure knowledge regarding the goals of the treatment, made me feel uneasy. As I have described earlier, I harbored doubts and felt insecure about my analytic goals in this case.

It was, however, quite clear to me what maturity required from my patient. Maturity, in this case, meant the giving up of her manic defenses—her infantile omnipotent fantasies—and her graceful acceptance of the limitations of age. But for Dina, maturity and growth could be achieved only by mourning for losses she felt were irretrievable (such as childbirth and youth). Acceptance of these losses meant full acknowledgment of the passage of time and the relinquishment of omnipotent fantasies and immortality. At certain points in analysis, I felt that not only was this an impossible task for Dina, but it was actually detrimental to her. As analysis progressed, it became clear that Dina's wish for parthenogenesis was a psychotic obsession that served as a manic defense against fragmentation. Not only was Dina denying reality, she was also trying to replace it with delusional fantasies that she felt compelled to enact. She used this enactment to avoid a psychotic breakdown that threatened her at this stage in her life. This became the source of a grave dilemma for me: Since pregnancy and childbirth seemed to be so vital for Dina's psychic survival, was I supposed to fight against this need of hers? Was it at all possible for Dina to give up her manic defenses, and if so, at what cost? And if my role was to put her in touch with unbearable psychic pain, could I take the responsibility for the outcome?

Today, looking back at this analysis after many years have elapsed, I wonder to what extent my questions about whether it was possible to achieve maturity in this case stemmed from the massive projective identification that the patient used throughout the treatment, and to what extent they were due to my own countertransference feelings, which were evoked by her intense encounter with a "mid-life crisis" (Jacques 1965). The painful issue of aging and relinquishing childbirth and youth was not foreign to me—it is universal to all women of this age. I became aware that Dina, who was only five years my senior, evoked conflicting feelings in me about the passage of time and its accompanying limitations. This was one of the main reasons why, at a certain point in analysis, I was almost persuaded that her manic defenses (becoming pregnant once more) might contain a positive element. In this regard, I wish to quote Grinberg, who so eloquently describes the impact of maturity and change on both members of the analytic couple: "It is a painful truth and one which has been avoided until then: that of the full recognition of the passage of time as much in the analyst as in the analysand, in which illusory timelessness is transformed into a real temporality with the limitation of the omnipotent fantasies and those of immortality. These limitations are experienced many times as a partial death" (1980, p. 29).

I believe that Dina's resistance to change, along with her fear of growth and aging, constituted part of an unconscious death anxiety that affected us both and was expressed through her obsession with generating life.

From another perspective, I could understand why Dina tried to postpone aging and death with omnipotent, magical, everlasting life-giving. She felt a tremendous pressure to achieve this concrete solution because she was unable to achieve sublimation and thus change her goal of pro-creativeness into creativeness. Sublimation as a process that underlies creativeness was inhibited and had failed. But sometimes I would wonder—

wasn't Dina's struggle to postpone aging and death a universal one? Aren't we all in the same boat, in this regard? Freud's wise words about our inability to consciously realize the existence of death come to mind: "We were of course prepared to maintain that death was the necessary outcome of life. . . . In reality, however, we were accustomed to believe as if it were otherwise. We showed an unmistakable tendency to put death on one side, to eliminate it from life. We tried to hush it up . . . as though it were our own death . . . in the unconscious everyone is convinced of his own immortality" (1915, p. 289).

## Manic Defenses

I would now like to examine the problem of termination and the extent to which the treatment goal of relinquishing manic defenses were met in this case.

The psychoanalytic literature that deals with the theoretical and technical problems related to termination of analysis offers a series of criteria that take into account the patient's development and his achievements in different areas of life. These criteria have been described in a wide variety of ways (Symposium 1937, 1948, 1950; Pfeffer 1963; Firestein 1969; Hurn 1973; Balkoura 1974; Robbins 1975) and have been reviewed on the basis of different theoretical constructs (Firestein 1982; Schachter 1992).

I will briefly mention some of these criteria. Weigert (1952) wrote that the appearance of a markedly increased capacity for candor on the part of patient and analyst was a harbinger of termination. Greenson (1967) believed that if the patient had never experienced an intense, prolonged angry reaction towards the analyst, then the analysis had probably not reached termination. Novick (1982) focused on the patient's ability to experience and to maintain an oedipal transference. Siegel (1982) emphasized the amelioration of a harsh, judgmental superego. Rangell (1982) was of the opinion that the terminal phase had been reached when the patient had achieved the capacity to choose.

The criterion for termination that has probably received the most attention is the capacity for self-analysis (Hoffer 1950; Kramer 1959; Siegel 1982; Schlessinger and Robbins 1983; Berenstein and Fondevila 1989; Kantrowitz 1990; Schachter 1992). Grinberg (1980) expanded on this topic, viewing self-analysis as an outcome of the "interminability" of the process of searching for mental growth and integration. According to him, the termination of the dynamic interaction between analyst and patient allows the analysand to reach a new "take-off" point, from which he can control the development of his mental growth and maturation by himself. The "interminability" of the process fits the current view that there is no such thing as an ideal termination; that the symptoms never disappear completely; that the patient does not achieve all of the structural changes one would like; nor does he manage to acquire a totally integrated personality. The literature of the last few years has dealt with interruptions, situations of "impasse," and reanalysis. This view supports Freud's early opinion that "We do not always achieve our aim to its full extent—that is, do not achieve it thoroughly enough . . . portions of the old mechanism remain untouched by the work of analysis" (1937, p. 229).

With these different criteria in mind, I wish to examine to what extent the treatment goal of relinquishing manic defenses was met in this case. For this purpose, I shall address the following issues: Did termination really take place? What were the satisfactory aspects of termination and for whom were they most satisfactory? What was the analyst's attitude toward the apparently successful outcome of the treatment at the end of this analysis, and has it changed now, many years later?

I believe that termination did take place in this case, and from the patient's point of view, as well as my own, some positive results were achieved. In my opinion, Dina's working through her disappointment and hatred in the transference inclined the prevailing balance between hate and love more toward love. She was able to recall deep, unconscious memories of hate toward the maternal object because they were mitigated by love. Her fear of death and destruction was somewhat moderated by her emotional experience in analysis, and by the work of mourning that accompanied the entire analysis. Dina felt she had been able to conceive as a result of feeling less threatened by death. Possibly, she was now able to become pregnant and give life because she experienced something in herself as life giving. From this angle, the treatment had a positive outcome for patient and analyst alike.

On the other hand, I frequently wondered what structural changes had taken place in my patient. The immaculate pregnancy, producing a baby without a man, was a manic defense with a successful outcome. As a result of her manic defenses, she had obtained her life's goal—the avoidance of pain and mourning inherent to growth. In contrast with the first time that she had become pregnant during treatment, this time she remained in analysis, stating clearly that she did not regard the pregnancy and the baby as a means of "filling her life with meaning." But could she ever complete the process of mourning necessary for accepting her monosexual destiny and the inevitability of her death, which she had begun before the birth of this child? To what extent did this "success" help her avoid her death anxiety? Could this success have been the result of an unconscious defensive collusion on the part of both of us in the face of the threat of intensive psychic pain? From this point of view, termination was less satisfactory for the analyst than for the patient.

Analysts' difficulties with the incomplete results of analysis have been reviewed by Schachter (1992). Ticho observed that "countertransference difficulties play a larger part in the termination phase than in other phases of the analysis" (1972, p. 328). Siegel stated that "The story of the well-analyzed patient is a myth which is told and retold by analysts and patients alike in the interests of hope or to justify the long and expensive treatment process or for other reasons associated with problems in self-esteem" (1982, p. 396).

Dewald (1982) similarly noted that the limitations of analytic treatment may evoke narcissistic injury in the analyst. This may lead to an indefinitely prolonged analysis in the attempt to avoid such injury. Cooper wrote about this as follows: "It is during the termination phase that we become most intensely aware of all the personal and professional hopes with which the analysis began. . . . We are likely to experience with a new clarity the disappointments, the unresolved, and even untouched issues of analysis, as well as the gratification of knowing how much was achieved" (1985, p. 1).

Over a long period of time I was unable to complete the recording of this interesting and apparently successful treatment because of my doubts as to its success. Some of the many questions that preoccupied me were: Did the patient understand herself better at the end of the work? Should this analysis be regarded as a partially successful one? If so, what would have been a fully successful outcome?

These questions were answered unexpectedly about a year ago when I ran into Dina by chance on the street. I was struck by the fact that although looking older, Dina was smartly and more femininely dressed than I had ever seen her before. She shook my hand warmly and, as if sensing my unvoiced questions, said: "I am all right, you know. I am working as a teacher and am very happy with my work. I like the high school children; teaching is creative, important for future generations, and it also satisfies my need for an audience. I am very happy with my family; my children are wonderful." She was quiet for a moment, then added, smiling: "I'm about fifty-four years old now and I know it, but I don't mind my age any more. I am not always in a euphoric mood but I'm quite satisfied with who I am and what I have. And I am very grateful to you for what you did for me."

Listening to Dina for just these few minutes on the street, I realized to my satisfaction that her analysis was not only terminated but, indeed, had been successful. Dina appeared to be clearly able to deal with the conflicts she encountered without me, by using what she had learned in analysis. I knew then that, at the end of the work, she understood herself better, and also had acquired the tools to enable her to achieve further growth. In her case this meant that she could, to a certain degree, realize her limitations and give up her perfectionist and infantile expectations, thus in great part overcoming her manic defenses.

Arlow's words about the experience of termination in analysis very much reflect what transpired at the end of this treatment: "The fantasies and conflicts involved in the experience of termination cover a wide range that not only recapitulates separation from the mother in early childhood but also activates fantasies about completion vs. incompletion, castrated vs. phallic, life vs. death, and disappointment over the fact that the analysis has failed to fulfill all those unconscious childhood fantastic wishes that the patient brings into the analysis under the guise of the wish to get well" (1970, p. 52).

The working through of these feelings by my patient and myself, which began during the closing phase of analysis and continued after it, enabled both of us to achieve some tolerance of the psychic pain contained in maturation and growth, and facilitated our ability to mourn. Both of us, patient and analyst alike, were better able to move on from our manic defenses and do the work of mourning necessary for continuing life in a creative way.

## NOTE

1. The issue of termination and analytic goals has been a relatively neglected subject in the psychoanalytic literature (Blum 1989). It was through my clinical

work that I became involved in this topic. Over a long period of time I was unable to complete the recording of this interesting and apparently successful treatment that ended some years ago. In trying to understand what was hindering my writing, I came to the conclusion that it was probably connected to my countertransference feelings about the patient's "treatment goals" and "life goals" (Ticho 1972). Ticho defines "treatment goals" as the removal of obstacles to the patient's discovery of his potentialities. "Life goals" are the goals the patient would seek to attain if he could put his potentialities to use.

In this paper, I defined "treatment goals" and "life goals" differently. I define "treatment goals" the way both analyst and patient view the aims of treatment; "life goals" will be defined as the way in which both partners of the analytic couple refer to the goals the patient would seek to attain in life.

# 3

# Lust for Love

*Touch, but no contact.*

—Rechy 1967, p. 57; quoted in Bollas 1992, p. 147

In this chapter I deal with the problem of the extent to which devices of analytic technique can be legitimately modified in order to facilitate some kind of change in a patient who uses homosexuality as a manic defense against suicide and psychotic dissolution. In the case under discussion, the manic defense was not completely relinquished, but the patient became more in contact with her feelings and less frantic in her search for a homosexual partner.

I have been plagued by questions and doubts concerning the partial results of this treatment. What can we hope to achieve from psychoanalysis in cases in which homosexuality serves as a "manic defense" (Klein 1935; Winnicott 1935) against fragmentation and psychic death? And what is the role of the analyst in these cases? Is it the analyst's role to help patients relinquish their homosexuality, which they may experience as essential to their psychic existence? Or should s/he help them along their path to self-discovery, which may or may not entail their letting go of the homosexuality that helped them avoid the pain and mourning inherent in trauma? I do not presume to have the answers to these difficult questions but I would like to tackle this issue by means of a case study.

In this case study, the patient's demand for touching and being touched by the analyst (the wished-for homosexual partner in the transference) was crucial for her to continue the analytical work. The discussion demonstrates the great difficulty involved in (1) helping such patients analytically and (2) withstanding the threat that they will act out violently and dangerously if the analyst does not acquiesce in some way. It also shows how a verbal interaction with the analyst that was experienced by the patient as physical touch enabled the continuation of analytic work and the working through of the patient's manic defense.

Before describing the case, I will review the topic of touch in the analytic treatment from a historical as well as a contemporary perspective.

For a long period of time, the subject of touch in analytic treatment was viewed not only as a sensitive and controversial topic but also as a forbidden one. After being an "untouched area" in classical psychoanalysis, it then became a hot topic, widely discussed in recent literature. For example, the *Psychoanalytic Inquiry* (20, no. 1, 2000) devoted an entire issue to the topic of touch in the psychoanalytic situation.

The interdiction against touching was codified with the development of the rule of abstinence. As early as 1910, Freud wrote, "The patient should be kept in a state of abstinence or unrequited love. The more affection you allow him, the more readily you reach his complexes, but the less definite the result" (Jones 1955, p. 448). This statement was further elaborated by Freud in 1915 and 1919. The theoretical rationale underlying this approach was that preventing the patient's instinctual drives from being discharged would force their transformation into verbal representations. The now-conscious repressed instinctual wishes could then be worked through to achieve their renunciation and sublimation.

On the basis on this model, Casement (1982) refused to hold his patient's hand, out of conviction that to do so would gratify the patient's longing for a good object (not infantile sexual wishes) and would interfere with the full reliving of the trauma, including the aggression generated by the trauma.

Despite the rule of abstinence, psychoanalysts have reported occasions of considered use of touch to facilitate treatment. Ferenczi (1953) would permit behavioral enactments that at times included affectionate kisses (Shapiro 1992). Fromm-Reichmann stated that "at times it may be indicated to shake hands with a patient or in the case of a very disturbed person to touch him reassuringly" (1950, p. 12). Searles indicated that "declining to provide physical contact" may be helpful, yet he mentioned the undesirability of "being neurotically afraid of physical contact" (1965, p. 701). Winnicott (1965) reported, in his own writings and in those by his patient Margaret Little (1990), that he would hold his patient's hand in an effort to create a sufficient "holding" environment. Little (1966) described a patient who despaired over his discovery that his "accidental" self-injuries were intentional, and needed the analyst to touch his hand. In a lecture, Kohut (1981) described offering his two fingers for a patient to hold when the patient was in a state of deep despair (also reported in Bacal 1985). Pedder (1986) as well described a deeply regressed patient who needed physical touch.

Although published reports typically address the use of touch with very disturbed or deeply regressed patients, Mintz (1969) has suggested that physical touch may also be useful with the "healthy neurotic" in periods of deep regression when the patient is temporarily unavailable for verbal communication. Balint still further expanded the circumstances of the emergence and meaning of touch, and described his patients' desire for touch toward the end of treatment when the patients are better integrated and better able to communicate affection, mutuality, and a deeper connection. Touch under these circumstances is not erotically stimulating but a powerful form of communication that leads to a deeper intimacy and a "tranquil quiet sense of well-being" (1952, p. 231). Breckenridge (2000) described a clinical situation in which allowing physical contact conveyed a sense of acceptance and helped modify a profoundly negative self-image. McLaughlin observed a general shift in the classical position on touch. McLaughlin noted being increasingly comfortable with holding a patient's hand, including when a patient on the couch reaches back for his. A patient may be reaching for "support, consolation, or for my presence in the face of the patient's not yet speakable yearnings" (1995, p. 441). He found that "this responsiveness facilitates, rather than hinders, the patient's consequent analytic seeking" (1995, p. 442).

The complexity of this topic has been eloquently described by Maroda: "What I have found is that the request for physical contact has many different meanings, and that the answer to the question of 'to touch or not to touch' lies in the adequate understanding of the patient's request and the analyst's emotional response to it. Understanding the patient's intrapsychic meaning, placing this in an appropriate emotional context, understanding how the current request for touch represents a re-enactment in the transference-countertransference interplay, and then making the right decision, are exceedingly daunting tasks. They require intellectual and emotional depth on the analyst's part" (1999, p. 143).

I will now describe a case study in which the patient experienced a verbal interaction as a physical touch in the psychoanalytic situation, an experience that led to direct emotional contact. This verbal interaction and the elaboration that followed it enabled the patient to partially give up her manic defenses and facilitated the process of mourning.

## THE CASE

### The First Encounter—Desire and Fear

Before quoting some fragments from the patient's analysis to illustrate the previously described theme, I will introduce her and provide a glimpse into our first meeting. Deborah, a forty-five-year-old woman, married with seven children (aged seven to nineteen), came to me for psychoanalytic help. The reason she turned to me for analysis emerged through the following story. Deborah was a career woman, the director of a private enterprise. Several years previously she went abroad with her husband and children, where she became interested in sex therapy and took some professional courses. During her stay abroad, she underwent psychological treatment, which escalated into a sexual affair with her therapist, a woman. This therapist initiated her into lesbianism.

For Deborah, the bond with her therapist became very strong, affectively and sexually. When she returned home with her family, Debora experienced their separation as tremendously difficult and painful. The relationship with her husband lost whatever affective meaning it had had before.

The previous summer, Deborah went abroad to take part in a sex therapy program for students. There, she had an affair with a female colleague from the group. She again was exulted by the love she experienced for this woman. Recently, she received a letter from the woman informing her that she had a new woman friend who was living with her. Deborah, confused, restless, and not knowing what to do, decided to seek help.

In the first interview, Deborah explained to me why she sought a female analyst: being familiar with the prohibitions of the profession, she was sure that I would not seduce her. She expressed a wish to do everything possible to prevent this treatment from becoming a love relationship, as had happened with her former therapist.

I observed the woman seated opposite me, speaking in a monotonous, quiet voice. She was of ordinary appearance, blond, plump, with regular features, and unsophisticatedly dressed. I noticed a certain lack of expression on her face, a lack of color and vitality in her demeanor. What struck me most of all was the gap between her lack of affective expressiveness and her description of the intense feelings that accompanied her lesbian love affairs.

I gathered from her story that now, abandoned by her second lover and trying to fill a void, she hoped to find in analysis a potential new lover, like the one she had found in her first therapy abroad. At the same time, I believed that she might be terribly afraid of the realization of her erotic wishes, especially as the fulfillment of her desires was connected to separation and pain. The conscious fear of her unconscious desires and wishes toward me was a theme that accompanied us throughout the entire treatment.

### Anamnesis

Deborah was the daughter of Sephardic Jews who had emigrated from South America to Israel before World War II. Her parents both came from large families, and each had several brothers and sisters.

Deborah had only one sister, six years her junior. She had virtually no recollection of her childhood years. She knew that her mother had suffered from depression while pregnant with her, having been told this during adulthood. When Deborah was twenty-six years old and already married with two children, her mother, suffering from psychotic depression, was hospitalized in a psychiatric ward. The sister became a professional in her field; she never married or built a life of her own.

Deborah's mother had a brother who was diagnosed as schizophrenic. He lived with his mother (Deborah's grandmother), who was considered an unstable person. Several months after the grandmother's death, this uncle committed suicide.

Deborah's father had been an important figure in the Jewish community in South America and was greatly admired by Deborah. She perceived him as a rational person and tried to identify with him.

Her husband, who was fifteen years her senior, was already a well-known industrialist when they met. It was a flattering match for Deborah. In spite of this, before her wedding she became depressed and had what she termed a "nervous breakdown." Then, like now, she felt the absence of an expression of his love in words. She regarded her husband, who was by now famous and successful, as a workaholic, always busy "saving humanity." Deborah viewed her marriage as unsatisfactory. She felt she was always searching for somebody to whom she could be genuinely close.

### Desire and Inner Deadness

After our initial meeting, I accepted Deborah for analysis and we began treatment four times a week, on the couch. I do not intend to describe the entire course of the analysis. However, I would like to refer to the first year of analysis, during which I became acquainted with Deborah's wounded self and her inner deadness, themes that preoccupied us over many months of analytic work. I learned about her inner deadness from the way she tried to revive it, by watching people in types of situations where they expressed feelings. For example, she used to go to the arrivals hall at the airport to watch people meeting and embracing passionately. She would watch for hours, never getting bored, thirstily drinking in the expressions of emotion from strangers.

This inner deadness infiltrated almost all the emotional spheres of Deborah's life, even her motherhood. When her children were little, she felt she could not relate to them. She would go to playgrounds where mothers watched their children and would observe the mothers talking to their children. Deborah tried to feel motherly feelings by identifying with and imitating normal mothers. She was not always successful in this endeavor.

Deborah claimed that the only two things that succeeded in reviving her inner deadness were giving birth and falling in love. Only these powerful experiences enabled her to feel emotionally alive.

Listening to Deborah describing her plight, I felt as if I were gazing into an abyss, a frightening black hole, a deadly wound that had opened up in the place where normal human emotions should have been. What was the terrible experience of lack, I asked myself, that had dried up the spring of feelings, creating a desert, an inner emotional deadness, which could not but make her life meaningless? Or was this the inner deadness of the mother, which was now part of the daughter's psychic life?

### Desire and Persecutory Fears

I now would like to explore Deborah's self-destructive tendency, as revealed through her associations and fantasies, mainly during the third year of analysis. First, I will present a dream from this period.

"In my dream" said Deborah, "you came up close to me, touched me and told me something personal about yourself. I looked at you—there was a woman dancing to the rhythm of jazz music, the woman didn't actually look like you, she was darker, had curly hair, another face. She was not somebody I knew, but I felt it was you."

Deborah's associations regarding the dream revolved around her children. Her two daughters, fifteen and twelve years old, danced jazz. She felt it was much more difficult for her to relate to her daughters with their budding femininity than to her sons, with whom she was much closer. A memory now surfaced about her younger daughter who, when frustrated and angry, appeared to Deborah as if she wanted to jump out of the window and commit suicide. We first attempted to explore Deborah's wish to get close to me, her longing to be touched by me, as well as the fear this closeness entailed. But where did her self-destructive tendency, which was expressed by how she perceived her little girl, come from? Was it possible, I asked myself, that the encounter with a female analyst who did not fulfill her erotic wishes provoked so much anger, frustration, and desperation that Deborah, who actually wanted to destroy me, turned the aggression inward and wanted to destroy herself?

Deborah's further associations continued to revolve around death. She described the way her uncle, her mother's schizophrenic brother, had committed suicide. When nobody was guarding him (shortly after his mother's death), he left the house, submerged his head in a swamp and inhaled the dirty water. He suffocated to death in the mud.

I understood the message Deborah was conveying to me through her story: I have to guard her against her self-destructive impulses, otherwise she might drown in them. But what was Deborah's "swamp," I wondered. Was she indeed threatened by psychosis, and to what extent would her defenses against psychic death prevent it?

The answer to these questions was revealed through the exploration of Deborah's persecutory fears, which were combined with her desire for erotic love. I illustrate this through an episode from the third year of analysis.

Deborah had worked abroad for several months in a sex therapy clinic run by a female therapist, well known in her field. Deborah claimed that the therapist was very fond of her. Childless and searching for a professional female heir, she even offered to adopt Deborah. The clinic employed women therapists as surrogates, whose role it was to help invalids function sexually. Deborah worked as a surrogate for a while. During this period, she was occasionally troubled by a secret fantasy that she didn't understand. Deborah sometimes felt like slashing her wrists. She had no idea where this feeling came from. Life seemed so very interesting. It was, indeed, a very strange thought.

Through her story, I realized how much Deborah had reenacted her unconscious conflicts and wishes regarding life and death in this kind of work. Functioning as a surrogate, she consciously fulfilled her wish to repair a damaged, sexually dead person by giving him the ability to make love. This required of her only erotic love without any emotional involvement, which suited her perfectly. However, in her unconscious fantasy, Deborah was herself the invalid who needed reparation of the vital ability to give and receive love. By being a surrogate, she was attempting to revivify the dead part in herself; but, as can be seen from her suicidal thoughts, she was unsuccessful in her attempt. Working through this episode, we understood that Deborah wanted to take her own life because the physical act of making love far from satisfied her emotional needs. At this point I realized that Deborah's manic defenses were not working for her. Giving and receiving love on a physical level had not made her inner deadness and the meaninglessness of her life disappear. I therefore began to interpret Deborah's needs and expectations to her, hoping to put her in touch with her feelings.

I pointed out to Deborah that, in analysis, she was the emotional cripple who needed revivification of her dead inner self. In this role, she was asking me to be her emotional surrogate who, by giving her feelings, was supposed to revive in her the ability to love and enable her to feel alive again.

Until now, there had been two things that had succeeded in revivifying Deborah's inner emotional deadness: giving birth (hence her large number of children), and falling in love with a woman. Now that she was older and no longer able to have children, Deborah's entire life revolved around the desperate need for a love relationship with another woman.

### Lust for Life

I explore the issue of Deborah's struggle for emotions through an episode taken from the fourth year of analysis. Deborah gave a detailed description of a farewell party she had attended when abroad with her

husband; the party was given in honor of a famous actor who was suffering from a terminal illness and was on his deathbed. She and her husband
had been invited along with many television people, actors, and friends.
The party, given at the actor's request, was a very special event. For seven
hours, people spoke to him and about him, each of them receiving a small
farewell gift from him. After the party, there was a program on television
in which the actor's doctor stood on the stage for more than an hour,
showing everyone slides of the actor's damaged organs and explaining
about his illness.

In the transference, I asked Deborah whether I was supposed to become
the doctor who publicizes his patient's internal state. Deborah furiously
rejected my interpretation. She often expressed irritation and anger whenever I referred to our relationship. "You are always pushing yourself into
things that belong to reality," she said. "This has nothing to do with you."
It was true that she wanted fame and recognition, she added; actually,
there was a journalist from a local women's magazine who had recently
been asking her for an interview about her successful career. Such a person
could bring her fame and advertise her business.

It was clear to me that in the transference Deborah regarded me as a
potential instrument for advertising herself, under which lay the hidden
need to exhibit herself in public. That was the reason that for many years
I had been unable to write about this case. Only now, years after the analysis ended, and after "dressing her up" in proper disguises, was I able to
describe this treatment and the difficulties I encountered in it.

Deborah's reaction brought to my mind what I already knew about her
perverse, exhibitionistic needs, revealed to me through her stories about
different courses in sex therapy that she had taken abroad and that she
described with great gusto. In one of these "experiential" courses, a group
of about twenty women sat in a circle with their legs spread apart, exploring their vaginas in front of each other. In another course, the students
were shown about two hundred slides of female genitalia. Deborah
claimed that these courses were intended to help the students overcome
their inhibitions.

In my countertransference feelings, I was aware that Deborah wished
to play a perverse game with me of comparing our genitalia, in order to
ensure that she was a woman. Apparently, only by exhibiting herself in

public (in the proximity of women) could she feel that her femininity truly existed.

Continuing her story about the actor, Deborah mentioned that she had been very impressed with the party, as well as with the actor himself, whose life story had become public knowledge at this stage of his life. He had arrived in Israel from Eastern Europe as an adolescent, after his parents had been murdered by the Nazis. He had lived a very creative though immoral life, being sexually promiscuous, mainly with women but also with men, losing contact with his family, his wife, and his children. It was rumored that he had been seduced by his mother when he was thirteen years old and that throughout his life he had exhibited antisocial behavior by seducing minors who were around the same age. Nothing had ever been proven against him, but the scandalous story of his life became a newspaper scoop and was then made into a television series.

Deborah expressed her admiration for the actor and for his way of life. She believed that he had achieved complete acceptance of his body and had derived a lot of pleasure from his sexual life. She also felt that, like him, she too sought powerful life experiences. I was aware that Deborah needed these manic defenses to feel alive.

The story about the actor being seduced in adolescence by his mother evoked in Deborah memories of herself as a child being molested first by a man and then by a woman. She remembered that when she was nine years old, a man who worked in her parents' house sat close to her and stroked her under her skirt. He asked her if she liked it; it was a pleasant feeling. By contrast, the second episode involved a woman, and was completely masked by a facade of love and affection. Only the context in which it was recalled hinted at sexual exploitation. At age eleven, Deborah was in a car with an aunt, her father's sister, a nurse by profession. Deborah put her head in her aunt's lap, and the aunt stroked her head. She felt she wanted more and more. The same experience was repeated later with her first female lover, her first therapist. Once, performing a Gestalt exercise, the therapist put her to sleep like a baby, by stroking her hair. It felt so good that Deborah wanted it to go on forever and ever. She felt that she had missed out on that kind of physical affection all her life. Much psychical work was needed in analysis to make Deborah aware of the traumatic elements of her molestation in childhood and its later impact on her life.

Deborah's oedipal longings surfaced later. Deborah was conscious of her oedipal attraction to her father, which was further transferred to her husband. She remembered that her father had given her love and caring in childhood, but she had always felt the tension of the physical attraction between them. She felt his seductiveness toward her when he sang love songs to her on his guitar. She believed that her love for her husband stemmed from his similarity to her father.

In the transference, I was suddenly placed in the role of the admired but rejecting father (husband)-analyst. Around the time of Holocaust Remembrance Day, Deborah chanced upon my name in a newspaper, along with other Israeli researchers who dealt with the Holocaust. This made her wonder: How important could she be for me, if my real interest lay in life-and-death matters, similar to those that preoccupied her husband or her father in the past?

Deborah believed that her preoedipal longings, which were lived out in her lesbian relationships, stemmed from the affective and physical lack of closeness that she had experienced with her mother. She was aware of the frustration she had experienced in childhood, and held her mother responsible for it. She felt that her longing to be touched and caressed by a woman had been evoked by the special relationship with her aunt.

In the transference, we got in touch with Deborah's anger and rejection of me, which were the result of her frustrated longing for physical contact in the analytic situation. Deborah vehemently claimed that she was aware of her "real" needs—she longed for a relationship that would combine sexuality and feelings and that would make her "whole." Deborah felt that she could achieve such a relationship only with a woman, the relationship with a man only partially satisfying her. It was clear to me that a physical relationship with a woman, and with me in the transference, was Deborah's manic defense against her inner deadness.

When I pointed out to Deborah that she was probably longing for closeness on an emotional and physical level with me in treatment, she was outraged. She believed that, again, I was pushing our relationship to the foreground, a fact that she found very irritating. What did her dreams and wishes, her anger and frustration have to do with me at all? She knew very well how barren and intellectual analysis was; she knew I would never fulfill her wish to be touched and caressed. "Why do I need such intensive treatment?" she asked. "I am aware of my strong need for a relationship with a woman. This urge bothers me more and more in analysis; it uses up a lot of my energy. I think if I had such a relationship, I wouldn't need treatment anymore. I wouldn't feel the longing and the loss."

At this stage in analysis, Deborah began to "flirt" with the idea of leaving treatment. I tried to show her how aggressive she was becoming toward me and our work. I reminded her that at the beginning of treatment, to avoid another failure, she had warned me not to seduce her as her first therapist had done. Now she was claiming that the treatment would be a failure unless it included a physical relationship, the only way to save her life. It seemed to me, I added, that she had wanted to destroy this treatment all along, even before it began.

The confrontation in the transference with Deborah's dead and deadening aspects remained unfruitful. My attempts to help her realize the cruel way she was treating me fell on deaf ears. I felt that my interpretations were becoming repetitious, lifeless, and ineffective. I began to wonder whether Deborah could ever give up her manic defense, the fulfillment of her homosexual wishes, which was supposed to revive her emotional life. If so, was the "holding"—the love, care, and understanding I gave her in analysis—enough to breathe life into her emotional deadness and to fight the death forces expressed through her self-destructive tendencies? To what extent was her homosexual solution vital for this purpose?

A particular dream that indicated Deborah's fear of feelings toward me in the transference elucidated certain matters for me. This is the dream: "I was traveling with my husband, one daughter, and the famous actor whose party I had attended. I had fantasies about the actor and wanted to be alone with him. It was a difficult situation; half of his body was paralyzed because of the treatment he was undergoing. My husband stated that I, too, was suffering from a terminal illness. He decided to bury me. The idea was to put me in a grave so that I would suffocate and not need to undergo this painful analytic treatment. I didn't take leave of my children, of friends. I didn't choke, I got up and continued living."

In her associations, Deborah mentioned that the actor's treatment had not only been unsuccessful, but it had also caused him damage. She, like the actor in her dream, came to analysis half numb (emotionally). But what if analysis would harm her more than it would help? She felt that since her emotional illness was fatal, she had to undergo a very painful treatment in order to recover. But, at the same time, she was afraid that the very treatment that was supposed to be life giving, by evoking her emotions, would be painful to the point of being life threatening. Deborah felt that she would rather be numb, paralyzed, choking, than be confronted with her feelings toward me. On the other hand, she wanted to get out of the grave, out from her inner emotional deadness—she wanted to feel alive.

What could I do to bring Deborah to life, I asked myself. I felt paralyzed, trapped between her aggressive behavior toward me and her destructiveness toward herself. Working through my countertransference feelings, it suddenly occurred to me that the actor, who suffered from paralysis in half of his body, might also represent me and my impotence in helping her realize her hostile aspects. And if this were so, how was I going to escape from the place where I was being suffocated by her rejection and hatred on the one hand, and by my fears for her physical and psychic survival on the other?

Since Deborah had never accepted my interpretations of her libidinal needs and wishes or of her aggression and hostility toward me, I had to find a different way of reaching her. I knew that I had to show Deborah that I cared, I had to recognize her needs and wishes, without linking them directly to me, without letting her feel that I was a separate human being. Finally, I had to touch her positive feelings through my words, so that she would be able to face both her love and her hatred toward me with less shame and humiliation.

A beautiful verse by Rainer Maria Rilke (1904, p. 27) came to my mind and I said, "You shouldn't turn away from treatment. Love consists in this that two solitudes protect and touch and greet each other." For some moments we were both silent and then I saw tears in Deborah's eyes. "I never knew that you really cared about me," she said. "Your words touched me."

This awareness was a breakthrough in Deborah's hate and a change in her transference relation to me. In the ensuing period, Deborah no longer wanted to leave treatment. We now began a long and difficult journey of discovering and exploring her feelings toward me. Much psychic work was needed to help Deborah realize that physical contact from me, though itself an erotic act and a token of my love, would destroy our treatment. Because feelings constituted a threat to her precarious sanity, touching was her way of avoiding feelings and thus remaining on safe, but barren, ground. Deborah had to understand that by using touching to survive psychic death, she was also keeping her emotional deadness intact. Though still very ambivalent about this painful realization, she had at least become aware of it. "It was always hard for me to have an emotional experience without turning it into something sexual. It was so frightening to have feelings that I needed sex to make it bearable. I wanted you to touch me, to caress me, but deep down I did not want to have any feelings toward you."

I could now point out to Deborah that her emphatic demand for an unacceptable form of behavior stemmed from her need to repeat her childhood trauma in treatment, by turning me into the sexual exploiter. Cognitively, Deborah understood this easily; it took us a long time to work through and achieve some "affective understanding" (Freud 1915) of this realization. During this period, Deborah had many dreams that indicated a heterosexual attraction as well.

A meaningful change occurred when, during the last year of analysis (the fifth), Deborah acquired a new woman friend, Eve. This friendship, though very intimate, never became sexual. Deborah had fantasies about what could become a "real relationship" between them, but she refrained from including sexuality. In analysis we understood that, for the first time, Deborah could bear to have feelings toward me. Via Eve, Deborah expressed how grateful she was to me in analysis: "I do not need to have an orgasm, for that I have a vibrator. Eve is alive, she is a person full of emotions. I was alive on many different levels, but on a deeper level I needed Eve, or you here in treatment, in order to feel alive."

In spite of her still-existing problems—her attraction to women and her inability to feel completely happy in her relationship with her husband—we were both aware of a change in Deborah's attitude toward life. Manic defenses expressed through powerful experiences were no longer vital for her psychic survival. She thus gave up her frantic search for a homosexual partner, no longer believing that it would solve all of her problems. She also stopped fighting social conventions—her marriage and her children, which previously she had complied with against her will. A kind of accommodation or compromise solution was reached between what she wanted to be and her family situation; she thus found her familial situation more satisfactory. Deborah was also able to have mutual (not necessarily sexual) relationships with women friends. Deborah felt that she came out from the desert, the inner emotional deadness that had made her life meaningless: "Now I know that I can't always be in touch with my feelings," she said, "but I don't feel an emotional cripple anymore."

## DISCUSSION

Now I wish to explore the hypothesis that a verbal intervention can be experienced as equivalent to touch, in light of the relevant contemporary literature. I will then discuss the issue of manic defenses and their function in cases threatened by fragmentation and psychic death. I examine what can be expected from psychoanalysis in such cases, and refer to the role of the analyst and to my doubts about whether or not it is possible to achieve a complete move from manic defense to mourning.

### Intervention as an "Interpretive Action" (Ogden 1994)

The case study presented in this chapter illustrates the great difficulties I encountered in the treatment of a patient, who, to my mind, may best be classified as the very disturbed hysteric described by Zetzel (1968/1972). Deborah demanded that I repeat her infantile traumata (to exploit her sexually) in treatment, regarding this as absolutely necessary for saving her life. My attempts to help her understand this demand and confront her with the cruel and hostile way she was treating me failed, as she was suffering from a kind of "malignant narcissism" (Kernberg 1992) and experienced all references to our relationship as humiliating and persecutory.

Since the most decisive factor influencing the patient's experience of the analyst's interpretations is the current status of the transference, I tried to alter the negative direction that the transference had taken. For this purpose, I resorted to an intervention that was completely different in form and content from the usual interpretations employed in analysis.

In his interesting discussion of this case, Reppen (1999) pointed out that the spontaneous, unplanned quality of the intervention I used in this case is reminiscent of the "interpretive action" coined by Ogden (1994). I used this intervention ("action") in order to unlock a deadlock and it was directed at the patient's physical and emotional needs.

The intervention consisted of two sentences. The first addressed the patient in a simple, concrete, direct way, asking her not to leave treatment. The second took the form of a verse of poetry—it was metaphorical, affect-laden, and dramatic. It shared the need for love existing in both patient and analyst. I believe that the statement conveyed a clear emotional message, and the tone of my voice, impregnated with affects, enhanced its impact. Perhaps my words and the way they were spoken functioned as a "sonorous bath" (Lecourt 1990), creating an association between touch and hearing. In contrast to insight, which is the outcome of a correct interpretation, my intervention resulted in a feeling. While insight correlates with seeing, feeling correlates with touching. It was only through this emotional "touching" that the patient felt it was worth her while to remain in analysis.

Patients seem to vary considerably in their capacity to comprehend the full implications of single interpretations. In this case, there was a single interpretation that had a major impact on the continuation of the analytic process. I believe that the emotional impact of the intervention described earlier prevented the patient from enacting her destructive and self-destructive tendencies, because she was willing to continue with analysis. Deborah's ability to get in touch with her feelings was the result of the long working through that ensued. The fact that every interpretation logically implies a number of other interpretations is important in considering the process of interpreting during the course of an analysis, since each interpretation can thus be seen as a member of an interpretative series (Rycroft 1986). In this case, the "interpretive action" was the beginning of a new series.

### Intervention as a "Moment of Meeting" (Stern et al. 1998)

The moment when I took the decision to intervene in an unusual way reminds me of the "now moment" (Stern et al. 1998), a "present moment" with a subjective quality that could alter the therapeutic relationship. The "now moment" forced me into a response that was novel to our habitual framework. Because at this moment I felt that I was at an impasse, but I also felt that I could seize it as an opportunity; it was a moment pregnant with anxiety as well as expectancy. The "now moment" occurred when the therapeutic frame was at risk of being broken. As described by Stern, it may have played a mutative role, since it implied an affective attunement and a cognitive reappraisal that stemmed from the newly created dyadic state.

### The Self-revealing Aspect of the Intervention

I am very much aware that the intervention described earlier was not only a commentary on my patient's deeper motivation, but it was also a self-revealing remark (Singer 1977). Renik claims that "anonymity for the analyst is impossible, not only complete anonymity but any anonymity at all" (1995, p. 468). Some authors claim that every intervention hides some things about the analyst and reveals others (Chused 1990; Greenberg 1991). In this case, I could give voice to the patient's longing for love without revealing my own longing for love. But the self-revealing aspect of the intervention made the patient realize that her hungry need for physical closeness and the pain and rage consequent to its lack resonated in me.

Only later in our work did we understand that underlying Deborah's unconscious wish to show me her vagina and to look at mine, was her deeper need for a mutual relationship in which she had to "discover" my feelings in order to get in touch with her own.

### The Psychic Equivalent of Touching by Means of Words in Analysis—Becoming an Emotional Surrogate

My verbal response to Deborah's need for love initially stemmed from my fear of her self-destructive tendencies. When the negative transference culminated in her threat of leaving treatment, I was aware of the implicit possibility of her becoming self-destructive if I were not to acquiesce in some way.

I therefore had to take a different course of action. I had to become an emotional surrogate, to offer her emotions to enable her to feel. To this end, it was not enough to use an "objective" interpretation (Gedo 1994), which named, in a kind of objective and neutral way, the feelings evoked in her in the transference (with or without linking them to emotions toward primary objects in the past). Instead, I had to "embody" the affective states by expressing them myself. Modell (1990) observed that in special moments in treatment it is virtually impossible to discern whether a specific insight originated with the analyst or with the analysand. Here, too, the statement I made belonged to both of us.

The loss of my separate individuality possibly began at the moment I attempted to render myself unconsciously receptive to being made use of. Unconscious receptivity of this sort (e.g., Bion's [1962/1989] state of "reverie") involves a partial giving over of one's separate individuality.

By becoming the patient's emotional surrogate, I made myself available to a new object relationship that facilitated some understanding and growth. Loewald has stated that new spurts of self-development may occur through the establishment of new object-relationships (1960, pp. 224–25). Grunes believes that a new object-relationship in therapy increases the patient's sense that "words do convey affectively alive experience and can also be experienced as expressions of volition and desire" (1984, p. 127; also cited in Reppen 1999). My view is that by becoming my patient's emotional surrogate, I responded intuitively to her regressive need for "primary love" (Balint 1968) from a primary object. Anzieu describes this eloquently: "It is only through his discourse that the analyst can touch his patient. Through the internal view of elaborating an interpretation, the analyst has to find words that are symbolic equivalents of what was missing in the tactile exchanges between the baby and the mother. Through these words, which involve the body of the psychoanalyst speaking on a pre-linguistic level, one can in fact touch the body of the patient" (1986, p. 86).

Because it became possible to work through my patient's demand for further gratification after I had met her need verbally, I could conclude that my response was necessary for turning the process that had begun in a malign form of regression—the craving for satisfaction—into a benign one—a "regression for recognition" (Balint 1968). By this I mean that Deborah was able to use my reaction to continue her internal dialogue.

### The Use of Words as a Means for Enhancing the Capacity to Feel

The use of a verbal interaction to overcome the unconscious self-limitation of the patient's capacity to experience being alive was an important factor in this case. The patient's deadness was expressed in the constriction of the range and depth of her feelings. By embracing this form of psychological deadness in order to avoid psychic pain, she sacrificed much vitality. Therefore, at a certain point in analysis I had to actively, and even passionately, find words to convey an emotional experience to her. These words were, in Ogden's poetic terms, not "lifeless effigies" but rather "living tissue" (1999, p. 5), and were intended to revive her inner deadness.

In this context I would like to quote Goethe who, in his play *Faust*, describes the yearning for the experience of being alive in the following way: "[A]nd I'm resolved my most inmost being shall share in what's the lot of all mankind that I shall understand their heights and depths, shall fill my heart with all their joys and grieves" (1808/1984, p. 46; also cited in Ogden 1999, p. 16). I believe that the analytic discourse in this case enhanced the capacity of the patient to experience the "joys and grieves" of human emotion.

### The Purpose of Manic Defenses

I would now like to return to the questions that I raised at the beginning of this chapter regarding the manic defenses that were the underlying issue in this case illustration. But I will first deal with Deborah's need for her manic defenses and the purpose they served in her life.

Kernberg (1975) pointed out that intense sexual strivings may prematurely develop in a child to deny frustrated oral and dependent needs. He emphasized that such development powerfully reinforces oedipal fears by pregenital fears of the mother, thus interfering with a positive Oedipus complex. Adult sexuality is then characterized by a sexualized search for the gratification of oral needs from an idealized mother, leading to homosexuality, as it shown by this case study.

Deborah used her homosexuality to deny gender and sexual differences. Freud (1927) believed that this kind of denial, together with the denial of castration and splitting of the ego, led to the formation of the perverse structure. Contemporary literature emphasized the omnipotence characterizing this defense. Chasseguet-Smirgel (1984) pointed to the omnipotent pretension inherent in denying the limits of sexual possibilities as a way of protecting oneself from the terrifying awareness of differences in gender and generation.

Deborah also used her homosexuality to deny an inner reality that was completely unacceptable to her. She fled from an internal reality filled with hatred and the repudiation of the maternal object, to an external reality in which there was an ideal maternal figure, embodied by a female lover. The "suspended animation" (Winnicott 1935)—the attempt to omnipotently control the bad internal object by denying its existence through the flight to this kind of external reality—obstructed her relationship with her children, husband, and close friends. As a result, Deborah was unable to experience warm feelings; she felt dead inside and her world became an emotional desert. Deborah's frantic search for a homosexual partner can be seen, in Kahn's (1979) words, as a compulsive attempt to conceal and partially substitute for the absence of the feeling of being alive. By means of this manic defense, she even tried to reverse the deadness into aliveness, but without much success. Using homosexuality, Deborah tried to create a sense of her self, though at the expense of the self, and her sexuality remained fragmented and infantile (McDougall 1978, 1986). Deborah's compulsive desire for a homosexual partner could also reflect the need to convert her own infantile trauma into an adult triumph (Stoller 1975). From Kohut's (1971, 1977) point of view, this was a desperate attempt to reestablish the self's integrity and cohesion in the absence of an empathic response from an important other.

## What Can We Hope to Achieve by Means of Psychoanalysis in a Case Where Homosexuality Is Used as a Manic Defense?

The analysis of this case shows the great difficulty in giving up homosexuality when it is used as a manic defense against fragmentation and psychic death. Nevertheless, we see that some important changes did indeed occur in this case.

A change occurred as a result of Deborah's working through her conflicting attitude toward her maternal introject, the "dead mother" (Green 1986) who, herself tremendously threatened by emotions, had prohibited the emotional life of the daughter. Deborah had to part from this castrated, as well as castrating, maternal representation in order to become emotionally alive and also to be able to appreciate the positive elements in her life. Her separation from her mother also led to the diminishing of her self-destructive, ego-alien tendencies, which stemmed from her interminable emotional frustration.

Another change was Deborah's increased ability to deal with the anxiety ruling her inner world, which resulted in her abandoning her frantic search for a homosexual partner. In her interesting paper "Womanliness as a masquerade," Riviere claimed that "what appears as homosexual or heterosexual character-traits, or sexual manifestations, is the end result of the interplay of conflicts and not necessarily evidence of a radical or fundamental tendency. The difference between homosexual and heterosexual development results from differences in the degree of anxiety" (1929, p. 303).

Deborah did not give up her homosexual identity; she continued to feel attracted to women, but, and this was the greatest change, she became sufficiently in touch with her emotions to appreciate what she had in life.

As a result, she was able to give up her manic defense—her frantic search for a homosexual relationship, the purpose of which was to mask her inner emotional deadness.

What is the role of the analyst in such cases? It is now widely accepted that analysis of deviant sexuality is not so much a matter of decoding and interpreting fantasies, anxiety, or unconscious defenses that are acted out or represented in this kind of activity, but rather a matter of understanding and interpreting the transference phenomena constructed on the basis of the patient's internal world (Meltzer 1973; Ogden 1996). I believe that in cases in which sexuality is uncoupled from its "natural" goals and serves mainly as a manic defense against fragmentation and psychic death, the analyst should use his countertransference feelings in a way that can help the patient feel more alive and whole. However, I have great doubts about the possibility of achieving a complete change in such cases. The relinquishment of manic defenses may threaten the patient's fragile psychic survival, and fragmentation and psychic death may be experienced as imminent. In the present case I had to reappraise my goals and accept that a compromise solution was the only solution acceptable to my patient. The treatment enabled Debora to be in touch with feelings without giving up her homosexual identity. Far from solving all of her problems, Deborah nevertheless emerged from the treatment better equipped to face life as well as her homosexual conflict.

**II**

# UNRESOLVED MOURNING AND ITS BEARING ON SOCIETY

# Introduction

Mourning is an individual phenomenon as well as an enduring group phenomenon. Group mourning, collective mourning, is a complex phenomenon, because the group is not simply a collection of individuals but the product of a combination of different characteristics.[1]

Volkan (1992) explored the phenomenon of collective mourning from the perspective of large-group psychology. He stated that large groups, like individuals and families, mourn too. Members of a group who share the same loss collectively go through a similar psychological mourning process. As with individual mourning, the work of collective mourning helps the group accept reality, adapt to the shared losses, and continue life.

Traumatic events, which exacerbate feelings of humiliation and helplessness and which can cause post-traumatic stress disorder (PTSD), interfere with the initiation or adaptive accomplishment of the work of mourning. Volkan claims that the influence of a severe and humiliating calamity that directly affects all or most of a large group forges a link between the psychology of the individual (his individual mourning) and that of the group (collective mourning).

Chapter 4 attempts to illustrate this link by integrating the analysis of a Romanian patient's unresolved mourning over the loss of primary objects and migration to another country with an examination of the unresolved mourning of Romanian society. Romania's societal mourning was largely due to the loss of its corrupt leader, who in the collective unconscious represented a father figure. The mourning stemmed also from the ideological migration of Romanian society from Communism to a Westernized society.

Groups, like individuals, struggle against feelings of pain and mourning. Groups may avoid mourning by transmitting feelings of pain, shame, and guilt from one generation to another. This phenomenon occurs when, in the wake of a traumatic event, the mental representation of it that is common to all members begins to take shape. This mental representation is the consolidated collection of the shared feelings, perceptions, fantasies, and interpretations of the event. Also included in the mental representation are mental defenses against painful or unacceptable feelings and thoughts. When mental representations become so burdensome that members of the group are unable to initiate or resolve the mourning, their traumatized self-images are passed down to later generations in the hope that others may be able to mourn and resolve what the previous generation could not (Volkan 1991, 1992, 1997, 1999, 2002; Volkan and Itzkowitz 1994).

Chapters 5, 6, and 7 deal with the transmission of trauma in cases of Holocaust survivors and their offspring. This phenomenon is primarily the outcome of the survivor parents' unresolved mourning, which is transmitted to the offspring. In this regard Barocas and Barocas (1979) state: "They [children of survivors] seem to share an anguished collective memory of the Holocaust in both their dreams and fantasies, reflective of recurrent references to their parents' traumatic experiences. These children wake up at night with the terrifying nightmares of the Nazi persecution, with dreams of barbed wires, gas chambers, firing squads, torture, mutilation, escaping from enemy forces and fears of extermination" (p. 331).

The clinical chapters on this topic attempt to deepen our understanding of two distinct methods used by Holocaust survivors' offspring in their endeavor to deal with the pain and mourning transmitted to them by their parents:

1) a substitute-for-mourning mechanism called *enactment*
2) a reparative defense of creative activity

The transformation of enactment into mental representations and the elaboration of creative activity in therapy enable differentiation between the parent's story and that of the offspring and facilitates mourning.

## NOTES

1. In "Groups psychology and the analysis of the ego," Freud (1921) distinguished between individual psychology—that is, concerns of the individual that relate to the gratification of and defenses against instinctual drives and wishes— and group psychology. Freud began by examining the late-nineteenth-century theories of the French sociologist Gustave Le Bon, who postulated that an individual within a group loses much of his distinctiveness and acts instead in accordance with the homogeneous urges that unite the group (p. 234). Freud stated that the group was different from the sum of its parts.

# 4

# Romania and Its Unresolved Mourning

*I would give all the landscapes of the world for that of my childhood. I must add, though, that if I make a paradise out of it, only the tricks of infirmity of memory can be held responsible.*

E. M. Cioran 1982, p.12; quoted in Amati-Mehler et al. 1993 and quoted in S. Akhtar 1999, p.89

In this chapter, I explore the phenomenon of delayed mourning due to migration, both on an individual level and on a societal level. While migration is the more general term, strictly speaking, to *emigrate* means to leave one's country and to *immigrate* is "to come to a country of which one is not a native, for the purpose of permanent residence" (Urdang 1968). I will first describe the phenomenon of delayed mourning for primary objects due to migration on an individual level, basing it on a therapeutic encounter between a patient who had just emigrated from Romania to Israel and a Romanian-born Israeli analyst. I will then examine the unresolved mourning of Romanian society, which was transplanted from one culture to another by means of its transition from a Communist dictatorship to the post-Communist era—another form of migration. This unresolved mourning was also expressed through the longing of many Romanians for their infamous leader, Nicolae Ceausescu, who functioned as a mental representation of a father figure. The longing is a clear indication that his followers internalized his image and therefore found it difficult to change their identification with this leader, even long after he disappeared. In Romania, the influence of Nicolae Ceausescu continued to have far-reaching effects years after his execution (Volkan 1998).

## AN IMMIGRANT PATIENT AND AN ANALYST OF THE SAME NATIONAL ORIGIN

Anna, a young doctor specializing in psychiatry, had emigrated from Romania to Israel several months before she was referred to me. Anna had completed her medical studies in Bucharest and was now completing her internship in a psychiatric hospital in Israel.

In the first session, Anna told me that she was referred to me by the senior psychiatrist of the locked ward where she was working. This psychiatrist, a woman who had also emigrated from Romania to Israel many years ago, befriended her and tried to help Anna adjust to her new country. Anna had been feeling quite depressed since her immigration to Israel, and she derived strength from their friendship. Lately, their conversations had revolved around having children, since Anna, although married for seven years had not yet tried to conceive a child. These conversations aroused much sadness in Anna, who claimed that she was not fit to have children of her own. It was in response to this that the friend suggested the possibility of therapy. Anna accepted the idea with the request that the therapist speak her own mother tongue. The psychiatrist friend then referred her to me.

Although initially hesitant about conducting analysis in Romanian because of my lack of fluency in the professional terminology of the language (I had emigrated from Romania as a child), I agreed to do it, because it is nonetheless my mother tongue, and I thought that it could be an enriching experience for us both.

Anna was a pretty woman in her early thirties. She had brown hair and brown eyes, an expressive face, and a feminine demeanor. Anna spoke to me in Romanian, and I was impressed by her sophisticated and beautiful use of the language.

From the very start of therapy, using my mother tongue had a strong emotional impact on me. I felt excited and somewhat intimidated. My mastery of the Romanian language is relatively good, so I am often told. But relative to whom? I now asked myself this question while listening to Anna. Relative to a twelve-year-old child, the age at which I had illegally emigrated from Romania together with my parents, I silently answered myself. I had not forgotten the language, since it was the language I had spoken at home with my parents in Israel throughout my adolescence, but I had never acquired a more sophisticated Romanian in adulthood.

I was aware that my feeling of intimidation stemmed from a very deep personal experience from childhood that echoed inside me from our first encounters. The Romanian language represented a world of purely private experiences for me. The story in the family was that although my parents spoke German at home, I preferred to speak Romanian, which I had learned from my nanny. The nanny was a very devoted Christian Adventist who had taken care of me as a child and had showered me with love.

Although I have conducted analyses in foreign languages that I learned to speak later in life, nothing was further from my professional world than the language of my childhood and adolescence. Would I be able to conduct analysis in this language, so distant from my professional work? It became clear to me that by accepting my patient's terms, I had lost the asymmetry necessary for a therapeutic relationship (Zac de Filc 1992). Moreover, my simple, unsophisticated language placed me in the position of a child, especially when confronted with the elegant language of my "grown-up" patient. I began to wonder whether this unusual situation, in which the therapist finds him- or herself linguistically disadvantaged, with all its emotional implications, might not have a negative effect on the treatment. What had I compromised by accepting, albeit with some misgivings, my patient's request, I asked myself. On the other hand, didn't my patient have a right to treatment, in spite of being a new immigrant to this country and not having command of the local language? Did I have the right to condemn her to silence and a childless fate, without giving her the opportunity to struggle against it?

I will not describe the entire course of this long and complex analysis. Instead, I will focus upon Anna's identity problem, which had become even more pronounced as a result of her immigration to Israel. I will then deal with the working through of her incomplete mourning for her parents, the postponement of which had been aggravated by her immigration.

From the beginning of her treatment, I was aware of Anna's nostalgia for the country she had left behind. Anna's memories centered more on places than on people. She recalled the houses, cafés, street corners, hills, and countryside of her homeland. During her sessions, my office was filled with the colors, sounds, and smells of places familiar to both of us from our childhoods. This made me understand why Anna wanted to talk to me in her mother tongue. She wanted to share her very early experiences of a place that she hoped was familiar to me from my own childhood. Anna was looking for a special kind of understanding.

The therapeutic relationship that emerged helped Anna, toward the end of the first year of analysis, disclose an extremely important secret to me. Anna spoke in depth about her feelings of estrangement in Israel. I could easily identify with this, remembering my own feelings of uprootedness and vulnerability as a new immigrant. The reason that Anna gave for feeling so foreign was unexpected: "I am not Jewish. I do not belong here," she said. "Nobody knows about this; it is a secret." I was very surprised indeed. If there is a typical Jewish appearance, Anna had it. It fleetingly occurred to me that her brown hair and beautiful brown eyes would have definitely endangered her life during the Holocaust.

The story that followed revealed that Anna and her husband had had a considerable struggle to get out of Romania. Since at that time this privilege of leaving Romania was given only to Jews, she and her husband searched for a Jewish connection. Anna's husband discovered that his mother's first husband was Jewish. This fact, in addition to a heavy bribe paid to the Romanian officials, enabled the couple to obtain the false papers necessary for being considered Jewish, thus enabling them to immigrate to Israel.

My gut reaction to Anna's story was the wish to console her. "Who cares whether you are Jewish or not?" I wanted to say to her. However, aware that my impulse to deny Anna's feelings of being a stranger probably stemmed from my own painful memories as a child in Romania, I kept quiet.

My first memory evoked by Anna's story was that of the complicated world of a Jewish child from a rabbinic family growing up with a Christian Adventist nanny, who faithfully took me to Adventist services on Friday afternoons (of course, without my parents' knowledge!). I remember loving Jesus and the beautiful pictures and sculptures of him. How great was my frustration when I discovered that, being Jewish, Jesus was not our God! Also, growing up among Christian Orthodox children I learned that we, the Jewish people, were accused of having killed Jesus and were therefore damned forever. My Hebrew name made the fact that I was Jewish, and thus a foreigner, obvious to everyone.

On the other hand, I remembered that coming to Israel, the country we had longed for, and living among Jewish people, did little to alleviate my feelings of being an outsider. In the new country, children looked and behaved differently; they spoke a language totally foreign to me. It took a long time for me to feel at home, and I never completely acquired the sense of belonging that I had so desired.

Based on my countertransference feelings, I asked Anna if she thought that her feelings of being a foreigner stemmed from immigrating to Israel. Anna reflected and said quietly, "Actually, I have felt a stranger all my life." Anna added that in her neighborhood in Romania there were many German-speaking people as well as Jews, and as a result, she understood both German and Yiddish. "I always admired the Jewish people and wanted to live among them. They are clever and witty," she said, smiling.

What a strange world, I thought to myself. As a child I wanted to belong to the Christian majority, which I felt was all-powerful, and Anna wanted to belong to the Jewish minority, which she imagined was superior. This childhood experience that we both shared, a longing to belong to another nationality, had an impact on me as well as on the therapeutic relationship. I realized that, as children, we unconsciously longed for a happier, better-integrated family, and we projected the qualities of strength of body and mind onto each other's ethnic group. Based on my own realization, I pointed out to Anna that she perhaps had always wished to have a happier family, and that she imagined this family to be Jewish.

Anna was able to accept this interpretation, which facilitated the further working through of the painful love-hate relationship that characterized her attitude toward her own family. We first elaborated upon the feelings that accompanied the loss of her parents. She recounted at length her mother's terrible suffering and death; her mother had died of brain cancer when Anna was twenty-one. Anna and her older sister lived with their mother, who devoted her life to the care of her daughters. Her parents divorced when Anna was around twelve years old. She witnessed many violent quarrels between her parents, and always felt that she had to protect her mother from her brutal father. She remembered the bitter day when her father left home and moved to the city. He was a well-known musician with many women friends. Her poor mother worked long hours as a cashier in a store and was barely able to support her children. Her dream was that her daughters would have an education and Anna, the brilliant medical student, fulfilled her mother's dream. Anna was very attached to her mother and did everything she could to make her happy.

When she was an adolescent, Anna occasionally visited her father. Anna liked him; he was very charming and seductive. He took her to concerts where he presented her as his young mistress and invited her to restaurants with his friends. After a while, her father became very depressed. He became an alcoholic and abandoned his work at the orchestra. Two years after her mother's death he was found dead in his apartment, probably as a result of alcohol and drugs.

During the year of her mother's illness, Anna took constant care of her. Though trying hard to study as well, she was unable to concentrate. Her mother died and Anna failed her final exams.

Anna left home after her mother's death and moved to the city. Her sister was already married with children. Anna felt completely abandoned and was unable to mourn her mother or, later, her father. She had an unhappy affair with a man she did not love, followed by an abortion. Anna was depressed, unable to continue her studies or find work.

In the midst of this chaotic, fragmented life, she regained control of her faculties and decided to reregister at the university to retake the courses she had failed. There, she met a young man, her future husband, who gave her much love and support. The relationship had parental aspects that Anna very much needed. She loved her husband, and they decided together to immigrate to Israel and build a new life.

Anna's maternal grandmother, who lived in Romania, died while Anna was in analysis. This event put Anna in touch with a great deal of grief and pain. Working through this powerful outburst of mourning in analysis made Anna aware that she had never actually mourned her parents. Anna expressed a wish to visit her parents' graves, as well as that of her grandmother, to whom she had been very attached. I felt that Anna had to go back to her country of origin in order to complete her work of mourning. She had to mourn her lost beloved ones, as well as the parts of her own self that had remained there. Anna longed to see the color of the trees, the familiar streets and houses, and her childhood home. She also wanted to visit her sister and family, to bring them presents from Israel, and to bring back some of her personal belongings that she had left behind. In analysis, I felt that Anna was asking me to give her the courage and support to undertake the visit.

When Anna returned to analysis three weeks later, after her visit, she looked different. The depression that had accompanied her before was gone, and it was replaced by a statement of loss and pain. During this period, we were able to work through her love and longing for her mother, as well as her anger at being abandoned by her when she was so young and helpless. We discovered that behind the bitterness toward her abandoning father were feelings of pity and sorrow, as well as love and admiration.

Much psychic work was needed for the completion of Anna's work of mourning. The elaboration on the visit to her parents' graves, its emotional meaning, and the separation from her parents preoccupied us for an entire year. At the end of this year, Anna came to her session smiling and asked me if I was ready for a surprise. Radiant with happiness, she broke the good news: "I am pregnant," she said, "and it took me only one month."

Anna was elated, and I rejoiced in her happiness. I accompanied Anna through her pregnancy, which included all of the normal anxieties and expectations of a young mother. Knowing that she would have a boy, she raised the question of circumcision. (Jewish males are circumcised at the age of eight days, this being considered a sign of the covenant between the God of Israel and his people.) In the end, she made her decision: "I want my boy to be circumcised. He lives in this country, and he will be like everyone else." Her husband was of the same opinion.

When her analysis ended some months later, Anna promised to come back and visit me sometime. She indeed came to see me two years later with a most adorable toddler. She had completed her internship, had begun working as a psychiatrist, and the family's economic situation had improved. She had recently heard from some colleagues that I was planning to go to Bucharest for work and she was very excited about that. "I would very much like to go with you, to take you around, to help you there," she said. "You helped me go back and find myself. You gave me a lot and I would have liked to reciprocate," she added in her beautiful, elegant Romanian.

In the autumn of that year, thirty-six years after leaving the country, I returned to Romania in a professional capacity. A colleague met me at the airport and, at my request, we immediately set out to find my childhood home. We reached my old neighborhood that was so familiar to me, and

I easily found my way around. I looked at the houses, churches, and streets that were imprinted upon my memory and walked about as if in a dream.

When I arrived at the square where my parents' house was supposed to be, I was struck by the strange sight that unfolded before my eyes: The left-hand side of the square looked the same as I remembered it, but the right-hand side, where our house once stood, had changed completely. Stunned, I stood in front of the square, asking myself over and over again, "But where is the house? Where is it?" My colleague, who had already warned me that parts of Bucharest had completely disappeared during the rule of Nicolae Ceausescu, patiently explained to me what I already knew. Ceausescu, the former dictator of Romania, had destroyed entire neighborhoods; beautiful historical buildings and churches that had given the city its very special character had been torn down indiscriminately. In their place, architectural monsters had been erected, their ugly grandiosity reminiscent of the Fascist era, as well as of Ceausescu's megalomaniacal wishes, ruthlessness, and oppression.

The same traumatic experience confronted me when I attempted to find my grandparents' house. The house, which had also served as a synagogue in the Jewish community and in which I had lived until the age of four, held some of my earliest memories. I still remembered the sun shining through the leaves of the tree in the big yard where I played. I also remembered the Torah scroll in the synagogue, as well as my grandmother's big kitchen where, as a young child, I enjoyed cooking with her. This house had been the container of feelings of warmth and love, and my memories of it had served as a source of strength and courage during difficult moments of my life.

Staring at the new surroundings for some time, I realized that both my parents' and grandparents' houses had vanished into thin air. Feelings of anger overwhelmed me. After working them through, they gave way to feelings of sorrow. I felt as if the houses were parts of myself that were irretrievably lost. I became aware that, although I had done much work of mourning throughout my life, it was far from complete. Working through my mourning, I thought often of Anna, my Romanian patient. I realized the impact that the treatment had had on both of us. Not only had I helped Anna in the search for her self but, by assisting her on her journey back to her homeland, I myself was better prepared for the visit back to my birthplace. Thus, Anna's wish to accompany me on my journey back to my country of birth was realized, at least in fantasy.

## THOSE WHO STAYED BEHIND—AN EMIGRANT SOCIETY

In January 2001, my book *The Cry of Mute Children*, which deals with the understanding and treatment of second-generation Holocaust survivors, appeared in Romanian, published by Editura Trei (Kogan 1995). The book's main themes are, first, the transmission of trauma from one generation to another and, second, the creation of hope and the reconstruction of the self-image. I feel that these two themes are relevant to Romanian society and to anyone whose life has been touched by the reality of war, violence, and trauma. The Romanian people suffered the trauma of living under a dictatorship that ruled by terror and violence. Not only did they live lives of sheer misery, but they had also been humiliated and infantilized. In my encounters with local Romanians, I have seen a lack of self-assurance, a derogatory attitude toward themselves, and a lack of belief in their ability to create a better future. The many years of oppression and terror left a deep imprint on their psychic make-up.

Over the past few years I have taken an active part in the establishment of the Psychotherapy Center for the Treatment of the Child and Adolescent in Bucharest, the first of its kind in Romania. Here is how this center came into being: On one of my visits to Romania in a professional capacity, to work with Romanian therapists, I was met at the airport by a colleague, Vera Sandor. It was December, the trees were covered with a heavy blanket of snow, and there was a thin layer of ice on the ground, which I was told was very slippery and dangerous. During our ride from the airport, I was deep in thought, looking at the beautiful patterns that the snowflakes created on the windscreen, patterns that reminded me of scenes from my childhood. At a traffic light, I saw a small dark figure banging on the window. Startled, I asked Vera, "What is that?" "A street child," she replied calmly. Then she went on to explain about the life of street children, which I was familiar with only from Western literature on Romania.

The traffic light changed, and we drove off. However, the face of that little child continued to haunt me for a long time.

It was during this visit that Vera talked about her dream of setting up the Psychotherapy Center for the Treatment of the Child and Adolescent in Romania. "There are houses for street children, but they usually run away from them. We should find better ways to deal with that, but it is also vital that we prevent others from becoming street children. As you know, there are lots of families in Romania with problematic children who are not on the streets, and these children have no place to turn for help," she said. This is very true, I thought, and I wondered what was happening to those children who did have families, food, and clothing, but who were also suffering from psychic problems. Their future is grim, and they may end up becoming thieves, criminals, psychotics, or drug addicts. Shouldn't we use our knowledge and experience to avoid such catastrophes that could affect their lives and the shape of an entire society?

Leaving Romania for Hamburg to work with my colleague and friend Professor Peter Riedesser, I shared with him the dream of setting up such a center in Bucharest. Peter, a man of vision, enthusiastically became part of this enterprise.

I will not go into the details of the long journey we both made in order to realize this dream. Suffice it to say that after the many difficulties and disappointments that we encountered along the way, there were people who had faith in our work and goals, and who helped us set up the center in Bucharest.

During my many subsequent visits to Romania, I supervised the work of the staff as well as the center's activities and goals, and I learned how Romanian society had reacted to the abrupt change from a totalitarian Communist regime to a Western lifestyle. Discussions with friends, colleagues, and students showed me that the general feelings toward the totalitarian regime were disappointment, hatred, and impotence. In spite of this, the Romanian people still felt some yearning for the past. This phenomenon is frequently found in many countries that become westernized. What is unique about Romanian society is that it suffers from a state of unresolved mourning for a dictator who they themselves eliminated. This pathological mourning for old values and for the image of the lost dictator made it more difficult for Romanian society to integrate the new attitudes and values of the new era.

Entering a new era, Romanians were first forced to reevaluate old principles and adapt to different values. They could envision promising opportunities, but these were accompanied by alien, burdensome requirements. They had to abruptly exchange the rituals and teachings of a familiar culture for a new, unfamiliar situation (Kahn 1997).

In addition, the totalitarian Communist regime had stifled the initiative for private enterprise as well as the motivation needed to achieve a higher work ethic and a higher standard of living. The state had provided a secure, albeit very low salary for the people, independent of the quality of their work. There was equality in this situation, since a miserable, poor life was almost everyone's fate. Basic needs, such as health and education, were taken care of by the state. This infantilized the population, making them unable to take responsibility for their own lives.

The new post-Communist era also created turmoil in peoples' lives. Despite the promise of freedom and opportunity, the immediate reality required skills that had not been developed for a long time and a motivation to work, to which they were unaccustomed. The Romanian people also experienced narcissistic hurt when comparing their lives to life in the West and in particular to that of the other westernized countries of Eastern Europe; this was accompanied by feelings of shame and humiliation. In comparison with the West, their own living quarters and attire took on a shabbiness that they regarded with the embarrassment of the newly poor. For the most part, they still considered themselves incapable of coping in a competitive economy; they were embarrassed by their inexperience in carrying out the complex practices fundamental to the democratic process.

As a result of these changes, the Romanian people came to feel the humiliation of the breadwinner's vocational worthlessness in the workplace and resultant loss of status within his family. The purchasing power of their savings and their modest pensions became insignificant. From my encounters with the group that initiated the center, I learned that Romanian society looked upon the West with awe and suspicion. When I told this group about the efforts made in the West to help them construct the center, they asked fearfully, "Why do they want to do this for us?" I then realized that one of my first roles would be to serve as a bridge to the West, one that would allow the people to build a future relationship of trust.

## DISCUSSION

In my discussion, I first focus on the impact that emigration had on the sense of identity and the mourning process of the patient described in the first part of this chapter. I then briefly relate this process to mourning processes on a societal level.

The capacity to maintain a sense of consolidated identity (sameness amid change) was first noted by Erikson (1950, 1956). More recently, Stern (1985), through his recent concept of "self-history" (i.e., a sense of continuation with one's subjective past), refers to this same capacity. In trying to clarify the concept of identity, Akhtar (1999) has noted that individuals with a solid identity retain genuine ties with their past while comfortably locating themselves in their current reality.

The drastic alteration of external reality resulting from migration from one country to another produces a profound psychic flux and has an impact on an individual's identity. Loss of familiar landscape, music, food, language, and customs mobilizes pain and mourning (Grinberg and Grinberg 1989). Such mourning and "culture-shock" (Garza-Guerrero 1974) cause a destabilization of identity, and it takes considerable time and intrapsychic work to settle and restabilize itself. However, in instances where the preemigration character structure is problematic, where the intrapsychic separateness did not exist before emigration, the consolidation of identity may be hindered all the more.

In the case of Anna, the patient came to treatment with conflicts that had already afflicted her sense of identity. As a child, her ethnic or national self-representation was laden with shame and she idealized the Jewish identity. When she became an immigrant in Israel, she felt as vulnerable as a child and her devaluation of her country of origin as well as of her own self was reinforced. Much psychic work was needed to change this devaluating attitude, which stemmed from early traumatic experiences as well as from her incomplete work of mourning.

Anna suffered not only the loss of her mother and father; by emigrating, she also lost the support she had drawn from the familiar climate and landscape, unconsciously perceived as the extension of the mother. Her wish to return for a visit to her native land, which emerged in analysis, was very much linked to her longing for lost primary objects as well as the need to give them up and build a life of her own. Revisiting her parents' graves helped her achieve this aim and held great psychic significance for her (Akhtar and Smolar 1998). By bringing back gifts to relatives left behind and by bringing some of her personal belongings back with her to her new home, Anna made the first attempts at separation, like a toddler in the rapprochement phase.

Before she began analysis, the patient had not yet given up primary objects or familiar places through the work of mourning, nor assimilated them in the ego through identification. This resulted in a temporal "fracture of the psyche" (Akhtar 1999). One of the aims of her analysis was to help her put together the different fragments of her psyche, as well as the various "pieces of her life" (Pfeiffer 1974). The "holding relationship" (Kogan 1995, 1996, 1998, 2000, 2002) in analysis helped her mobilize forces and go back and face the "mental pain" (Freud 1926) incurred in the acknowledgment of her losses. This dynamic shift helped Anna continue her work of mourning in analysis.

Working through feelings of idealization and anger toward her lost objects facilitated the possibility of meaningful living. This helped her transform a devalued self-representation into a new self-representation, as a resident of her "adopted" country. The search into the past and the attempt to complete the work of mourning facilitated the creation of a sense of future that, in this case, was expressed through the creation of a child.

The "sonorous wrapping" (Anzieu 1976) of the treatment conducted in our native language had an impact on Anna, as well as on myself. It connected us both to the early maternal image and to early childhood experiences. For the patient, and for myself as well, migration had caused a ruptured self-experience, which was mended by the emotional refueling of revisiting the native country. From this point of view, we both emerged from this analysis with better-integrated selves.

On the societal level, the temporal "fracture of the psyche" caused by the incomplete work of mourning, is a phenomenon that characterizes Romanian society as a whole. The people belonging to this society were not forced to relocate. No one had to leave home. Romanians were neither forced to cross the borders of their country nor give up their mother tongue. They did not have to part from their families, or bid farewell to their friends and neighbors. They did not have to learn a new language, get used to new customs, eat strange food, or find new friends. In spite of this, through my acquaintance with Romanian society due to my work as a psychoanalyst in that country, I realized that emotionally they were immigrants, people transplanted from one culture to another. The loss of the old cultural environment threatened established identifications and the ensuing self-image, and was followed by mourning that has not been completely resolved even today.

The great disparities between their lives before and after the fall of

Communism, as well as the abruptness of the change, left people yearning for what they had left behind. In this new situation, which had its uncomfortable and painful aspects, many felt nostalgic for the past Communist ideals, and even dared to secretly express a longing for the lost dictator. The corruption, betrayal, and terrorization by the former Communist government were partially experienced as an idealized parent who had been exposed as corrupt or inhuman. The experience of loss of the old culture intensified, accompanied by anxiety, hostility, and a "sense of discontinuity of identity" (Garza-Guerrero 1974). The destruction of former identifications, as well as the loss of the accustomed life, brought with it depression and feelings of loneliness. The prolonged despair was due in great part to the difficulty of working through processes of mourning.

Freud defined mourning as "the reaction to the loss of a loved person, or to the loss of some abstraction which has taken the place of one, such as one's country, liberty, an ideal and so on" (1917, p. 243). For the individual, mourning is an obligatory psychobiological process. In normal situations, if someone dies, we have to do much work to let that person die psychologically. Without going through the work of mourning, we cannot genuinely accept the reality that something is lost. And if the lost person is needed for our psychological well-being, or if he or she forms a part of our own ego-ideal (Joffe and Sandler 1965; Sandler, Holder, and Meers 1987), we may slip into a state of pathological mourning.

Romanian society was for a long time marked and characterized by unresolved mourning for their dreadful leader, Nicolae Ceausescu. Volkan (1998) convincingly bases his analysis of the relationship between Romanians and their dictator on Freud's (1913) psychoanalytic understanding of primitive man. Volkan claims that although the Romanians killed Ceausescu, they allowed him to live on in many ways—most important, through the actions and policies that followed his death. Their pathological mourning was expressed through the fact that they never eliminated the image of the leader (the father figure) but kept it alive through hatred as well as nostalgia.

Romanians rejoiced over the removal of their dreadful leader but after the initial excitement, most eventually felt that little had changed. Many considered the National Salvation Front (NSF) merely an anti-Ceausescu faction within the Romanian Communist Party and regarded the new regime simply as the replacing of one group of Communists with another.

The Romanian people never fully realized that, although the reign of Nicolae Ceausescu had ended, his "sons" had not only "murdered" him but also kept him alive. Having ruled the Romanian people for two decades, Ceausescu had become a part of them. With his death, a part of each Romanian also died (Grinberg 1964), but their shame of being associated with him and their hidden guilt for "killing" him had to be denied. However, through their identification with him they were also keeping the dictator alive.

In June 1990, nationalists launched a weekly publication called *Romania Mare* (*Great Romania*), a reference to the centuries-old traditional rallying cry of Romanian nationalists before Ceausescu's rise to power. The paper, which developed the largest circulation of any Romanian weekly newspaper, succeeded in keeping Ceausescu "alive" through an undisguised nostalgia for his regime. In the year 2000, the head of this weekly publication, Corneliu Vadim Tudor, became the head of the largest opposition party to the new government, almost endangering its existence. The party received a great number of votes, promising to "purify" Romania of the gypsy population, the Hungarian minority, and the Mafia, while emphasizing Romanian nationalism. Despite the fact that the NSF was reelected, the rejection of democracy by many Romanians and the longing for the past dictatorship became quite obvious. By identifying with the aggressor, the Romanians had internalized the image of the dreaded leader and made it part of themselves (Volkan 1998).

As in the case of my patient and myself, the efforts and willingness of my Romanian colleagues to accompany me on my journey back to my childhood may perhaps be viewed as an expression of their own need to search for their past in order to complete their own work of mourning.

# 5

# From Enactment to Mental Representation

Over the last twenty years I have dealt with the subject of intergenerational transmission of the Holocaust trauma and its impact on the lives of Holocaust survivors' offspring, approaching it from different angles. In this chapter, I focus on a substitute-for-mourning mechanism expressed through enactment (termed *concretization* by Bergmann [1982]). This phenomenon is often found in cases of children of survivors, especially in the initial stages of their analysis.

I first define enactment, and then discuss it within the context of the existing literature. I show the aspects of it that are unique to Holocaust survivors' offspring, highlighting its function of avoiding mourning and pain. I illustrate this with clinical material taken from some of the case studies that I have published (Kogan 1987, 1989, 1993, 1995). Finally, I offer some technical suggestions that may be used by analysts to help patients understand the origin of enactments connected to their parents' traumatic past and facilitate their road to mourning and to the achievement of a better integrated self.

## DEFINING ENACTMENT

*Enactment*, putting into action, is a nonverbal behavior that reflects what occurs between patient and therapist in the analytic situation, with the emphasis on the way the analyst participates in the process. This may be compared to acting out and acting in. *Acting out* is the attempt to avoid painful knowledge in treatment by means of acting instead of remembering and communicating. *Acting in* is defined as acting in the transference;

it may be the only way available to the patient to relive an experience and to convey it to the therapist. The fact that the term *enactment* was coined only during the last decade and a half (much later than the other two terms) reflects the development and change that took place in psychoanalytic thinking in this regard. Eshel (1998a) refers to these changes in her excellent review of enactment, which I briefly summarize below:

> Freud, who considered psychoanalysis to be a talking cure, regarded nonverbal activity as a problem in analysis. He believed that acting out (*agieren*) was an expression of resistance to remembering and communicating, thus constituting an obstacle to treatment (1905, 1914), as evidenced by the following statements: "The patient does not remember anything of what he has forgotten and repressed, but acts it out. He reproduces it not as a memory, but as an action; he repeats it, without, of course, knowing that he is repeating it" (1914, p. 150). But, further on in the same article, Freud indicated that he viewed acting out in a much more complex way than in his above description in that article. Apparently, he regarded it not only as resistance to treatment, but also as a way of remembering: "As long as the patient is in treatment, he cannot escape from this compulsion to repeat, and in the end we understand that this is his way of remembering" (1914, p. 150).

Freud's dual attitude to acting out has been dealt with by other psychoanalysts. For example, Etchegoyen (1991) agrees completely with Freud's earlier notion of acting out as resistance to treatment. On the other hand, Boesky views acting out as totally necessary for the working through process, which he believes "can never happen without acting out since in this sense the whole transference is 'acting out'" (1982, p. 43–44).

Toward the end of his life, becoming more aware of the close relationship existing between transference and acting out, Freud showed evidence of a more positive attitude toward acting out. He indicated that communicating through acting was at least as valid as communicating through remembering: "Another advantage of transference, too, is that in it the patient produces before us with plastic clarity an important part of his life story, of which he would otherwise have given us only an insufficient account. He acts it before us, as it were, instead of reporting it to us" (1940, p. 175–76).

This newer attitude of Freud's, as well as the more recent attempt in psychoanalytic literature to give greater legitimacy to acting in psychoanalysis, led to the appearance of two new concepts, *acting in* and *enactment*. These two concepts viewed acting in analysis as a way of remembering and expressing, and as a nonverbal way of communicating, rather than as a way of avoiding painful knowledge, as in the case of acting out.

Defined as "acting in the transference" or "acting in the analytic situation," acting in has been considered a useful concept by some analysts (Hinshelwood 1989). A problematic aspect of this concept, however, is that it is defined by a local or technical situation rather than by a theory or metapsychology (Etchegoyen 1991; Laplanche and Pontalis 1973). Consequently, a further concept was coined in the last decade—*enactment*. First suggested by Jacobs (1986), enactment was accepted as a far more useful concept than acting in, which was contaminated by the negative connotations involving resistance to treatment that were attributed to acting out. Enactment differs from acting out in that it is primarily an interactive concept, reflecting what occurs in the relationship between patient and analyst, and stressing the analyst's participation in the process (Schafer 1982).

With the continuing development of psychoanalytic thinking, the connection that was postulated between acting out and early, traumatic, nonverbal experiences reinforced the communicative aspect of this phenomenon. In cases of trauma, for example, acting out was seen as the expression of an inner experience. This connection between acting out and trauma was first made by Fenichel (1945), followed by Greenacre (1950, 1963), Bion (1962), Rosenfeld (1965), and Meltzer (1967). Kinston and Cohen linked acting out with trauma and "primary repression," seeing it as a manifestation of a "catastrophic, unthinkable, past-but-ever-present trauma and associated confusion, terror and hopelessness" (1986, p. 339).

I define enactment, in the context of the Holocaust, as a general term that includes the attributes of both acting out and acting in. In this sense, enactment may serve the purpose of avoiding painful knowledge and memory (similar to the objective of acting out), while at the same time it is the only way available to the patient to relive an inner experience that he wants to convey to the therapist (as in the process of acting in).

My usage of the concept enactment in the context of the Holocaust differs from that of analysts' who primarily stress its interactive aspects. These analysts believe that enactment (or *actualization*, as it is termed by Sandler and Sandler 1978) reflects what occurs in the relationship between patient and analyst and the analyst's part in the process (Schafer 1982; Chused 1991; McLaughlin 1992; Renik 1993; Jacobs 1991, 2000). I am defining enactment as the compulsion of Holocaust survivors' offspring to recreate their parents' experiences in their own lives through concrete acts. Thus, enactment refers only to the externalization of traumatic themes from the past and not to what occurs in the relationship between patient and analyst in the analytic situation.

## THE ROLE OF ENACTMENT

Children of survivors often carry their parents' unresolved mourning for their lost loved ones, and therefore engage in a variety of displacement mechanisms, which can be called "substitute-for-mourning" mechanisms (Bergmann 1982). One of these mechanisms is enactment, the function of which is the avoidance of psychic pain. In this sense, it is similar to the phenomenon of "pensee operatoire" (Marty and de M'Uzan 1963), which is defined as a restricted, pragmatic way of thinking about people and events, and implies a lack of emotional response to crucial moments or traumatic losses in the lives of the people concerned. In trying to avoid psychic pain, both enactment and pensee operatoire have the quality of acting out.

In cases of Holocaust survivors' offspring, enactment includes some aspects of manic defense, which are expressed through mechanisms of denial, omnipotence, and idealization. Enactment is expressed through symbolic, displaced actions, which are lived out with current objects, but are unconsciously addressed to lost loved ones. Shared fantasies of parents and children are concretized by the children, in the sense that they are grafted upon the environment and woven into current reality rather than verbalized. As long as fantasies are active, both parents and children can omnipotently deny that members of the parents' families were killed. Idealization of the dead often takes the place of mourning; archaic fantasies regarding the dead continue to exert an influence on affects and actions. Keeping the dead alive in fantasy necessitates enactment in a concrete way to prove that they are still alive. This kind of enactment leads to living in two realities, that of their parents' traumatic past as well as their own present reality.

Another aspect of enactment in cases of Holocaust survivors' offspring is expressed in the fusion of past and present, which is another form of denial of reality. In such cases, an individual causes another to act toward him in a certain way by imposing fantasies upon the relationship that are linked to the parents' traumatic past. Such enactment expresses a striving toward the realization of object-relationships with both real and fantasized objects. In this sense, enactment is a subcategory of actualization (Sandler and Sandler 1978), a process through which an individual, instead of verbally asking another person to fulfill his wish, causes that person to act in a certain way in order to fulfill it. It is thus similar to actualization in its wish fulfilling aspects, but it differs from it in that it applies only to traumatic themes from the past, which gives the need a particular urgency.

These enactments, especially those appearing in the first stages of analysis, constitute the patient's only means of reliving an inner experience that he or she wants to convey to the therapist. In this sense, enactments include the attributes of acting in, which can eventually be used to help the patient realize the origin of the fantasies that led to the enactment.

## THE SOURCE OF ENACTMENT

For children of survivors, there is no memory of a time when the Holocaust did not exist in their awareness, whether articulated or unconscious. The remembrance of the Holocaust is constructed out of materials or stories—those spoken aloud, told and retold, as well as those silently borne across a bridge of generations (Axelrod et al. 1978; Barocas and Barocas 1973; Kestenberg 1972; Klein 1971; Laufer 1973; Lipkowitz 1973; Rakoff 1966; Sonnenberg 1974; Laub and Auerhahn 1993; Auerhahn and Laub 1998; Brenner 2000). This remembrance marks those who carry it as secret bearers (Micheels 1985). Children who become burdened by memories that are not their own (Auerhahn and Prelinger 1983; Fresco 1984) often echo the dramas existing in their parents' inner worlds by enacting them in their own life (Krell 1979; Phillips 1978; Laub and Auerhahn 1984; Kogan 1995, 1998a). These often violent enactments involve an intermingling of death wishes with potentially dangerous situations (Kogan 1998b). In many cases, they are caused by persecutory anxieties that grow into delusional fantasies of paranoid proportions, anxieties that include a lack of differentiation between self and others, past and present, and inner and outer reality.

At the core of the compulsion to enact the parents' traumatic experiences in their own lives is a kind of identification with the damaged parent, which is termed *primitive identification* (Freyberg 1980; Grubrich-Simitis 1984; Kogan 1995, 1996, 1998). This identification leads to a loss of the child's separate sense of self and to an inability to differentiate between the self and the damaged parent. I find this phenomenon similar to the identification that takes place in pathological mourning. Freud (1917) described this identification as a process whereby the person in mourning attempts to possess the object by becoming the object itself, rather than bearing a resemblance to it. This occurs when the mourner renounces the object, while at the same time preserving it in a cannibalistic manner (Grinberg and Grinberg 1974; Green 1986). It is this type of identification that is at the core of the offspring's inability to achieve self-differentiation and build a life of his or her own.

The coexistence of the offspring's global identification on the one hand, and the denial or repression of the parents' trauma on the other—a coexistence present in many of these cases—creates a gap in the child's emotional understanding, a gap I have labeled a *psychic hole*. The psychic hole can be seen as a state in which conscious ignorance of the Holocaust (the hole) is one side of the coin, while unconscious knowledge of it is the other. In order to convey more vividly the meaning of the psychic hole, I will use a metaphor from the world of astrophysics—the phenomenon of the black hole. This term, reviewed by Eshel (1998b, p. 1115), is pregnant with meaning in psychoanalysis as well as in astrophysics.

I first define this concept as it appears in both fields. I then refer to various hypotheses regarding the way such a hole is formed, pointing out its uniqueness in cases of Holocaust survivors' offspring. In the world of astrophysics, the black hole is defined as a body that sucks into it all the forces of gravitation. It is described as a "region of space-time where infinitely strong gravitational forces literally squeeze matter and photons out of existence" (Penrose 1973; cited in Gribbin 1992, p. 142; cited in Eshel 1998b, p. 1115).

In psychoanalysis, the term *black hole* is used to describe the nature of early traumatizations caused by physical separateness from the primal mother, which lead to primitive mental disturbances. This concept was first applied clinically by Bion (1970) in reference to the infantile catastrophe of the psychotic. It was further developed by Tustin (1972, 1986, 1990, 1992) with regard to psychogenic autism of children and also by Grotstein (1986, 1989, 1990a, 1990b, 1990c, 1993) to psychotics and borderlines. As opposed to these authors, who were referring to mentally ill patients, Eshel (1998b) used the term metaphorically regarding individuals who seem to function in their social and professional life; in these cases, Eshel sees the black hole as the product of the impact of a "dead" parent, particularly the "dead mother" (Green 1986).

The psychic hole, as I see it, is also a body, as is the black hole of space; it is the encapsulation of all the fantasies regarding the parents' traumatic past, an encapsulation that has an impact on the patient's entire life. My usage of the term *psychic hole* differs from the formulations of Kinston and Cohen, who consider it to be an "absence of psychic structure" (1986, p. 338), or that of Laub and Podell, who define it as an "empty circle" (1995, p. 992). It does not belong to the category of blankness (negative hallucination, blank psychosis, blank mourning, all connected to what Green [1986] calls the problem of emptiness or the negative), or to Quino-doz's nonexistent "hole-object" (1996).

I believe that the psychic hole in cases of Holocaust survivors' offspring is formed in a different, quite unique way: It is created through the denial or repression of the trauma by the parents (a trauma that, by means of "primitive identification," the offspring attribute to themselves), as well as through the offspring's repression of the traces of the trauma. In cases in which parents have succeeded in working through the feelings of mourning and guilt connected to their traumatic past, and in conveying their history to their children in a healthier way, the children are much less likely to experience a psychic hole in their psychic reality.

Let us try to understand how the psychic hole was formed. Even in those families where a pact of silence prevails, a child would still be able to guess some of the details of the parents' severe traumatization. When cognitive development is sufficiently advanced, he or she will begin to investigate the parents' past. At this stage, the parents' wish to deny or repress the traumatic events could force them to unconsciously convey to the searching child that the object of their investigation is not something that really happened in their lives. Rather, it is the child's wicked thought, a bad dream, something that ought to be forgotten (Grubrich-Simitis 1984). Thus, the parents' redefinition of the traumatic events in their lives as something horrible emanating from the child's inner world, resulting both from what they tell the child as well how the child experiences it, makes the reality of the trauma unreal.

Through these processes, what was known or almost known becomes unknown. It is the unknown, or that which cannot be remembered, that becomes the source of the child's unconscious fantasies about his or her parents' traumatic past, and the compelling need to enact them in his or her present life.

I now present some examples of the enactment of delusions that stem from the "unknown" past of parents.

## CLINICAL EXAMPLES

### Rachel[1]

Rachel was the daughter of a man who had survived the Holocaust, but whose first wife and child had perished. Rachel's father kept the loss of his first family secret from his second wife and children. He never spoke about his bereavements and injuries, but worked hard and advanced himself. At the age of twelve, Rachel became anorectic. By means of her anorexia, she enacted a fantasy world belonging to her father's traumatic past: She attempted to starve herself and survive, just like the people who had survived the concentration camps (Kestenberg 1982).

At the age of thirty-one, Rachel went to Israel, where she fell in love with a painter who was on the verge of divorce. This man was the father of a two-year-old child whom he had left with his wife in another country. In choosing a man who had left his wife and small child in a faraway country, Rachel was attempting to reenact an aspect of her father's past in her own life.

The following episode of enactment, which occurred during Rachel's analytic treatment, illustrates her identification with the roles of victim/killer (belonging to her father's traumatic past) as well as the meaning of this enactment in therapy. Rachel had adopted a kitten that served as a substitute child for her. As she was planning to be out of town for a day, she cancelled her analytic session, locked the kitten in the bathroom, and left the heater on so it would not be cold. When she returned home, she found the animal lying dead near the heater. Rachel thought that since the kitten had recently suffered from diarrhea, it had died of dehydration from the heat. She buried it, thinking of the many soldiers who had died in battles. That night she forgot to turn off the gas heater in her living room. She awoke the following morning to a strong smell that made her aware that the gas had been on all night.

We attempted to understand this morbid episode of enactment through the transference relationship and in view of the impact of her father's traumatic past. Rachel identified with the kitten that was desperately searching for warmth. When I wasn't there for her, she burnt herself and dehydrated to death, thus becoming my victim. At the same time, she was also the murderess who killed the baby inside herself by putting it into the furnace. Through the enactment of this role, she was punishing herself by dying in a gas chamber, like those who died in the concentration camps. In the transference, the unconscious meaning of the enactment was that Rachel perceived me as a source of warmth and protection (the heater), as well as of destruction. Thus, when separated from me, she felt totally insecure and lost, but when reunited, she felt swallowed, absorbed, and threatened by the loss of her individuality.

Over the course of five years of analysis, we worked through—among other things—the details of her father's traumatic story, which Rachel had just discovered before beginning analysis, causing her to reenact his past in her own life. We elaborated upon her feelings of mourning and guilt, which belonged to her father and had been transmitted to her in nonverbal ways through the atmosphere prevailing in her home. The realization of the meaning of her enactments and their working through during later stages of analysis enabled Rachel to free herself from the burden of the past and build a life of her own.

## Hannah[2]

Hannah was a foreigner living in Israel who sought analysis because of feelings of derealization and an inability to cope with life. She was the daughter of a Holocaust survivor whose first wife had perished in the Holocaust and who had spent much of the war in hiding. He had suffered from masked depression throughout his life, and had never disclosed his past to his new family. But during the first year of analysis, Hannah heard through a cousin about his first wife and how she had died. The secret was at long last revealed to his wife and children, and Hannah's father donated a sum of money to an institution in Israel in his first wife's memory.

Following this, there were many episodes of enactment, which expressed Hannah's unconscious attempt to re-create the fate of her father's first wife in her current reality. Furthermore, the fact that she was living in Israel, surrounded by Arab hostility, was very much connected to her fantasies about her father's past. A description of one of her enactments follows.

Hannah rushed back to analysis from a trip to Europe in a state of panic and tremendous anxiety, and related that she was in great danger because "an Arab is after me." It turned out that she had met an elegantly dressed man in the lobby of her hotel, who appeared to her to be an Arab spy. Despite the fact that she did not have Israeli citizenship and that she had been living in Israel for only a few months, she immediately told him that she was an Israeli citizen. After going out together to dinner and a film, Hannah went with him to his room, where the two had sex without uttering a single word. Suddenly Hannah realized that she didn't even know his name, and panic-stricken, she immediately made up an excuse that she had to go to the toilet, dressed hurriedly, grabbed her handbag and left the room. Two hours later she was on a plane to Israel.

Upon arriving home, Hannah phoned the hotel where she had stayed to inform them that she had left a pair of shoes there, and gave her address so that the shoes could be forwarded to her. Immediately afterward she came looking for me in desperation, convinced that the "Arab spy" would pursue her.

Hannah connected this episode to the film *The Night Porter*, which she had seen many years before. She related that the film took place some time after the Nazi concentration camps had been liberated, and it described an encounter between a Jewish woman who had been imprisoned in a concentration camp as an adolescent and the Nazi officer who had been her tormentor there. In this encounter, the past prevailed over the present, and the protagonists, propelled by a force greater than themselves, resumed their concentration camp roles of victim and persecutor. The man sexually abused the woman, and then—unable to return to reality—killed her.

Attempting in the transference to understand Hannah's need to enact her unconscious wishes and fantasies related to her father's first wife (the psychic hole), I pointed out that she was assigning me the role of her savior, while attempting to bring this woman back to life by becoming her. But, I added, she was trying to kill her father's first wife by placing herself in danger of being killed by the Arab/Nazi.

During this phase of treatment, Hannah achieved some "affective understanding" (Freud 1915) of her enactments. Without my describing this phase in detail here, suffice it to say that, following the above-mentioned episode, and feeling supported by her analyst, Hannah plucked up the courage to question her father about his traumatic past. Their discussions produced an unexpected result. Concerned that he was nearing the end of his life, her father decided to write an autobiography, and asked Hannah to be his editor.

In analysis, we understood that by accepting this work, Hannah was demonstrating her readiness to become acquainted with concrete details of her father's trauma and, moreover, place it in a past that was not her own. Only then could we work through feelings of mourning and guilt that belonged to her father, which had been transmitted to her in nonverbal forms of communication. This long process of working through eventually enabled Hannah to achieve a better differentiation between herself and her father, between past and present, between reality and fantasy.

### Kay[3]

Kay was the stepdaughter of a Holocaust survivor who had been castrated by Mengele's doctors. Kay communicated with me (in the first phase of treatment) through infantile drawings. One of her pictures, bearing the title "Electricity," depicted a man with a wiry flower emerging from his head. Only at a later stage in analysis, when Kay was able to communicate with me verbally, were we able to understand her unconscious fantasy: The flower of death symbolized her stepfather's traumatic experience of having to avoid death by spending an entire cold night standing naked between the electric wires of the concentration camp.

Kay was referred to treatment after attempting to jump from the eighth floor of a building. In analysis, we were able to understand her attraction to death by jumping off high places as an attempt to enact the torment associated with her stepfather's survival and close encounters with death. For her stepfather, falling would have meant touching the wires, electrocution, and a horrible death. When Kay went up to the eighth floor, intending to throw herself out of the window, she was convinced that she would survive. Her delusional, paranoid fantasies of magically and omnipotently conquering death were endangering her life.

The following episode illustrates Kay's compelling need to enact the reparation of her stepfather's castration upon her own body. After my summer holiday, she informed me that she had undergone breast surgery during my absence. She stressed the fact that she had chosen to do it when I was away because she did not want to cancel her sessions after I returned home. Elaborating, she explained to me that the operation was the fulfillment of a wish she had had since she was young—to enlarge her breasts with silicone implants.

Kay had visited a doctor who examined her breasts, after which he described them as empty rather than small. He indicated that an operation was possible but was not without risks. She was warned of the possibility of her body rejecting the silicone, a condition that is accompanied by tissue inflammation, fever, and pain, and one that would necessitate further operations. She was told that she might never be able to breastfeed a child. Despite being terrified of these prospects, Kay nevertheless decided to go ahead with the operation. She was referred to a shop where she was measured for implants and selected them from a catalogue, choosing a medium size, which she felt would make her look much more like a whole woman.

Kay came to analysis on the appointed date, two weeks after her operation. She entered the room walking upright and, pulling her blouse against her breasts, asked if I could see any change. Only afterward, when lying on the couch, did she tell me the whole story. She was overjoyed and stressed her satisfaction with her ability to conquer her fears.

In my countertransference feelings, I felt a heavy weight burdening my heart. This made me aware that Kay was not in touch with her sadness, which was conveyed to me by massive projective identification. Attempting to understand what had compelled her to do this deed during my absence, I pointed out to Kay that she had begun feeling that her breasts were empty only when I was not around, when she wasn't getting the feeding and support from our regular sessions. Kay laughed a short laugh and then confirmed my hypothesis in an angry voice, "I don't need you; I don't need anybody. I want to depend only on myself."

I showed Kay that her need to "fill" her breasts stemmed from her anger and frustration at feeling abandoned by me. Gradually, she became aware of these feelings and accepted them. Working through these feelings in the transference led her to reveal her fantasies of flirting with death on the operating table. She had undergone the operation in order to repair her femininity, but thought she might die as a result. Of course, she now felt that she had once again overcome a terrible danger.

Kay associated her victory over possible death on the operating table with a story from her stepfather's life. After the war, he had met one of the few other men who had survived castration in the Mengele experiments. The man told Kay's stepfather about a Jewish doctor in Paris who performed restorative surgery on these people—that is, implantation of testicles—free of charge. Her stepfather decided to go to Paris and have the operation. It was successful and he was able to resume sexual relations with women, though he remained infertile.

Kay and I then began to find out what was filling her psychic hole, the unconscious fantasies that compelled Kay to enact her stepfather's life story on her own body. I pointed out to Kay that she might have been trying to implant her femininity into her breasts in the same way that her stepfather had had his manhood implanted into his empty testicle sacs.

A pregnant silence filled the room as Kay absorbed my words. Then, understanding the meaning of her choice to undergo surgery, she was overwhelmed by a powerful surge of emotion. It took us a long time to work through the feelings of fear, depression, and pain that replaced her euphoria. Furthermore, we tried to elaborate on the complex needs she had expressed through her deed. Consciously, she was trying to attain a better, repaired sexuality. Unconsciously, she was attempting to endanger herself in a concrete way, to come as close as possible to an imagined death in order to omnipotently overcome it.

Kay did not know many details of her stepfather's experiences during the Holocaust, because he kept them mostly to himself. The atmosphere at home was one of silence, concealing a past full of terror and violence. Her stepfather had been writing his memoirs of the Holocaust for the last twenty years, but Kay had never had the courage to ask to see them. In analysis, after working through her fear of discovering what had really happened to him, and encouraged by my supportive attitude, she decided the time had come to do so. To her great surprise and excitement, her stepfather sent her his complete autobiography, which he had dedicated to his adopted children. Kay read it avidly, and brought it to me so that I too could read it. I did that, feeling that I had to participate in this action; thus, I "actualized" (Sandler and Sandler 1978) her wish to make me her partner in "the search for the self through family secrets" (Gampel 1982).

The elaboration of this episode enabled us to begin an exploration of the way Kay had communicated with me during the first part of treatment, and the way she had lived her life until then, using her body to express unconscious fantasies pertaining to bodily sensations, anxieties, and emotions that were experienced by her stepfather during the Holocaust.

We could now understand her constant preoccupation with her body—physical fitness, weight, and muscle tone—as part of her survival complex. It was based on her unconscious fantasy that "I feel my body, therefore I exist."

All through her treatment, Kay complained at length about her defective sense of smell. Only now could we make the connection to her stepfather's story about the awful stench emanating from people dying in their excrement and vomit, not being able to make it to the public latrine. Thus, impairment of the olfactory sense became a survival mechanism for him. Kay's constant state of hunger, as well as her suffering from cold and her inability to find suitably warm clothing, were primary aspects of her stepfather's wartime experiences as well.

Kay had a fear of incontinence (which she showed by often running to the toilet during sessions). In this regard, she brought up a story of woe and humiliation from her stepfather's memoirs: "Father stood for hours at roll call, peeing in his pants, knowing that any movement could incur the death punishment." Urine was the substance used by her stepfather to treat a wound on his leg caused by a brutal kick from a German soldier.

During this phase of analysis, in which she recounted these stories, Kay felt that she was treating the wounds in her soul with bits of information from her repressed consciousness, things that she had known but had forgotten over the years.

## FROM ENACTMENT TO MENTAL REPRESENTATION

I believe that the most effective way of transforming the compulsion to enact (the defense against mourning) into a cognitive mode is by helping these individuals find the meaning of the trauma in their parents' lives and bind[4] it in a meaningful context, thus consigning it to the past of the parents. During the first phase of analysis, the analyst deals with cognition and emotions that were severed by the parents' repression of the trauma, leaving traces of the repression in the child. Finding the parents' "unknown" story and lifting this repression, followed by a process of working through, transforms the possible enactment into an "affective understanding" (Freud 1915). This kind of understanding links thoughts and feelings, greatly decreasing the need to repeatedly enact the parents' stories in the children's current lives.

The quest for information—the purpose of which is to enable the patient to give up these enactments—is a difficult experience for the survivor's offspring. It is my view that in the initial stages of analysis, only a supportive, nurturing environment, which includes a holding relationship (one that decreases the patient's tremendous anxiety) and holding interpretations (those that help the patient mobilize his or her forces to find the meaning of the trauma in the parents' lives) can strengthen the patient's mental organization to the point that the flow of fragmenting, potentially life-threatening reenactments is halted (Kogan 1995, 1996, 1998, 2000, 2002).

The quest for information also serves the purpose of differentiation and the creation of a new and separate self. On this level, it might be accompanied by torment and anxiety. Consciously, the child is afraid that his questions about the past will force the parent to relive painful, traumatic memories that may threaten his psychic survival. Unconsciously, the child experiences the wish to know his parent's history as a step toward differentiation and a relief from the burden of the past, which he feels may be potentially destructive for the parent. This search is usually facilitated by the holding atmosphere in analysis and by the patient adopting the analyst as an ally in his quest.

Treatment often does not end here, and there is much psychic work to be done in further stages of analysis. It is only after the initial phase of holding, in which the patient's self is strengthened, that interpretations of his or her unconscious life become not only acceptable but also necessary. During these later phases, it is possible to work through the missing piece of the parent's history, which is often connected to the child's feelings of shame and guilt.

In some cases, the parent's story does not emerge easily, but has to be actively sought. The therapist's supportive attitude facilitates the patient's discovery of that part of the parent's history that will fill the hole through the acquisition of concrete details from the parent's past. Examples from the cases described earlier are Kay's request to read her stepfather's book of memoirs in order to learn—among other things—about his castration by the Nazi doctors and Hannah's agreement to become the editor of her father's autobiography of his Holocaust past.

The construction of an unbroken narrative—one that fills the gaps in the child's knowledge, that makes it permissible to mention the unmentionable, that interweaves the awareness of the realities and horrors of the Holocaust with the present—enables the offspring of survivors to gradually gain some comfort from the split-off knowledge, which has been accompanied by unacknowledged affects and fears. The events and narratives that formed the starting point of the child's traumatic wound can be reconstructed, so that the split-off and diffusely reenacted memory fragments from a persecutory world are elucidated. Thus, the interpretation of fragmentary, defensive reenactments leads patients to an awareness of the reality of the trauma—an awareness that becomes part of their flow of life. Although, this is only a beginning phase of treatment, the patient will now be able to at least partially relinquish his struggle against mourning. The work of mourning that continues during the latter phases of analysis will eventually free him from the burden of the past and will enable him to achieve a stronger, better integrated self.

## NOTES

1. See Kogan (1989, 1995) for additional descriptions of this case.
2. See Kogan (1993, 1995) for additional descriptions of this case.
3. See Kogan (1987, 1995) for additional descriptions of this case.
4. The concept of binding was first described in Freud's (1920) theory of why certain events have a traumatic effect upon the mind, and how the personality takes account of and adapts to the resulting changed internal conditions. The concept appears in connection with his famous metapsychological explanation (1920, p. 31) of trauma as an "extensive breach made in the protective shield against stimuli," which occurs only when the mental apparatus is not prepared for anxiety, that is, the parts of the system that are to receive the excessive stimulation are not properly hypercathected and therefore "the inflowing amount of excitation could not be *bound*." It is hard to be sure what precisely Freud meant by binding, since he used the term at different stages of his work in different ways (Laplanche and Pontalis 1973). However, by 1920 it had taken on the general meaning of a defensive operation that restricts freeflowing excitation. Once the catastrophic breach in the protective shield has taken place and mental functioning is in turmoil and disarray, the problem is one of "mastering the amounts of stimulus

which have broken in and of binding them in the psychical sense, so that they can then be disposed of."

In the recent literature (Garland 1991, 2002), binding is described as a process by which the ego creates links between the freeflowing excitation and functions of the mind. In this way the ego attempts to recreate structures of some permanence in which ego functioning is possible.

# 6

# Trauma, Resilience, and Creative Activity

*Unlike play, artistic creativity involves much pain.*

—Segal 1991, p. 108

## THE NATURE OF RESILIENCE

The immediate and long-term effects of the massive psychic trauma incurred by different ethnic groups have been studied primarily from a pathological perspective. It has become almost axiomatic that individuals who experience persecution and multiple losses are more vulnerable—they suffer from post-traumatic stress disorder (PTSD) and continued manifestations of annihilation anxiety, such as lack of trust, a tendency to isolation, and a numbing of feelings.

Nevertheless, many such individuals appear to lead productive lives and have even forged intimate relationships. Recent years have been witness to a new approach, one that examines the resilience of those survivors of trauma and their descendants, who have succeeded in making something worthwhile of their lives in spite of its ravages.

Resilience, according to the dictionary, means recoiling or springing back to the original shape after bending, stretching, or compression. Psychosocial resilience implies a similar springing back after subjection to severe stressors (Valent 1998).

Resilience—which may be regarded as the opposite of vulnerability—is thus a new concept. It originated in observations of children who seemed to emerge relatively unscathed from even the most adverse social conditions. These observations gave rise to the initially rather optimistic concept of invulnerability (Anthony 1974), which, with time, gave way to the concept of resilience. This concept was further explored in recent literature by Boris Cyrulnik (1993, 1997, 1999, 2001, 2003, 2004), the president of the International Observatory of Resilience at the University of Toulon, France.

Resilience, which reflects the strength of the human spirit, is an objectively useful concept that may also include elements that can mitigate the long-term effects of severe stressors, as I discuss in this paper.

How can we explain resilience in the face of adversity? Endowment, temperament, and familial or environmental factors that preceded persecution may be advanced to explain resilience-producing traits. An individual's intrapsychic structure may also contribute to this resilience. It is important to note that resilience in one area of functioning is not necessarily indicative of resilience in all areas (Rutter 1993). Rutter (1987) maintains that resilience is not a fixed attribute, but rather that it hinges on a balance between the mechanisms and processes of protection and vulnerability. The factors affecting a person's resistance to adversity are both environmental and constitutional and may change over time, making it impossible to distinguish between what may be attributed to the environment and what is constitutional.

In this chapter, I explore one of the pivotal factors of resilience—creative activity—as it is manifested in the analysis of a Holocaust survivor offspring and its connection to mourning. The intimate relationship between creativity and resilience in stressful situations is such that the more we master creative problem-solving skills, the more we will be able to respond to stressful situations (Flach 1988).

In the case of offspring of Holocaust survivors, I define resilience as the offspring's ability to acknowledge and work through the guilt and mourning deposited in them by their parents. Managing emotional pain is most difficult, calling for such survival forces as faith, hope, and the will to live. Creativity may serve as a tool to facilitate acknowledgment of the painful feelings transmitted by the parents. By working through the hidden truths discovered through creative activity, the offspring are able to bind it (see note 4 in chapter 5) in a meaningful context.

Vulnerability, as I define it here, includes the denial and repression of cognitions, emotions, and meanings inconsistent with survival and hopeful attachment figures, which may lead to the failure to recover from trauma. Herein, I first relate briefly to the generation of the parents, touching on their vulnerability and resilience. I then consider in greater depth the generation of the offspring, focusing on their resilience. I discuss one of the important factors of resilience—creative activity, which leads to the elaboration of mourning—as it is illustrated by segments of an analysis of a Holocaust survivor's daughter.

## VULNERABILITY AND RESILIENCE IN THE GENERATION OF THE VICTIMS

The first studies of the vulnerability of survivors were conducted by Niederland (1964) and Eitinger (1964). These researchers insisted that persecution had left long-lasting, perhaps permanent effects on survivors; the end of the war, the liberation of concentration camp inmates, and the resettlement of refugees did not mean an end to the effects of Nazi atrocities. Subsequent articles stated that the intense depression felt by survivors led to complete social withdrawal, seclusion, and profound apathy (Lifton 1978). It was further hypothesized that survivors had difficulty "reinvesting in life" and were deeply ambivalent about founding new families (Krystal 1968). Vulnerability and resilience of survivors were explored in depth by Danieli (1998).

A characteristic trait found in survivors, which has been mentioned in Holocaust studies, is the shallow quality of their emotional response, referred to as "psychic numbing" or "psychic closing off." Experiencing overwhelming losses and stress during the Holocaust, along with the resultant intolerable anger and fear, survivors blocked out all capacity for emotion in the interest of continuously adapting to a changing, hostile environment. Emotional awareness would have carried with it the potential for demoralization, and would have distracted them from the task at hand—of surviving one day longer. Although this defense was invaluable at the time and contributed to their resilience, its lingering deployment was obviously maladaptive (Lifton 1968; Hass 1996).

Kestenberg and Brenner (1996) did important research in the realm of the impact of trauma on the lives of child survivors. They found that the disruptions of rules and regulations in the lives of infants and children, born during the Holocaust, left as an aftermath a recurring affecto-motor or somatic state of feeling bad, which is conceptualized as being bad. The younger the child, the more likely he was later in life to reexperience trauma as feeling bad, whereas feelings of emotional relief were remembered by things that made the child feel good, such as milk or sugar. The superego that is built to a great extent on feelings of comfort and discomfort, on pain and pleasure, that come and go unaccountably, could become fragmented. In analysis an ego strength was revealed, which showed that the ego of the child survivor could be quite resilient and flexible.

A famous example of the resilience of child survivors is found in Sarah Moskovitz's *Love Despite Hate* (1983). This book described the story of a small number of orphaned child survivors who came to England after the war from Terezin, Auschwitz, hidden in private homes or by nuns, and from orphanages. These children, ranging from toddlers (also described by Anna Freud and Sophie Dann) to young teenagers, were cared for by a caseworker named Alice Goldberger, herself a war-time refugee, and her small staff with funding from British and Jewish sources. These children did remarkably well as a group, especially those few who survived with their siblings. Some of the most competent group members drew comfort from their religious ties, whether Christian or Jewish. Goldberger had the talent to foster each child's individual interests, and thus make each one feel worthy and special. This volume is a valuable source of information with early documentation of the severity of childhood trauma, follow-up interviews showing the resilience of most individuals, and evidence about the unique importance of one person who made a helpful connection with all these children.

As a result of my extensive professional experience with offspring of Holocaust survivors, I am constantly overwhelmed by the richness of the many avenues of resilience with which their survivor parents dealt with trauma. The qualities needed by them to endure, cope with, adapt to, and survive massive atrocities and mass murder have been referred to variously as psychic strength, fierce determination, inner resources, perseverance, life-affirming acts and attitudes, indomitable spirit (Lee 1988), and defiance, as well as a stubborn determination not to give up (Hogman 1983).

Resilience factors that contributed to these qualities were mental attachments to good objects and the hope of retrieving them (Brenner 1988), the wish to live life, to create it, to hope in the face of adversity. Love of life itself, a spirit of survival, stamina, courage against fear, the sustaining quality and power of love, and capacities of repair and integration are all factors of resilience. Higher mental and spiritual levels of resilience emerged from the resourcefulness developed under these traumatic

conditions. Creativity, whenever possible, helped with survival by expressing hope. Creativity was expressed through drawings made in the ghettos
and concentrations camps, even in games. Developmental drive, creativity, and curiosity, which were maintained against all odds, helped survivors conquer the destructive and self-destructive forces unleashed by
massive traumatic experience.

The vulnerability and resilience of the parents, which I have touched
upon only briefly, is a major part of the background against which their
children grew up. I now discuss resilience in the generation of the offspring, focusing on creativity as one of its important elements.

## VULNERABILITY AND RESILIENCE IN THE GENERATION
## OF THE OFFSPRING

Many investigators assume the inevitability of transmitting pathology
from survivors to their children (Kestenberg 1972; Trossman 1968; Brenner 2002). They claim that since Holocaust experiences negatively affected
the survivor's capacity for human relations, he or she is unable to be an
effective parent, and this disability has had damaging psychological ramifications for children raised by these adults. Barocas and Barocas (1973)
state: "[B]ased on clinical experience with such patients (children of survivors) our impression is that these individuals present symptomatology
and psychiatric traits that bear a striking resemblance to the concentration
camp survival syndrome described in the international literature" (p.
821).

The legacy handed down to the second generation is that they often
carry in themselves the denied mourning of their parents. Denial of
mourning was part of a long-term post-Holocaust process of adaptation,
which for most included earning a living and raising a family. The energy
needed to live life did not allow much time for grieving. Forgetting traumatic memories was an adaptation in the service of life, but it also served
the forces of Thanatos by causing a loss of parts of the self that belonged
to the past (Laub and Lee 2003). Thus, although there was resilience in
the survivors' adaptability, they and their offspring paid an emotional
price. The feelings that survivors deposited in their children created vul-
nerabilities in the next generations—feelings of pain, shame, and guilt,
and the compelling need to reenact the story of their parents in their own
lives in order to master the trauma.

These offspring often echoed what existed in their parents' inner worlds through the reenactment of the past (Bergmann 1982; Kogan 1995, 2002). Reenactment precludes symbolization of the past and thus prohibits memory via symbolization or representation (internal images). The past is endlessly respun and no resolution of the trauma is possible.

There is a space, however, between reenactment and representation. This can be regarded as a transitional space in which symbol formation begins to unfold. In Winnicott's terms, this is a "potential space" (1971a), which allows for the emergence of representational modes, transitional phenomena, and creativity. Creative activity of offspring who "have always known" about the Holocaust, yet whose parents could not speak about their experiences, often contains symbols of the Holocaust that reside in this transitional space. These symbols tell the story through their unverbalized meanings. Creative activity thus becomes a kind of shorthand—a language beyond words—that evokes the texture and embodies the meanings of the past. As opposed to works of art that are unrelated to treatment, which may at times mask the as yet unworked-through and unknown aspects of trauma (Laub and Podell 1995), I believe that creative activity during treatment is a means of unmasking hidden truths. It thus helps fill the psychic hole, the gap in the offspring's emotional understanding of the parents' traumatic past. Creative activity facilitates resilience by serving as an important tool that enables the offspring to reveal and work through the history of their survivor parents, and to elaborate feelings of pain and guilt transmitted to them. Thus, they are eventually able to integrate their parents' suffering and mourning—which had become their own—into a bearable experience for themselves.

I will present a vignette from one of my case studies to illustrate how creative activity leads to the discovery of feelings of pain and guilt transmitted from one generation to the other, and how it facilitates the work of mourning in treatment, enabling the patient to integrate the parents' trauma into his or her own life.

### The Case

Shelly, a thirty-two-year-old woman, sought professional help because she had lately become unhappy with her life and work. She had been married for seven years, had two sons (aged four and six), and worked as a scientist in a large institution. She disliked the institution where she worked, and regarded her professional dissatisfaction as the main source of her unhappiness. She also felt that she was a big disappointment to her parents, who ever since her childhood had expected her to become rich and successful, something she could never achieve.

Shelly was the younger daughter of scientist parents. Her older sister, who had not obtained a higher education but worked as a hairdresser, was considered a disgrace to the family. Her brother, who worked in a high-tech company and traveled a lot abroad, was the one who brought the family "fame." Compared to her successful brother, and compared to her mother who had been a physicist and a feminist, Shelly felt that "she never made it." She considered herself a good mother to her children, the only realm in which she believed she had surpassed her mother.

Shelly's fear of analysis was enormous. When I greeted her at the door the first time, she turned as if to run away. During the initial process of analysis, I realized that Shelly was unable to lie on the couch while I sat behind her. That position left her feeling abandoned and overwhelmed by paranoid fears. I let her choose a position that would be suitable for her; and after trying to sit up in a chair, she lay down and asked me to sit facing her so that she could maintain eye contact with me.

At the beginning of analysis Shelly spoke about the way she had often endangered herself when she was younger. On her frequent travels abroad she hitchhiked with strangers. Once she slept in a farmer's house; at night he came into her room and tried to touch her. She ran away from him, climbed up to the roof of the house, and jumped. She was lucky to fall on a pile of hay and was only badly bruised. In Israel, Shelly used to walk at night in dangerous neighborhoods. Once, she was attacked by a man who tried to rape her; she screamed, and fortunately the man ran away. Throughout her adolescence she abused drugs and alcohol, was often bulimic, and would induce vomiting.

I will not go into the painful and complex analytic journey of the last seven years. Instead, I will proceed to demonstrate how the impact of the Holocaust was expressed in analysis through Shelly's creative activities (poems and paintings) and the role of these activities in her healing process.

At a certain point during the first phase of therapy, when I informed Shelly that I would be going abroad for several days, she began bringing to therapy paintings and poems that reflected her feelings about our upcoming separation (see drawing 1, "Airplanes that take you away from me" and drawing 2, "Shelly with the ropes").

Shelly wrote a poem about these two drawings:

> You are my savior
> I am pulling on invisible ropes
> And try to climb up to you
> To hold on to you
> But I remain down here with
> A bunch of ropes that cover almost all of me
> And I try to pull again and again
> On the ropes—towards you
> In my fantasy—I see you in your room
> I pull on your strings
> You inflate like a balloon
> And get up and fly out the window of your room
> Out and up—up—up.

Shelly associated these ropes with the umbilical cord. Through these poems and drawings, as well as through her dreams from this period, we came to understand that Shelly was reacting to our separation with tremendous fear and anxiety. Recurrent themes in her dreams revolved around her children who were in danger of being hurt or lost. Shelly felt that my going away meant leaving her alone to cope with death and destruction.

Some of the drawings she brought to the sessions enabled us to discover the damaged child within herself (see drawings 3 and 4, "The damaged child" and drawing 5, "The child's head—a pot filled with earth and a tree growing out of it").

These drawings helped Shelly recall once more the various episodes of self-destructiveness from her youth described by her at the beginning of the treatment, her attraction to death, and her fear of it. Only later on in analysis could I help Shelly become aware that the pot filled with earth could indeed symbolize death, but the tree growing out of it, the symbol of life, showed her resilience.

In the transference, Shelly's aggression and wrath, which had been evoked by my plans for going abroad, had no limits. An episode from this period illustrates this. Shelly referred to a Band-Aid I had had on my cheek some weeks prior to the current session, following a skin operation, and said, "Two weeks ago I saw a Band-Aid on your cheek and I decided that you were going to die; now you are going abroad. I would rather have you dead than going away!"

In my countertransference, I felt that Shelly had intruded into my "perimeter of safety" (McLaughlin 1995), especially since my skin operation had actually been a biopsy that had turned out to be benign. What a cruel, ruthless love this is! I thought to myself.

I first had to work through fears of my own evoked by her "need-relationship" (Winnicott 1964) in order to enable Shelly to elaborate upon her feelings toward me, which were a reflection of her painful and complex relationship with her mother. After much psychic work, Shelly arrived at the following conclusion, which she expressed through a poem. "You said that behind this big love for you there is a lot of anger. I wrote a poem about devouring love."

> A fish swallows a fish that
> Swallows a fish that swallows a fish.
> A mother swallows a child that
> Swallows a mother that swallows a child

This poem expressed Shelly's feelings about the mutual engulfment of a mother and a child generation after generation. By elaborating upon this phenomenon, we discovered its connection to Shelly's relationship with her mother and Shelly's bearing the painful legacy of the Holocaust for her.

Shelly's mother was a child during the Holocaust and fled Eastern Europe with her parents when she was twelve. Shelly's grandmother, the sole survivor of her immediate family, was a bitter, angry woman. She never forgave her husband for tearing her away from the members of her family who were left behind and who perished in the Holocaust. Nor did she ever forgive her daughter, Shelly's mother, whom she regarded as the reason the family left Europe and came to Israel. Shelly's mother grew up with the double message of being her parents' savior as well as the perpetrator of her relatives' death. She developed paranoid traits and often felt guilty for being "bad." She attributed her mother's wrath and unhappiness to her own "poisonous" qualities, and later in life feared that she was "poisonous" to her own children. The grandmother, who had suffered many losses, might have been projecting her burden of depression and guilt upon her daughter, who bore this burden for her. Shelly's mother, unable to contain the guilt and pain within herself, projected it onto her own child, thus turning the daughter into a container of pain (Bion 1962). This can be seen in particular in one of Shelly's drawings (see drawing 6, "Mother, child and the demon") and the poem that she wrote about it.

> As if I fought a huge demon
> All day long
> And I fell asleep
> And dreamt
> Of wars and bad people
> And dangers and gas chambers.

Shelly connected the demon inside her head, which was persecuting her mother, to the Holocaust. She felt that this demon was now engraved on the child's arm (here came to mind the numbers engraved upon the arms of concentration camp inmates). Thus, Shelly saw herself as this child who was bearing the mother's feelings of mourning and guilt. (Upon rereading my original wording of this family history, I observed that I had written it in a rather confusing way, and I realized that there was no differentiation in my own mind as well between mother and daughter.)

Shelly brought to the sessions a drawing of a woman with one face superimposed upon another (see drawing 7, "Woman with two faces, one superimposed upon the other").

In the transference, Shelly referred to her ambivalent perception of me. "Sometimes I think that you are the best analyst around, that I was lucky that you accepted me in treatment; other times I think you are worthless, and that maybe you are crazy, like my mother." Elaborating upon our relationship in the treatment, we discovered that in this painting she had superimposed the successful outward facade of her scientist mother upon a sick woman. Her mother suffered from many physical illnesses and had undergone several operations. There were times when she experienced what could very probably have been psychotic episodes. Shelly described occasions when her mother had been totally unkempt, wearing dirty clothes, and leaving sanitary napkins around the apartment. Her mother would dismantle kitchen utensils in order to clean them, and could never put them back together again, thus giving concrete expression to her feelings of fragmentation. There was little communication between Shelly's mother and her children. Whatever needed saying was communicated via the father. The mother was often haunted by paranoid delusions; she was afraid that she was feeding her children spoilt food that would poison them, that hereditary illnesses might destroy them. Catastrophe and death were always looming on the horizon. Shelly often felt abandoned by her mother, both physically and emotionally. These situations left her feeling terrified, threatened by annihilation. As a result of her childhood experiences, Shelly was extremely afraid to leave her own children for even a short while. For her, leaving as well as being left meant abandonment and destruction.

The drawing of the woman with one face superimposed on the other enabled us to discover that Shelly, too, had more than one face. Shelly was not only the damaged child, as seen in the previous paintings; by completely identifying with her mother, she herself became the poisonous, destructive mother. Her paranoid fears often changed into paranoid delusions about destroying her own children, and she was terrified that she might harm them (see drawings 8, 9, and 10, "The castrated child").

The "primitive identification" (Kogan 1995, see previous chapter) with her mother included a state of pathological mourning (Freud 1919). The long journey of working through this mourning began with the discovery and elaboration of the hidden truths embedded in her paintings.

We elaborated upon Shelly's morbid feelings by reexamining her paintings from earlier stages of analysis. An example of this was the painting of the child with a pot of earth in its head and a tree growing out of it. Shelly now connected it to a grave, to death, and the Holocaust. She felt an abandoned child, helpless and overwhelmed by archaic fears, because the child inside her, like the one inside her mother, bore the death and destruction of an abandoned family upon its head.

By elaborating upon her poems and pictures we were able to discover her longing for fusion with me (her mother in the transference) as well as her fear of it. Shelly became aware of her special link with her mother that enabled the transmission of feelings of anxiety, anger, and destructiveness as if through a permeable membrane. Shelly realized that these might have been her mother's feelings, which became her own.

Through other drawings, we discovered Shelly's terror and guilt about having been born into this world (see drawings 11 and 12, "Terror and birth").

The main questions that preoccupied her about these drawings were: "Should I have been born or not? Should I be living in a world where so many have perished?" Searching for an answer to these questions, we attempted to reconstruct her parents' history and the impact it had on her life.

Shelly's feelings regarding the legacy of the Holocaust were also expressed through her dreams. An example follows.

"I dreamt that my grandmother isn't dead, and she and my mother are attending a funeral. They are both wearing enormous hats, very elaborate ones, and they are wearing big, black mourning dresses. They appear short and grotesque in these clothes. I don't want to be like them." Through this dream, Shelly expressed her wish to be free of the burden of mourning, aggression, and guilt that had clad her mother and grandmother throughout their lives.

Working through her Holocaust-related pain and guilt in her present life enabled Shelly to better differentiate between herself and her mother: "My biggest fear was that I would be like my mother! Now I know that we are different; we lived in other times, different realities. I have my own life and I have to make the best of it."

This differentiation was followed by a long elaboration of her complex relationship with her mother. In this period, a dream about a former boyfriend reflects this relationship. In her dream Shelly saw her former boyfriend and, realizing how much she missed him, felt a powerful longing for him. The dream was triggered by the fact that several days earlier she had heard an interview with him on the radio. Apparently he had become quite famous; he was now a neonatologist. Shelly recalled how this man had evoked strange reactions in her. Once, in the middle of the night, she had asked him to bring her ice cream, and he had obliged. His love had made her angry. She had behaved aggressively toward him, treated him badly, humiliated and offended him. Trying to understand her longing for this man, Shelly raised several possibilities: Had she treated him the same way her mother had treated her as a child? Or perhaps she was now allowing herself to long for the love that in the past had frightened her and made her so angry? In the transference, I pointed out to Shelly that perhaps I was the doctor who was treating the infant inside her, and that she was allowing herself to long for my love now that she was less afraid of this longing.

This elaboration led to an upsurge of loving feelings toward her mother. On the occasion of her mother's birthday, a close friend of the family brought some letters Shelly's mother had written to her from the United States. She was then a young woman with three little children, working hard for her Ph.D. in physics. Shelly read these letters avidly and was very impressed by the fact that her mother loved and cared for her, a fact she had not realized before.

Memories about the mother of her childhood were evoked, and with them feelings of admiration for the talented woman her mother had once been. Shelly remembered that, in addition to being a gifted scientist, her mother had had a great talent for architectural design, with no formal studies in this field, and she had created beautiful interior designs for their house as well as for their friends' houses. Shelly now raised the possibility that she might have inherited her talent for painting from her mother.

At one point Shelly's mother was hospitalized for a hip operation. It was then that Shelly became aware that her anger toward her mother partially stemmed from her fear of losing her. After she recovered from the operation, though still on crutches, her mother insisted on visiting Shelly, in spite of the fact that this meant climbing three flights of stairs. Shelly appreciated her mother's effort and regarded it as a sign of her love.

Shelly brought to the session a diary that she had kept when she was ten years old. In this diary she found a story that she had written about her mother. The mother, who was a little girl in the story, and the mother's little sister went on an outing in the forest with their parents. Shelly's mother did not watch over her sister carefully enough, and the sister got lost in the forest. Her mother grew up and remained sad over losing her sister. In her story, Shelly tried to repair this traumatic event: Her mother went back in time and became anew the child who went with her family on outings to the forest. Shelly warned her mother to take good care of her sister. Thus, the mother got a second chance to save her sister and became much happier.

Shelly's story expressed her childhood wishes and fantasies of curing her depressed mother and making her happy. In her associations, Shelly talked about her mother's family that had disappeared in the Holocaust, and the burden of guilt that lay upon her mother. Shelly was aware that even as a child she had wanted to relieve her mother of this guilt. I asked Shelly whether perhaps her mother had lost not only her sister in the forest, but also the happy aspect of her personality. By giving her a second chance to save her dear ones, Shelly had tried to bring her mother back to the place where she could find this lost aspect of her own self.

Through her creative activity, Shelly allowed us entry into the painful terrain of the past, where we found clues to the plight of two generations that had been marked by the Holocaust. Therapy helped Shelly give up her manic defenses and touch the pain that had been transmitted to her, often without words. A poem written by Shelly illustrates this most eloquently:

> In my heart there are capsules of pain
> That were carefully packed many years ago
> By my mother and grandmother,
> Capsules full of little pills of pain
> In various colors
> Packed in transparent wrapping of orange and blue.
> There are days when the wrapping melts
> And a slight twinge of pain spreads through my body.
> There are days when
> There is no capsule breaking.
> And yesterday, in your room,
> Many capsules suddenly broke.
> And the pain began to stream through
> My body and overwhelmed me and passed
> From my center to my sides.

## FINAL WORDS

The most systematically worked out psychoanalytic views of artistic creativity have been those of Freud (1897, 1908, 1916) and views that are based on Kleinian ideas of art as a reparative activity that emanates from the depressive position (Segal 1952; Klein 1930). Segal's view of creativity, in Kleinian terms, is more positive than Freud's. Whereas Freud regards the need to create art as a defense, which a person who is freer of neurotic conflict would not require, Segal relates it to a universal process of development.

Airplanes that take you away from me

Shelly with the ropes

The damaged child

The child's head—a pot filled with earth and a tree growing out of it

Mother, child, and the demon

Woman with two faces, one superimposed upon the other

The castrated child

The castrated child

Terror and birth

Terror and birth

In line with Segal's ideas, described previously, I have attempted to show that creative activity of an offspring of Holocaust survivors during treatment is an element of resilience that facilitates the work of mourning and an ensuing developmental process. I will summarize it as follows:

1) Creative activity represents movement, by which reenactments shift to metaphors. In this sense, the movement is a transitional object and embodies "betweenness." What constitutes an object is the unfolding of a process (Parsons 2000).

2) Creative activity introduces a playful element into the reality of the trauma, thus enabling some distancing from the traumatic event. The imagery of the trauma becomes more colorful and plastic, the event is no longer recreated as if it were the offspring's own story, and it becomes more of a metaphor. This enables the working through of processes of mourning, which occur unconsciously in silent modes of expression such as enactments.

3) Creative activity is based on a reparative impulse, the patient seeking ways to repair the damage caused by fantasies shared with his traumatized parents. In these cases, creative activity may serve as a means for controlling regression (thus becoming a "regression in the service of the ego" [Kris 1952]) and for making use of primary processes, rather than compulsively reenacting these shared fantasies.

4) Creative activity is the moving force behind the search for an appropriate vehicle of expression. It stems from the need to master external historical reality, as well as from the need to reorganize the internal experience of this reality (Auerhahn and Laub 1998).

5) The parents' *Mythos of Survival* (Klein 1981; Klein and Kogan 1986), which consists of conflicting emotions and unconscious wishes about living and dying, has a great impact upon the offspring, intensifying their own conflict over life and death. Children of survivors who attempt to create during therapy are often struggling not only against neurosis or danger to internal objects, but also against the threat of not being. Creative activity expresses the conflict and the union between life and death instincts (Grinberg 1992), and therefore is of utmost importance in these cases. Since, as Winnicott has so eloquently stated, "There is a link between creative living and living" (1971b, p. 81), creative activity is mobilized in the struggle for life.

In the case illustration that I have presented here, the creative activity in the analytic situation was the first step in the patient's efforts to search for her internal source of anguish. The second step was the elaboration of her feelings of mourning and pain, which enabled her to integrate, restitute, and achieve resolution of the burden of depression and guilt transmitted by her mother.

The evolution of creativity moves toward the psychological healing of traumatic memory (Laub and Auerhahn 1993). Creative activity that involves the legacy of the Holocaust (as we often see in cases of Holocaust survivors' offspring) is thus a quest for mastery and redemption. By appearing in the transitional space between reenactment and representation, creative activity ultimately allows the patient to be in touch with mourning and enables its working through. It affirms the forces of life, thus overcoming silence and death. As an act of imagination, it is a path to hope and a profound beginning.

# On Being a Dead, Beloved Child

*Only his children Job did not receive again double, because a human life is not a thing that can be duplicated.*

—Kierkegaard 1941, p. 126

In this chapter I explore the impact of unresolved mourning of parents on the emotional and cognitive development of their offspring. I will illustrate this theme with a detailed case study of a replacement child, born to parents who had each lost a child during the Holocaust. The mother used various defenses to deal with her loss, denying its reality and omnipotently wishing to resurrect the dead, beloved child by means of the living one. I demonstrate the effect of the bereaved mother's unresolved mourning on the mother-child relationship and on the character structure of the child. As a result of the long process of therapy, the offspring's obsessive-compulsive symptoms diminished and were transformed into reparative defenses against pain and mourning. Creative activity helped the patient differentiate between herself and her mother, and facilitated the work of mourning.

## INTRODUCTION

Children of Holocaust survivors are born into families in which their parents experienced the sudden disintegration of their normal world, a world replaced by one in which appalling cruelty, loss of loved ones, and constant fear of death became the everyday norm. When the survivors are also parents who lost a child in the Holocaust, one or both of them often view a new child as a replacement for the one who was lost. This has profound effects on the development of the new child, who then concretizes the parents' unconscious fantasies and expectations in his or her life goals and practices. The replacement child's self-perception is often as a loved and narcissistically valued being, but only on the condition that he or she fulfills the destiny of the child who was lost. Since it is impossible to compete with an idealized rival whose sins have been paid for by death, the dead child becomes a hated "sibling" who destroys the autonomy of the surviving child's ego ideal.

The child of survivors, whether primarily neurotic or afflicted by a more damaged psychic structure, often exhibits anxieties whose origins lie in the effort invested in fulfilling the role assigned by the parents or in attempting to undo the destruction wrought by the Holocaust. When parents encounter their children's antagonism or hostility—a result of the pressures they themselves have put upon the children to fulfill this task—they tend to treat the children as though they were reincarnations of Nazi oppressors. The underlying reason for this behavior is the parents' identification of the child with an introjected aggressor (Kestenberg 1982). This phenomenon results from the parents' attempt to externalize disavowed aspects of their own self-representations, which were internalized under extreme stress when identification with the aggressor was the only major adaptational means of survival (Bergmann 1982).

For the child of the survivor, empathy and identification with the parent as a persecuted victim or as a Nazi aggressor lead to splitting in the ego and superego representations. In cases where the child is assigned a role of restitution in the parents' fantasies, which cannot be fulfilled, difficulties in thinking and reality testing often ensue, since it is unclear what is real and what is not. I wish to illustrate this theme through the presentation of a case study.

As a result of the obstacles I encountered in the attempt to make the unconscious conscious in this analysis, I will also focus on the special countertransference problems resulting from the fact that the analyst and the patient shared the same large-group identity (Volkan, Ast, and Greer 2002). In such cases, analyst and patient may collude in the attempt to avoid feelings of aggression and guilt, which are connected in both their minds to dreadful historical events.

## THE CASE

Nurit, a scientist, married, and the mother of three, sought help because of her compulsive behavior, which affected her everyday life. She was generally satisfied with her life and content with her family and work. She never had difficulty making important life decisions; she loved her husband and children and was happy with her profession and lifestyle. Her problematic behavior expressed itself in minor details of her life: in the need to check and recheck that she had turned off the gas stove, or that she had closed the refrigerator door, the garage doors, or the little bottle of talcum powder she kept in her bathroom. Other daily tasks of minor importance, such as setting her alarm clock and writing addresses on letters, had to be repeatedly inspected to ascertain that they had been performed correctly.

In our first meeting, Nurit described her symptoms as time- and energy-consuming; she wished to be rid of them as they were ruining her self-image of a mature, self-assured woman, which in many respects she felt she was. Also, she had recently had some fierce clashes with her older daughter, an adolescent, and her symptoms worsened. This led her to seek professional help to overcome her problems. Some years earlier, she had undergone behavioral therapy but had derived little benefit from it.

Nurit was an attractive woman in her early forties. She was tall, slim, neatly dressed with an elegant touch, her silvery white hair adding a regal quality to her appearance. To me, she appeared an intelligent, talented woman. Her manner of talking revealed the sophistication of a person who had spent her life in different places around the world. She had mastered several languages almost to perfection. "I like languages and they like me," she told me smilingly.

Listening to Nurit during our first encounter, I was struck by the tone of her voice, which was completely devoid of emotional inflections. Her voice had a metallic quality to it, as if it were a metal shield preventing emotions from breaking through. "What a painful wound must be hidden beneath these metallic sounds!" I thought fleetingly.

I recommended psychodynamic psychotherapy to Nurit as the treatment of choice at this stage, so that we could establish some emotional contact before embarking upon a long and painful analytic journey.

## Anamnesis

Nurit was the only child of two Holocaust survivors. Her mother came from a middle-class Polish family with several siblings. Her mother had always described her family as warm and loving, and Nurit believed that her mother had derived a lot of strength from this. Her mother's entire family (a brother, a sister, and their children) had perished in the Holocaust.

At nineteen, her mother married a man considerably older than herself, and they soon had a little girl. When war broke out, the rumor spread that Jewish men were in danger, while women and children would be safe. Many Jewish men therefore fled to Russia, leaving their families behind. Her mother's husband also fled to Russia, and she remained in Warsaw with her child until they were forced to move into the ghetto. One day, on her way back from work to her little girl, who was looked after by a caretaker, she was told that both child and caretaker had been killed in an "aktion." Nurit's impression was that the girl had been approximately seven years old when this happened.

After a while, Nurit's mother was transported to Bergen-Belsen, where she was held for several years. When the war ended, her mother came to Israel and met Nurit's father. As had her mother's husband, he, too, had fled to Russia during the war, leaving his father, his wife, and his little daughter behind. They were all murdered in his absence. Nurit thought that her father's daughter had been about the same age as her mother's daughter when she was killed, perhaps even in the same "aktion."

In Israel, her mother and father fell in love; however, the mother was still married, as her husband had survived and was living in Poland. The mother traveled to Poland to obtain a divorce from her husband, remaining there about a year. Nurit believed that this might have been an unsuccessful attempt on her mother's part to renew the bond with her husband. The story told in the family was that while there, her mother received a Bible that had been smuggled in by an acquaintance, and among its pages was a sum of money and a note from Nurit's father that read "Come back home!" Mother made her decision. She obtained a divorce, returned to Israel, and married Nurit's father. Nurit was born when her mother and father were approximately forty years old.

The family lived in Israel until the child was two years old. After the father established a successful business, they moved to Europe, living in different countries. Nurit had wonderful memories of her childhood. She was loved and adored by her parents, her governess, and her paternal grandmother, who lived with them. She did well in school, was popular socially, was adept at learning new languages, and adjusted easily to new places and people.

At the age of eighteen, Nurit left home and returned to Israel to live with her grandmother, who had moved back some years earlier. She completed her studies in science, married a man who provided her with constant love and support, and who succeeded professionally. Nurit viewed her successful marriage and her three children, two daughters and a son, as important life achievements.

**Phase 1: Learning a Forgotten Language**

During the first months of treatment, Nurit filled the sessions with stories of her terrible experiences and suffering at the hands of her mother from age eleven until she was eighteen, when she left home. These stories stood in stark contrast to the wonderful memories of her early childhood. They conveyed an oppressive, persecutory style of parenting, the impact of which was still present in the patient's life. The striking feature of these stories was that, in spite of their painful content, they were told in a manner completely devoid of affect. Nurit never mentioned the pain, humiliation, and fear that accompanied her terrible experiences. She also had great difficulty expressing emotions in the here and now of the analytic situation.

In spite of what appeared to be a good therapeutic relationship, it was difficult to help Nurit disclose the feelings that I felt were lurking beneath her defensive armor—her vulnerability, dependency needs, deeper fears, and longings. The transference had a shallow quality. I felt that I was not really able to touch her emotions. To help overcome this obstacle, I had to make Nurit aware of her difficulty in expressing her feelings. In addition, since I felt that the face-to-face nature of psychotherapy was not facilitating a spontaneous expression of feelings, I suggested that the form of treatment be changed to psychoanalysis, which I believed would help stimulate spontaneity in her.

After asking me several questions about this, Nurit agreed to undertake psychoanalysis at the frequency of four times a week, on the couch. She cooperated with the requirements of the process and free-associated with ease. However, the obstacle of my inability to touch her emotions seemed as insurmountable as ever. I realized that my commenting on the lack of affect in her speech would not enable her to express emotions. Instead, I explored the reasons underlying this lack of affect. I shared my feeling with Nurit that the root of her problem might be her long-continuing anxiety over being hurt, abandoned, or destroyed, and that together we would have to discover the reasons underlying her inability to express emotions, as well as its adaptive purpose. She acknowledged the existence of a protective shield that concealed her emotions, and we embarked upon the long, arduous journey of discovering the circumstances that had forced her to construct this heavy armor that, I believed, enabled her to cope with life. Only much later in analysis could Nurit express feelings of appreciation for my approach, which had encouraged introspection rather than feelings of inadequacy and guilt.

Though devoid of affect, Nurit's accounts of the atmosphere at home during her adolescence were horrifying. She described her mother's unexpected outbursts of anger, her habit of ignoring Nurit and not talking to her for days, her accusations that Nurit was the cause of her unhappiness. The idyllic childhood relationship had evidently changed into a complicated, painful one during the patient's teenage years.

Nurit declared that she had felt totally alone in the face of her mother's unexpected fury and senseless resentment. At first, she had tried everything possible to appease her mother's wrath and win back her love, but to no avail. To ward off her mother's aggressive attacks and outbursts, as well as her own feelings of helplessness and humiliation, she learned to hide her feelings from her mother. We came to the conclusion that the shield Nurit had constructed to protect her vulnerable young self had been vital for her psychic existence. But although irrelevant to her present life, it was still part of her.

Listening to the account of her adolescence, trying to imagine the hurt, humiliation, and anxiety caused by her mother, I considered another angle: the part that Nurit herself might have played in constructing her wretched life. This thought, which would have been totally unacceptable to Nurit at this stage of treatment, kept recurring to me throughout the analysis. It would be a long time before I could investigate it in the transference relationship.

During this period, by identifying her emotions and labeling them for her, I felt I was teaching Nurit a language once known to her but long forgotten. With her talent for languages, she was willing to relearn the language of feelings, which she had erased in her adolescence because of her fears of hurting her mother or being hurt by her. Relearning how to express emotions would hopefully result in Nurit's being less afraid of hurting me or being hurt by me in the transference.

An episode described by Nurit in the second year of analysis reflected her difficulty in expressing her feelings. She spoke of a recent experience she had had while in Europe: a visit to a hospitalized acquaintance, a young man, who after discovering his Jewish origins, had gone to Israel for a visit. During the visit, he was badly injured in a terrorist attack, and the explosion made him a quadriplegic. He returned to his native land in Europe for medical treatment, and Nurit's visit was welcomed by the hospital staff, who asked her to translate the patient's words to the Israeli specialist who had been invited for a consultation. Nurit was very impressed with the young man who, though almost totally paralyzed (he could move only his head), still wanted to return to Israel to build a life of his own and not be dependent on his parents.

In the transference, I told Nurit that she would need to translate her feelings into words for me so that I, in the role of specialist, would be able to understand her and help her become inwardly independent of her own parents. However, I added that this might be difficult for her because of her terrible fear of my leading her into an explosion of emotions on our analytic journey. Nurit rejected the second part of my interpretation, vehemently denying any fear, either of me or of analysis. I then asked Nurit whether she identified with the young man, the quadriplegic, on those occasions when only her head was working, while her emotions were paralyzed. Nurit's reaction was that she had recently learned to ride a motorcycle in spite of her fears, because her teacher was there behind her, guarding her. I pointed out that perhaps, since she knew I was behind her, she was hoping to gradually master her fear of expressing emotions.

Nurit's insecurity with regard to her perception of reality was a complex phenomenon that was related to her doubts about her sanity. I shall illustrate how we began working this through with an episode from the third year of analysis. Nurit was asked by friends to arrange the hospitalization of an acquaintance, the daughter of a friend of the family whose mother had died of a brain tumor. The mother, a survivor of Auschwitz, had been hospitalized on and off in psychiatric hospitals throughout her life. The daughter had studied and held a job when younger, but later gave up everything to care for her mother. She never married or had a family of her own; instead, she lived with her mother in a situation defined by Nurit as a "total symbiosis." When the mother died, the daughter apparently fell apart and had to be hospitalized.

In analysis, Nurit became aware of the anxiety caused her by the encounter with the psychically ill woman whose history was different yet similar (their mothers were both Holocaust survivors). I suggested to Nurit that this woman, though obviously mentally ill, might be a reflection of herself. At this stage, Nurit was able to accept this without resistance, even referring to the weak, dependent, fragile woman as "my alter ego." It was clear to me that Nurit's newly acquired ability to openly and undefensively acknowledge her weaker aspects was an indication that she was becoming stronger.

However, the attempt to understand the meaning of "total symbiosis" of mother and daughter brought to the surface the problems that still remained. I considered various ways of understanding the situation, such as when I asked Nurit whether she felt she might be as unstable and depressed as she believed her mother was. The patient vehemently rejected this possibility. Following her rejection, I silently asked myself whether the feelings of hatred and aggression that she attributed to her mother were actually her own. In addition, I wondered whether she was afraid of becoming so attached to me that she would fall apart if I were to disappear or die. In order to broach this subject, I frequently inquired into her feelings about my occasional trips abroad. My inquiries were always met with a consistent denial of any emotional reaction to our separations. This denial made me aware that, despite becoming stronger, Nurit was still encumbered by tremendous fears.

**Phase 2: Remembering the Unknown**

During her childhood, Nurit was told very little about her parents' pasts, but this was no less traumatic for her than the stories she did hear. Her mother's undue anxiety over Nurit's getting lost in the street, over the eventuality of illness, or that catastrophe might strike, undoubtedly conveyed to her her mother's fear and dread of violence and loss.

A transferential incident—finding a hair on the pillow on the analytic couch—enabled us to elaborate upon some painful memories. I illustrate the attempt to work through these memories with accounts of two consecutive sessions from the third year of analysis. These sessions also demonstrate the difficulties I experienced in working with Nurit's feelings in the transference.

*Session 1. Nurit walked into my office, arranged the pillows the way she always did before lying down, and suddenly said, "There's a hair on the pillow. Whose hair is it? Who are your other patients?" After a moment of silence, she continued by relating a memory.*

> Nurit: I remember a time in my childhood when I first noticed a picture of a little girl on my father's desk and asked who she was. I was told that it was a picture of my sister, who had died a long time ago. I thought this meant that she was Father's daughter. When I was older, I found out that she was actually Mother's daughter. This made me feel very insecure. I used to wonder, "Who does the child belong to—Father or Mother?"

I listened to Nurit in silence.

> N: (continuing) You know, sometimes, when I was walking down the street and saw a cat or a dog that was run over, I tried to look away.
> I: Do you think your reaction might be the same as your reaction to your sisters, who were run over by the Nazi machine?
> N: Well, yes. When I was younger, I would try to block out the stories of the dead. I wanted to grow up without letting them affect me.
> I: It couldn't have been easy growing up in the shadow of the dead.
> N: The truth is, I enjoyed being an only child. I had so many privileges.
> I: Today, when you noticed a hair on the pillow, you asked me who my other patients were.
> N: Right. I never actually thought about the others. For me they just don't exist, even though of course I know that they come here.
> I: You wish you were an only child, and like with your sisters, you try to ignore my other patients so that their existence won't affect you.
> N: [after a silence] When I first came to you, I was so worried about my oldest daughter. She is such a talented girl, but she was an under-

achiever in school. She also had this awful boyfriend from a low-class family; maybe he was even on drugs. She was always rebelling against us—her successful, achievement-oriented parents. I always felt that what she was doing was directed against me; she was so angry with me.

I: Perhaps you were angry with your mother and your sisters in the same way your daughter was angry with you?

N: [After a moment of silence, she spoke nonchalantly.] That's an interesting piece of information.

I was struck by the remote, intellectual nature of Nurit's reaction. I felt that my interpretation had fallen on deaf ears, that I was not really touching her. It seemed that there would be no point in inquiring in the transference about a possible parallel between her daughter's way of relating to her and her way of relating to me, as this would likely result in an immediate rejection.

N: I never did that to my mother [i.e., got angry with her]. I was a good girl, a good student in school. My parents never had to worry about me. But, as soon as I became a teenager, my mother was no longer pleased with me. She accused me of being egoistic and selfish. I was terrified by her threats. She told me that I would never have any friends because I was so cold and inconsiderate. I remember my mother saying, "You'll see—your child will do exactly the same thing to you that you're doing to me!"

I was struck by the way the patient experienced her mother's reaction. Aspects of my own mother, her aggression and critical attitude toward me, sprang to mind.

I: You probably felt she was cursing you.

N: Yes, definitely. Today I know that I have good relationships with people; a lot of people like me. But then I didn't know that and I believed her. It completely shook my self-confidence. You know, when I was around eleven years old, Mother became so demanding—everything had to be done perfectly! I remember the first time it happened, it left such a strong impression on me. Mother accused me of not turning off the light in my grandmother's room. I was so sure I had turned it off that I argued bitterly with her about it. But in the end, I felt confused and wasn't really sure anymore. This began happening so often that I no longer knew when I was right and when I was wrong. Maybe this caused the symptoms that I'm suffering from now.

Nurit's distress left a deep impression on me. Evidently, years of being told that she was completely untrustworthy had left her feeling that she could not trust her senses.

N: [speaking suddenly] This plant in your office, wasn't it much smaller two days ago, or am I imagining it?

There were various ways to react to this question. I could have inquired further about what she thought of this. I could have tried to link her anxiety over the replaced plant to her anxiety and guilt over being a replacement child for her parents (Brenner 2001)—but this was an idea that we would be able to deal with only later in the analysis. I chose instead to reassure the confused child revealed in the analytic situation. At the time, I felt that this was the only way to help her regain faith in her perception of reality.

I: Your question about the plant brings into the room the confused child who could not trust her senses. Yes, you are right, the plant was much smaller. I brought in a new, larger one yesterday.

In this session, we can observe my avoiding the attempt to touch upon unconscious, "dangerous" subjects, such as Nurit's wish that her siblings had never existed and her hatred of her mother. Instead, I totally accepted her conscious feeling of being the victim of a mother who had undermined her child's perception of reality. Nurit was afraid that I would not believe her version of the reality of life in her parents' home, just as her mother had not believed her reports of reality.

On the other hand, I felt something was missing in this analysis, and that was the work of making the unconscious conscious, due to my fear of arousing Nurit's anger and becoming her victim. The following statement by Nurit showed that she, too, felt something was absent.

> N: In the beginning of analysis, I expected you to ask me all sorts of questions so that you would know more about me, but you never did.

Since from the start, I had explained the role of free associations to Nurit, I speculated over the deeper meaning of her remark. Was she referring to questions regarding her feelings toward me in the transference that I did not dare to bring up? Or perhaps to elements hidden in her story that I did not know about? I chose to pursue the latter, feeling that it would be more acceptable to her (and possibly safer for me, as well, at this stage of the analysis).

> I: Perhaps you see me as yourself, the little girl who wanted to know so much about the secret past of her parents, but never dared to ask?

We were both silent and the session ended.

*Session 2.* Nurit entered the room, lay down on the couch, and immediately began talking:

> N: You know, yesterday I paid a visit to Hanna, Mother's close friend from Bergen-Belsen. I took the opportunity of asking her some questions about Mother's past.

Nurit had told me about Hanna, who had a traumatic story of her own. After her little boy was killed in an "aktion" in the ghetto, Hanna discovered a little girl at Bergen-Belsen, a cousin's daughter who had lost her parents. She took the child into her care, thus saving her life.

> N: Yesterday, Hanna described to me her first encounter with Mother at Bergen-Belsen. When Mother initially saw Hanna with her little girl, she exclaimed, "You're so lucky you saved your daughter—I couldn't save mine!" "How wrong you are," Hanna had answered, and painfully recounted the loss of her son. Comparing their similar

fates, the two women discovered that their children, both approximately eleven years old, had been killed in the same "aktion" in the ghetto. "There were no words to describe the bond between us," said Hanna.

Hanna and my mother became soul mates. They supported each other physically and emotionally and raised the little girl together. And I found out that my half-sisters were killed at around the age of eleven, not when they were seven, as I had always thought. So Mother lived alone with her daughter for four years.

We were both silent.

> N: I picture my mother as a lonely, frightened woman, living with her child in dreadful circumstances, under the threat of death and destruction. I can imagine the special closeness between mother and daughter in this terrible situation. They probably existed for each other. I envy their closeness, but I also feel sorry for them.

This was the first time I had heard Nurit express any sympathy for her mother.

> N: Something else left an impression on me in my meeting with Hanna: the fact that now, fifty years later, Hanna is still haunted by painful memories of her son's last moments. For example, Hanna continues to be tormented by the fact that her little boy was cold and was wearing uncomfortable shoes when he was snatched away from her and taken to his death. I think that this irrational, gnawing pain that still torments her also tormented my mother throughout her life. [After a moment of silence, Nurit continued.] I recently saw a movie about a Holocaust survivor who destroyed his relationship with his son when the child turned nine. The survivor himself was nine years old when his parents were taken away, leaving him alone in the world.
> I: Do you think this movie might reflect something about your relationship with your mother?
> N: Yes, it could; I never actually thought about it. My problems with Mother began at around the age of eleven, the age when my half-

sister was murdered. Mother loved and adored me as a child. That changed completely when I grew up. Mother wanted me to be a copy of herself, her double. [Then, without the slightest hint of emotion, she added the following.] I lived and her daughter died.

I: [I was amazed by this statement.] Her daughter? Aren't you her daughter?

N: I was Father's daughter. Mother always said that I was like Father and his family. I got along better with him. Mother was very jealous that I lived and her daughter perished. She never forgave me for that. [Silence.] Mother made me feel that I wasn't connected to reality, that I couldn't perceive it correctly, that I couldn't possibly be trusted. I felt I'd done terrible things, that I was apologizing all the time. I think my only crime was that I grew up instead of her daughter.

Following this session, myriad thoughts passed through my mind regarding this last comment of Nurit's. How horrible it must have been for the mother—the disappearance of her little girl, followed by the news that the girl and her caretaker had been killed in an "aktion." And then another separation, when the daughter who was slated to replace the lost child grew up and entered adolescence. By leaving childhood behind and becoming different from the person the mother had destined her to be, the daughter was no longer able to fulfill her mother's unconscious fantasy of resurrecting her dead, beloved child. Nurit felt that in her mother's eyes she had become the embodiment of her father's daughter, and, as such, Mother envied and resented her existence.

And what about this child, I further wondered, who had failed in the competition with her dead, idealized sibling and who was also unable to fulfill her mother's unconscious wish that she repair her grief? How she must resent her dead sibling and how angry she must be toward the mother who made her feel a complete failure and as though she were the cause of her mother's unhappiness!

Also, Nurit's persistent claim of a clear conscience, stating that her only crime was that she grew up instead of her mother's daughter, made it very difficult for me to delve into her unconscious wishes and her guilt over the "terrible things" her mother had accused her of. Consciously, Nurit remembered that her mother had regarded her as the cause of her unhappiness. Consequently, throughout adolescence, she saw herself as a bad, egotistical person, and felt guilty about it. I believe that, unconsciously, Nurit felt guilty about her aggressive wishes toward her little sister—Mother's child—and toward Mother herself, wishes that stemmed from feeling wronged by them. But if this were so, why wasn't I able to touch her hateful, murderous feelings toward me in the transference, I again asked myself. Was I so afraid of arousing her anger and thus becoming her victim? Or was I afraid of becoming her persecutor, who, by interpreting her aggressive wishes, would inflict even more pain and humiliation upon the victim? This dilemma preoccupied me at length without my being able to solve it. Only later on in analysis would I be able to deal with this issue.

Nurit continued to share with me her painful feelings over her lost place in her mother's heart. Her associations regarding the refugees who lived in DP (displaced persons) camps near her childhood home in Europe reflected her feelings of alienation from her mother. Nurit described the DPs as refugees: poor, uprooted people who belonged to no place in the present world, and who could not return to their past, nonexistent world. In analysis, we understood that Nurit had identified with these DPs during her adolescence. Not only had she been divested of her role as her mother's beloved child in the present, but she felt she could not go back to her loving mother from the past. Nurit was the DP who had arrived in place of her mother's "real" daughter, but who had not succeeded in replacing her. From a transferential viewpoint, Nurit felt like a poor, uprooted, displaced person, rejected by her mother, searching for a new home in analysis.

Another memory from Nurit's adolescence surfaced in analysis: Her mother, bitter and dissatisfied, had frequently spoken of adopting a child. This wish never actually materialized. However, her mother had a special relationship with Dina, an acquaintance, a young woman who had been a child during the Holocaust. Nurit believed that, on a fantasy level, her mother had found her "real" daughter in the "adoption" of Dina.

Nurit's accounts of her present-day visits abroad to her parents enabled us to elaborate upon her complex relationship with them. These visits were never easy or pleasant for her, and in spite of now being a mature adult, she still felt criticized and unwelcome in their home. She often asked her husband or one of her children to accompany her, to serve as a buffer between herself and her mother. Nurit felt that her visits to her parents were important to them so that they could show the world what a good, devoted daughter they had. However, her mother's complaints about the additional work for her cleaning woman made Nurit feel that her visits were a bother for her mother.

Nurit described in detail an episode from one of these. The following exchange took place between mother and daughter behind closed doors, at her mother's insistence. Mother began the discussion by saying, "You are a courageous person, aren't you? So, why do you hate me so much?" Completely overwhelmed by this question, Nurit asked, "Who says I hate you?"

"Everyone knows you do," answered Mother, and to prove her point named three cleaning ladies who had worked in the house some thirty years earlier. "The first one," said Mother, "told Grandmother that one could easily see that you're Father's daughter from his first marriage. The second one said that it's obvious from your behavior that you don't love your mother. I overheard the third one repeating the same statement."

At this point, Nurit said she realized that time had stood still for her mother and that the past was totally alive in her present world. Nurit's denial of her mother's accusation was to no avail. Mother began recounting Nurit's sins, beginning with her childhood. The list was interminable: When she was four years old and mother took her to a department store, Nurit said that she wanted a mannequin she saw there to be her mother, which her mother took as evidence that already at that fragile age, Nurit wanted to exchange her for a different mother. At age twelve, Nurit said she hated her mother's handwriting. Afterward, she wrote a note and apologized for that, but the note got lost. Mother went on and on in this vein, ruminating about Nurit's offenses.

Trying to bring her back to reality and to connect her to some feelings of love, Nurit said to her mother, "I am forty-six years old and I am your daughter. Can it be possible that this is all you remember? Don't you have any good memories of me?"

In spite of her efforts, Nurit claimed her mother could not be swayed. Firmly entrenched in feelings of hatred and persecution, her mother continued, "You threw me out of your house!" Nurit was stunned. "What!" she said. "When did this happen?" Mother mentioned an incident when she had come to Nurit's house in Israel to visit Nurit's father, who had been hospitalized there at the time. "I put my things away, but you told me not to make such a mess. You threw me out of your house." Mother's logic could not be disputed. "During that same visit," she said, "I slept in your double bed. You always grabbed the blanket away from me during the night. I could have died of cold. And I never had lunch when I visited your father at the hospital—you never asked me if I had eaten. I could have died of hunger and you wouldn't have cared."

Nurit recounted the enormous effort she made to interrupt her mother's tirade: "What a pity that this is all you remember after forty-six years! Mother, I do not agree with your accusations. I want to remember the good things we had together, the things I learned from you. I am leaving and taking those memories with me. I wish I could leave the others behind. Thank you for your nice presents." Nurit kissed her mother on both cheeks and walked out.

In analysis, Nurit tried to work through the feelings caused by this painful encounter. At first she was dumbfounded; her adolescence, and indeed, her life with her mother, were revivified in her mind. Nurit told me she now realized that her mother was living in a totally different reality, where Nurit was her Nazi persecutor. "This time Mother actually explained to me why she hated me," said Nurit. "Not only did I grow up turning into Father's daughter, but I also made her feel homeless and deprived her of heat and food. I denied her the most basic necessities of life and was so cruel that I didn't even care."

I pointed out to Nurit that she felt persecuted by her mother no less than her mother felt persecuted by her. Nurit agreed that each of them had projected the Nazi aggressor upon the other.

Nurit claimed that the way she now perceived her mother brought her a measure of relief and strengthened her belief in her perception of reality. Expressing her gratitude to me, she said, "When I listened to Mother, I thought about my treatment. I now see things in a totally different light. It was worth every penny I've spent on analysis," she added.

### Phase 3: Finding Hidden Truths

During this third stage, we both, analyst and patient, attempted to uncover the truth of Nurit's internal representation of her father and to work through her complex relationship with him. Until recently, Nurit had greatly idealized him. He was not only clever and successful, but had shown her much love throughout her childhood. They used to enjoy walking and talking together; her father had always been proud of her.

Nurit's oedipal attraction to her father, her love and admiration for him, stood in sharp contrast to her attitude toward her mother. In analysis, we worked through her oedipal conflicts at length. I will now describe an episode from the patient's adolescence that illustrates her unconscious attraction to her father and the place she wanted to have in his life.

Nurit related that when she was around seventeen years old, Father confessed to an affair with his secretary during his travels abroad. Nurit believed that this confession had been forced upon her father, as her mother had confronted him with a letter to his secretary that she had found which implicated him, followed by information she had obtained from a private detective whom she had employed for this purpose. Father acknowledged his guilt, but claimed that the relationship was over and promised to be loyal to his wife from then on. Mother had raved madly about father's betrayal and had even considered the possibility of divorce. To her mother's great surprise, Nurit took her mother's side and supported the idea of divorce, pointing out that she did not want her parents to stay together on her behalf.

Nurit remembered being very involved in the story of her father's betrayal. One day, she walked into his office and asked him if he had had only one lover or many. Father, totally surprised by the question, claimed that he had had only one relationship, which was finished. Nurit walked out of her father's office, satisfied with his answer.

In analysis, we tried to discover and work through Nurit's unconscious wishes and fantasies. She remembered feeling hurt by her father, as if she herself had been the woman who was betrayed. We understood that by favoring the idea of divorce and attempting to find out intimate details of his love life, Nurit had unconsciously wished to become his fantasized partner. Much psychic work was needed for Nurit to realize the impact that her oedipal attraction toward her father had had on her clashes with her mother, as well as on her defenses. Only later did we understand that her emotional detachment in analysis stemmed not only from the protective shield she had developed against being hurt by her mother, but also from her identification with her father.

Nurit was able to acknowledge some of her negative feelings toward her father, such as the fact that, even though he was loving and admiring of her, he had been of no help to her during her difficult adolescence. She claimed that he had preferred to ignore his wife's emotional state—her unexpected outbursts of anger and her cruel ways of handling Nurit. She remembered that, when she had initially found herself at the mercy of her aggressive, persecutory mother, she had turned to him for help and support. But father never took her side, in spite of seeing how upset and helpless she was. Nurit quickly learned that she was on her own in her fight for survival. Aware of her plight, father would sometimes softly utter, "It isn't really so terrible!" But he never actually dared to comfort her or to argue on her behalf with his bitter, spiteful wife. His repeated comment to Nurit was, "You have to understand your mother—she has been through so much suffering!"

In analysis, we tried to work through Nurit's feelings of anger and frustration at what she experienced as her father's emotional abandonment, feelings that until now she had denied. Attempting to understand his behavior, she expressed the belief that his guilt feelings—not only regarding his lover, but also over his former family—were at the core of it. He had fled to Russia during the war, leaving his father, wife, and child behind, and they had all perished in his absence. Nurit never saw him exhibit any feelings of mourning or guilt over the loss of his family. Father always kept his feelings under control. Nurit now believed that his life had been dedicated to her mother's well-being, which helped him make reparation for his lost family. She came to the conclusion that he had sacrificed her, Nurit, as part of a "peace treaty" with his wife. The patient believed that by never interfering with his wife's "methods of education" and leaving Nurit to her mercy, her father had gained the freedom to do as he pleased in his profession, his hobbies, and even in his relationships with members of his family whom his wife did not accept. When he did quarrel with his wife, she would express her anger by shouting and accusing him of being inconsiderate, egoistic, and lacking in feelings. She would then move on to Nurit, accusing her of being his daughter, resembling him and his family: hard, cold, and egocentric.

The following incident caused Nurit to realize her ambivalent feelings toward her father. When she opened the door to leave the room at the end of the painful encounter with her mother described earlier, her father passed by on the way to his room and closed his door. Although he had just seen the two women together in an unusual situation and had probably observed the flustered expression on his daughter's face, he did not pause to ask about it. "That's what he always used to do. I remember now," said Nurit. "I once thought that he loved me. I clung to him and had to believe in his love even if it wasn't true. I know now that he was never there for me when I needed him. He sacrificed me for his own well-being."

In connection with this episode I remembered that Nurit had reproached me, as well, for never asking her enough questions. Was it possible, I asked myself, that she felt that I, too, had abandoned her to carry her pain and suffering alone? I did not dare bring up this idea, feeling that she would immediately reject it. I later realized that at this stage, Nurit had projected onto me the role of her father, and I had identified with it.

The elaboration of her disappointment in her father highlighted the oedipal rivalry and envy that existed between Nurit and her mother. Nurit felt that her mother envied her everything she had ever achieved. I tried to point out to Nurit the extent to which she envied her mother for the love bestowed upon her by her father. Nurit acknowledged that for a long time she had felt that this love was given to her mother at her own expense.

Realizing how much she was affected by her parents' past, Nurit said, "I used to think that my parents' stories belonged to their past and I didn't want to know about them. Now I know that my parents' stories are my own stories. I am struggling to know, to understand. I am struggling to live."

**Phase 4: Confronting Her Own Wrath**

During this stage of the analysis, Nurit's mother, who was eighty-four years old, developed breast cancer, underwent an operation, and lived for another eighteen months. I will not describe this phase in detail; suffice it to say that at the start, her mother refused treatment, apparently concealing her illness for about two years.

Nurit reacted strongly to mother's behavior: "That's suicidal! If she had sought treatment from the start, she would still have a good chance of living. Mother told me on the phone that there was nothing to be sad about; at her age, this is normal. I separated from my real mother a long time ago. I can only pity this woman and hope that she suffers as little as possible. If that's what she wants, that's what she'll get!"

I pointed out to Nurit how angry she was at her mother. Nurit readily agreed: "Mother couldn't save her daughter, so she had to pay for it by suffering. This is her way of appeasing her feelings of guilt."

Nurit continued to settle her account with her mother. She claimed that by not seeking treatment for breast cancer, her mother was trying to destroy her breast, the symbol of motherhood. From her last discussion with her, she deduced that her mother had erased Nurit's happy childhood from her memory. "She lost her first child and erased the memories of the second," said Nurit. "She doesn't need a breast anymore." Was this really so, I asked myself, or was it Nurit's anger resurfacing at the moment of separation from her mother that made her see the tragic event from this perspective? Had her mother erased all memories from her mind or had Nurit erased her loving mother, the one who held happy memories? And if so, was it not because Nurit wanted to protect herself against the feelings of loss and pain that would be incurred by her mother's death? This hypothesis was confirmed by the events that followed.

Despite her opposition to receiving treatment, the doctors convinced Nurit's mother to undergo an operation. Nurit and her family visited her and sat for hours at her bedside. Nurit recounted that her mother recovered quickly from the operation and behaved very lovingly toward her husband and grandchildren. Nurit felt that it was only toward her that her mother acted coldly. Though hurt, she expressed some relief, confirming my hypothesis as to the defensive quality of her anger. "I was afraid she was going to bestow a lot of love and affection on me. I separated from a loving mother once before in my life. If she had shown me affection, I would have had to go through another painful separation."

I asked Nurit if it were possible that she had already separated from her loving mother, but not yet from her persecutory one. Nurit acknowledged the truth in this. When confronted with situations where she felt a lack of self-confidence, she would hear mother's voice inside her, undermining her trust in her senses. Evidently, this voice was now part of her. It was apparent to me that reparation of the split mother figure should be one of the objectives of analysis.

Nurit's mother died a year and a half after the operation. I now describe how, at long last, we revealed and worked through Nurit's aggressive feelings toward me (her mother) in the transference. For this purpose, I use material taken from two consecutive sessions in the fifth year of analysis.

*Session 1.* Two years after her mother's death, Nurit's persecution at the hands of her mother still remained a topic that constantly preoccupied us. There seemed to be no room in Nurit's mind for anything else. The image of the critical, persecutory mother accompanied us through entire sessions. I felt as if we were never alone in the room, but always in the presence of a threatening third figure. I was flooded by Nurit's obsessive thinking, angry and helpless to stop it. Feeling impotent and frustrated I said:

> I: Your mother is always here with us; she never leaves us alone. Lately, I feel that she is persecuting both of us.

Silence. What was it, I asked myself, that I could no longer tolerate? Nurit's never-ending obsession with her persecutory, present-though-absent mother was unbearable. Was it possibly connected to how, throughout her life, she had experienced the presence of her absent sister? Was this connected to my feelings about my own mother or about myself as an analyst? Or did it represent Nurit's sadistic, aggressive aspect, which I had never succeeded in working through in the transference? Nurit's ensuing remark and my reaction to it made me realize how angry she was with me.

> N: Well, lately, I've seen you looking exhausted, especially toward the end of the week. I thought, "She looks so tired—what can I possibly expect of her!"

I was astonished and ashamed, as if caught doing something wrong. True, I had lately been suffering from a state of physical exhaustion, which fortunately had been diagnosed and was being treated successfully. I was making an extreme effort to overcome it, hoping my patients would not be affected by it. The blow of Nurit's aggressive words left me speechless. I felt impotent, humiliated, vulnerable, afraid that my weak state had been exposed, that I had become totally useless to my patients. Her anger is so bitter, I thought to myself. With great effort, I addressed Nurit:

> I: If you felt I wasn't doing you any good, you must have been extremely disappointed and angry with me.
> N: Only for a short while. [This was stated in an unperturbed manner.]

I silently observed that in the previously-described situation Nurit no longer asked me whether her perception of me was correct. I neither confirmed nor denied it. Nurit no longer needed that from me.

*Session 2.*

> N: I wanted to tell you something I'm very proud of—the way I handled a difficult situation. My beloved cat, Kotul,[1] went outside and hunted down a little bird. He came back into the house, holding the bird firmly in his teeth. I was so upset at seeing the captive little bird. I thought that if I shouted at him, he would only hold the bird even more tightly in his teeth. So I decided to speak to him softly. Then I gently put my hands around his neck and squeezed; the pressure made him open his mouth for air and the bird was freed.
>
> I: You're saying that you had to strangle the fierce, attacking cat to free the little bird?
>
> N: [She laughed.] Actually, I love Kotul very much, but it was the only way to free the bird. I didn't want Kotul to feel that I was angry with him; I handled him with love.

There was a silence. My thoughts revolved around the ferocious cat and the vulnerable little bird as the Nazi-persecutor and Jewish-victim images, which were always lurking in the background of the analysis and which represented aspects of Nurit's self. But immediately, a question crossed my mind: Am I still so afraid of my patient that instead of interpreting the experience in the transference, I have to go back to Holocaust history and intellectualize?

> N: My mother held me in her clutches, the way my cat clutched the poor bird brutally in his mouth. For a long time, I felt that Mother was my Nazi persecutor, even though she felt it was the other way around. She always accused me of being the cause of her unhappiness. When her accusations first began, I was furious, mad with rage; I tried to argue with her. Later on, feeling there was no point in arguing, I stopped displaying any emotion whatsoever. I was like a smooth wall—just try and climb it! I gave my mother nothing to hold on to.

I: Here, too, you were like a smooth wall for a long time, not allowing me to get hold of your feelings. It made me feel that I was a weak, ineffective therapist who couldn't give you the necessary foothold. I became the inoffensive little bird and you hated my ineffectiveness. It was only when you opened your mouth and expressed your anger that you set me free. But perhaps you felt that I was putting pressure on you so that you would open up and express your anger toward me, and this eventually helped you to release the bird, the tender, loving part of your being. You finally felt that you had to open your mouth—actually, your heart—and express emotions.

N: Remember that long talk I had with Mother? I wish I could have told her that I didn't really hate her, but that I was terribly angry with her for so many years! Actually, all that time, all I wanted was her love.

I: You are telling me how much you needed my love in spite of being angry with me for sometimes appearing weak and ineffective.

N: True. I sometimes asked myself whether we touched on everything we could touch on, conscious and unconscious, if we asked every possible question. But the relationship with you was always very important to me—your understanding and acceptance, your sympathy. The fact that you looked at the reality I experienced through my eyes gave me a lot of strength. [There was a silence, after which she continued.] I always loved my mother; I always needed her love. I can now appreciate the positive things about her: her sense of humor, her ability to enjoy the small joys of life. She loved me, too, I know, but as the years passed, the relationship became complicated, difficult. I often miss the good things she could have given me—simple, direct support and understanding. But now that I understand her suffering better and realize that I wasn't its only cause, I feel less angry than I used to be. The anger and pain are less acute. I see her in a different light.

Through the elaboration of these feelings, the obsessive quality of the sessions revolving around her mother's persecution decreased. Nurit began to recount a succession of memories of the doting, loving mother of her childhood. She began to realize that she had inherited some of mother's better qualities, such as an appreciation of good food and of running a fine home. She even began to wear the beautiful jewelry she had inherited from her mother, something that she had previously been unable to do.

As a result of the analytic process, Nurit began writing short stories with a passion that overshadowed everything else. Her stories often resembled still-life pictures, moments frozen in time. This creative activity helped her free herself from her internal persecutory mother, and her obsessive symptoms diminished greatly. Below is an excerpt from one of her stories, which describes her mother's life in Germany after the war, before she moved elsewhere in Europe—and, in Nurit's opinion, on to a different stage in life.

### "Regina Schuhe"[2]

*Her life is easy, comfortable, filled with things she likes to do, people who like and respect her. She belongs to an elite group of outsiders enjoying a special status, and she also speaks the local language. She now has more than she ever did, and she enjoys it all with a wonderful lust for life. She mentions the recent past: the deprivation, the hunger, the dirt, the promiscuity, the constant struggle to remain decent and civilized, the bonds of friendship, of solidarity, and the sudden emergence of natural leaders: "wise ones," comedians. She never speaks of her murdered daughter, and never acts as though she could be meeting the men who killed her child. She is very normal, very adequate, well adapted to her new situation. She should perhaps never have moved on.*

The analytic process facilitated the sublimation of Nurit's obsessive symptoms into genuine creativity (Chasseguet-Smirgel 1971). The creative process, in turn, facilitated recovery, helping Nurit achieve a better differentiation between herself and her mother, between her present life and her mother's past experiences, between reality and fantasy. Creative activity also reinforced Nurit's sense of self-worth and self-confidence, strengthening her perception of reality. At this stage in the analysis, we both felt that we were heading toward the end of our analytic journey.

### DISCUSSION

I wish to examine this case from two different aspects. I shall first explore the patient's emotional and cognitive development in light of her parents' Holocaust experiences, with particular focus on the impact of the moth-

er's traumatization and unresolved mourning on the mother-child relationship and on the character structure of the child. I will then discuss
some of the transference and countertransference problems encountered,
particularly the unique countertransference challenges resulting from the
analyst's sharing a similar traumatic experience, as well as from the fact
that the patient and analyst belonged to the same traumatized large group.

### The Impact of the Mother's Traumatization on the Child

The patient came to therapy at the same developmental stage in life at
which her mother had experienced her own trauma, and upon undergoing
an experience akin to that of her mother's: the separation from and poor
relationship with her adolescent daughter. It is possible that the inability
of the mother to work through her horrific loss did not allow for a normal
separation between mother and daughter, and this reverberated in the
next generation in the relationship of the patient to her own adolescent
daughter. Afraid of reenacting her own traumatic experiences vis-à-vis her
daughter, the patient decided to undergo treatment and open up the
wounds of the past, the pain of which continued to haunt her present-day
life.

I wish to speculate about certain aspects of the mother-child relationship that preoccupied me throughout this treatment. First, how can we
explain the transformation of the "good-enough mother" (Winnicott
1965) of the patient's childhood into a persecutory figure so many years
after the trauma of having lost her first child? The patient remembered her
childhood years as joyful ones, with her mother apparently happy, loving,
forgiving, full of *joie de vivre*, knowing how to enjoy the simple things in
life. The change that the daughter experienced in the mother's personality
and behavior was singularly incomprehensible to her.

Lorenzer (1968) writes that pseudo- or super-normality, based on a
split in the ego, may explain the phenomena of symptom-free intervals
and may provide an explanation for the late decompensations or depressions resulting from extreme emotional traumatization, after a prolonged
intermediate phase of apparent health. Such a split in the mother's ego
could account for her ability, after her traumatic loss, to muster sufficient
strength to find a new love, divorce her first husband, remarry, and have
another child.

I wish to suggest that the mother found a compromise solution that enabled the healthy part of her ego to function. On the one hand, she denied the death of her beloved child, as it was simply unacceptable; on the other hand, denying the loss entirely would have caused her to lose touch with reality and to become psychotic. Her solution—that of living in a world where her first child was not really dead, having been resurrected by the second child—was, in my view, what has been termed a "manic defense" (Klein 1935; Winnicott 1935). However, the normal process of her adolescent daughter's separation may have been experienced as traumatic by the damaged mother (Freyberg 1980), causing the mother's bitter, depressed aspect to surface.

As for the daughter, I believe that the trauma of the Holocaust, which affected both her parents, intertwined with her own developmental problems, had an impact on her relationship with her mother, as well as on the relationship with her own daughter. In analysis, the patient and I dealt extensively with her oedipal conflicts, but I will not expand on this topic here. My goal is to deal primarily with one particular aspect of the analysis: that of growing up as a replacement child to parents who were Holocaust survivors.

In considering how the mother's traumatization affected the psychic make up and defenses of the child, we might note that the intermingling of former parental nurturing with current aggression can give rise to confusion in a child, who may then begin to doubt his or her sense of reality (Auerhahn and Prelinger 1983). Hence, the persecution that the patient experienced at the hands of her formerly loving and nurturing mother left her totally baffled; it had a disorganizing effect on her life that even influenced her perception of reality. Furthermore, the patient was torn between the fears of losing her mother and losing touch with reality, leading to terrible internal conflict (Olagner 1975).

The patient developed obsessive-compulsive symptoms in performing her chores, which she endeavored to accomplish with utmost perfection in order to appease her mother. Auerhahn and Prelinger (1983) state that a child who has been confronted with a vision of a world gone out of control may have an intense need to keep matters under total control, both in the environment and in the self, and to defend against feelings of helplessness or aggression. Thus, the patient's obsessive-compulsive behavior may have served to keep difficult emotions at bay.

The daughter's obsessive-compulsive behavior can be understood from yet another angle. She had internalized the image of the persecutory mother, and the mother's voice followed her throughout her everyday adult life. The moments of confusion about reality, in which the patient heard her mother's voice in her present life, could be regarded as moments in which separation had not yet occurred. The daughter may have tried to preserve the relationship with her persecutory mother even at the cost of her own health. Guntrip writes eloquently about this problem: "Why do human beings maintain an internal object-relations world at all, especially if it is a bad one? What greater danger is being avoided in electing to face the dangers of internal bad objects experience?" (1968, p. 207). Apparently, losing oneself in a vacuum of experience would be even more frightening (Fairbairn 1943; Green 1974; Guntrip 1968). The patient's inability to differentiate between her inner world and external reality, between past and present, between her mother and herself, came to the fore at these moments of confusion. Her compulsive behavior grew out of an attempt to master this confusion and to reaffirm her grasp of reality. The years of being regarded as totally untrustworthy, of being accused of terrible deeds that she could not possibly have committed, had left her feeling that anything at all was possible. She could not trust her own perception of reality, nor could she be a reliable relayer of information.

In reconstructing her mother's story and attempting to understand her, Nurit speculated upon the possibility that during the Holocaust, the perfect performance of everyday tasks might have been of vital importance for her helpless, lonely mother. Her mother must have believed that these compulsive rituals would protect her from the terrible events occurring around her. The daughter came to the realization that, by imposing this form of behavior on her, her mother was actually trying to save her, an act belonging to the reality of the Holocaust.

Thus, her mother, who had accused her of not being capable of perceiving reality correctly, may herself have been living in a chaotic world, one in which past and present were confused. As a result, the daughter often felt transposed into an unknown, persecutory world as well—this, too, affecting her perception of reality.

But what might have been the source of the mother's confusion? The mother never actually knew how her first child had been lost. We can speculate that this fact shook her belief in herself and in her perception of reality (she never totally believed that the child *was* lost), causing terrible feelings of guilt. The crisis of her daughter's adolescence as well as later on her husband's betrayal must have reinforced her confusion. In an attempt to master her depression and guilt, she may have projected her insecurity and confusion into the daughter, who—through "primitive identification"—identified with it (Freyberg 1980; Grubrich-Simitis 1984; Kogan 1995, 1996, 1998a, 1998b, 2000, 2001a, 2001b, 2002, 2005). The daughter, too, may have borne feelings of insecurity, which often felt ego-alien to her, primarily because they belonged to her mother and not to herself. In this way, the child probably became a container of pain that could not be encompassed intrapsychically within the mother's personality structure (Bion 1959), and this, in my opinion, was vital to her mother's psychic survival.

The moments of confusion in the patient's present reality, when the voice of the mother shook her trust in her senses, were moments of self-imposed terror. The punishment inherent in this situation may have been related to the patient's unconscious feelings of guilt. I wish to examine some of the sources of these guilt feelings.

Nurit, born after two children who had perished, was a replacement child for both her parents. Blum (1983) describes the so-called replacement-child syndrome: What is deposited by the parents in the new child's self-representation is not only the image of the lost child but the image coupled with the unconscious fantasy that this will repair the parent's grief. Thus, failing in this regard, Nurit may have been tormented by feelings of guilt and, as punishment, unconsciously brought upon herself the critical voice of her mother.

Freyberg (1980) writes that the offspring of Holocaust survivors tend to experience their individuation as destructive toward their bereaved parents, who cannot sustain any further "losses" in their lives. Thus, it is possible that the patient, who on a conscious level rebelled against the role she had been assigned, on an unconscious level felt guilty for becoming an individual and building a life of her own.

From a different angle, the patient felt guilty over wishing to erase the memory of her sibling from her mother's mind. Failing in the competition with her mother's dead, beloved child, she was overcome by anger and death wishes toward her deprived mother. The mother, unable to contain her daughter's angry feelings because of her own traumatization, accused her of "terrible deeds" and assigned her the role of the Nazi aggressor.

She thus confirmed the daughter's murderous fantasies and enhanced her guilt.

### Special Transference and Countertransference Problems

In the case of Nurit, special transference and countertransference problems were encountered. Many of the countertransference problems were linked to the fact that analyst and analysand shared a common traumatic historical experience on a personal level, as well as belonging to the same large group whose parents were affected, either directly or indirectly, by the Holocaust.

Roth (1993) and Moses (1993) list the barriers to making conscious what has been unconscious among Jewish patients who have been through the Holocaust. These include, inter alia, a sense of shame and difficulty in taming aggression. In the transference, I encountered Nurit's powerful resistance to becoming aware of her unacceptable feelings of guilt and shame. These feelings were linked to her unconscious aggressive, murderous wishes toward her sister and her mother. As she was ashamed of these feelings, she used massive defenses that were designed to avoid any emotional understanding of her unconscious wishes. Only after becoming aware, through her emotional experience in analysis, that her aggression would not kill me, could the patient become aware of her aggression toward the primary objects in her life, and as a result, achieve better integration of self- and object-representations.

As for the countertransference, it, too, was problematic. It was clear to me that my feelings, perceptions, and attitudes with regard to the patient were, in part, displacements from my own early-life situations (memories about my relationship to my mother) onto the patient. My own personal history demonstrates this quite clearly. My father, upon completing his studies in pediatric medicine in Vienna, returned to Eastern Europe, where he married my mother. When war broke out, my paternal grandparents and two of my father's siblings, along with their families, were taken to concentration camps. My grandfather, as well as my aunt's family, perished there. In the meantime, my mother contracted tuberculosis, which at the time was regarded as a fatal disease.

Because of the war, as well as due to my mother's illness, my parents decided not to have children for thirteen years. It was an oft-repeated comment at home that "Nobody should be born during such times." I was born at the end of the war, when my parents were in their mid-thirties. The story I grew up with was that I was the only one of my mother's thirteen fetuses that she did not abort or miscarry. My mother disregarded the doctors' warnings that she would be endangering her life by having me.

Throughout her life, my mother mourned the first child she had aborted, a boy. This absent child was always present in her life—as well as in mine. And, as with my patient, I never fully succeeded in competing with my mother's idealized, beloved son. On a conscious level, my mother gave me the love she had for twelve additional unborn children, but on an unconscious level, I always felt that she was never totally satisfied with me. Although she was proud of my success and achievements in life, I felt I never succeeded in resurrecting and replacing her lost son.

It was this difficult lifelong experience that was evoked in the analysis with Nurit. When the patient obsessed about her mother, this brought my own mother and my complex and painful relationship with her into the room. Although elaborated upon over long years of my own analysis, it nevertheless had an impact on my countertransference feelings, and, as a result, on the patient's transference and the enactments created by both of us.

In addition, in this case, I believe my countertransference feelings were also the result of the fact that both the patient and I belonged to the same traumatized large group (Blum 1985; Volkan, Ast, and Greer 2002), whose unconscious fantasies included imagery of the Holocaust. Although I was, of course, very much aware of the difference between a live child murdered by the Nazis during the Holocaust and a fetus aborted by a mother because of her fear of the Nazis, the images, identifications, and unconscious fantasies involved in being a replacement child of parents traumatized by the Holocaust affected me to such an extent that for a period of time, I completely identified with Nurit and fell under the spell of her internal world. The trauma of the Holocaust, the havoc and destruction it wreaked upon the lives of our parents, affected both of us, patient and analyst alike.

This may be the reason why, in spite of my awareness of the patient's massive defenses against aggression and guilt, I found myself temporarily powerless in the face of her efforts to control my feelings as well as her own. Afraid to arouse her anger, I became the helpless, frightened little

Jewish girl, while the patient became the omnipotent Nazi persecutor whose murderous rage I did not dare arouse. At the same time, I was afraid that by interpreting her unconscious aggressive wishes in the transference, I would become the Nazi perpetrator and inflict further shame and humiliation upon her (Oliner 1996). Only after working through my feelings, which led me to the realization that my apprehension was permeating the therapeutic relationship and hindering the patient's progress, did I disidentify myself from the Jewish-victim/Nazi-perpetrator images, recover my analytic function, and help the patient get in contact with her unconscious aggressive wishes and anxieties.

In spite of the fact that, for a period of time, out of my countertransference feelings, I had colluded with the patient in keeping the threatening material out of analysis, I believe that my regression during this period was actually a "regression in the service of the other" (Olinick 1969). The fact that for some time I had accepted Nurit's view of reality as objective helped strengthen her belief in her perception of reality and her psychic sanity. This cemented our therapeutic relationship, which became the background against which we could later attempt to make the unconscious conscious.

I feel that the moment in analysis when I experienced Nurit's direct aggression toward me constituted a "crucial juncture" (Klein 1929), in which her love and hatred toward me converged. The patient's aggressive attack expressed itself through her encroachment into my "perimeter of safety" (McLaughlin 1995). Unlike in other situations, where "getting real in analysis" (Renik 1998) had not posed such a problem for me, in this case I felt crushed by the violence of her attack. The fact that I survived her assault without retaliation (Winnicott 1971) turned me into a good object for the patient, enabling her to finally release the bad object from her unconscious (Fairbairn 1943, p. 336; Guntrip 1968, p. 345). This also helped her accept the ordinariness of her aggression, which then became dissociated from the Jewish-victim and Nazi-perpetrator images that were tormenting her. Working through this experience in the transference, the patient was then better able to integrate self- and object-representations and associated polarized affects. It helped her mend the split in the internal maternal figure, as well as the rupture in herself.

Other important achievements that resulted from the analysis were the patient's experience of an easier separation from her adolescent daughter and an improved relationship with her. In addition, the patient's anal struggles for control were transformed into creative activity (Chasseguet-Smirgel 1971). Through her creativity, the patient attempted a double reparation: to repair her mother—the object whose retaliation was feared (Klein 1929)—and to achieve self-reparation by mending what her ego had done to itself in fantasy.

## NOTES

1. The word *hatul* in Hebrew means *cat*. In Polish, Nurit's mother tongue, the word *kot* means *cat*. Apparently, the name *Kotul* was a combination of the Hebrew and Polish words for *cat*. In addition, the root *katol* in Hebrew means murder, destruction; thus, the name *Kotul* has the connotation of a ferocious animal.

2. The name of the story is also the name of a store where the patient's mother bought shoes.

# OBSTACLES TO MOURNING IN AN AGE OF TERROR

# Introduction

In this section I will explore defenses against mourning during the Holocaust (chapter 8) and during current episodes of terror in Israel (chapters 9 and 10).

Chapter 8 examines massive defenses, including the erasing of one's history, the denial of reality, and the absence of mourning in extreme life-threatening situations. These defenses are illustrated through a psychoanalytic examination of the life of Solomon ("Solly") Perel—the hero of the movie *Europa, Europa*. Solly is a Jewish adolescent who, during World War II, attended a Hitler Youth School, and this saved his life. Solly's mechanisms of repression and denial of mourning helped him survive physically, but at the cost of an enormous emotional price—the disintegration of his identity.

In recent years, Israel has continued to experience times of terror. Chapters 9 and 10 refer to the *intifada*, the Palestinian guerrilla war against Israel. When it broke out, most of us were in a state of shock. We were so close to peace, or so it had seemed to us. The *intifada* brought with it continuous gunfire in Jerusalem, murder on the roads, suicide bombers blowing themselves up in public places, terrible destruction, and the death of children and youth, adults and the elderly, sometimes even of entire families.

When acts of terror become part and parcel of our everyday life, and the threat to the security of each and every one of us increases, traces of the Holocaust may be reactivated in the unconscious of those who have been directly or indirectly affected by it. The reactivation of the traumatic past may have an impact on the defenses of both patient and analyst alike. Chapters 9 and 10 present cases in which manic defenses were reinforced

(Klein 1935; Winnicott 1935) as a result of the encounter with external traumatic reality, and analysis became difficult under the shadow of terror. Theoretical issues such as the relationship between external and internal reality in a situation of terror and the goal of analysis during such times are discussed in chapter 9 but apply to chapter 10 as well.

Both chapters illustrate the reactivation of the Holocaust trauma in the unconscious. Chapter 9 deals with the problem of the analyst's role during times of chronic crises and the impact of a shared life-threatening situation on the defenses of both members of the analytic couple. Chapter 10 focuses on the impact of external traumatic stimuli on the perception of reality and on the defenses of Holocaust survivors' offspring.

# Who Am I? Trauma and Identity

*So, we turned to the victims, the survivors. They were asked to bare themselves, to delve into the innermost recesses of their being, and tell, and tell again, to the point of exhaustion and beyond: to the delirium that follows. How it had been. . . . And you, how did you manage to survive? Had you known the art of survival from before? And how were you able to keep your sanity?*

—Elie Wiesel, 1972

## INTRODUCTION

Up to this point, the different chapters of the book have related to defenses against mourning in the context of a normal external reality. This chapter, by contrast, explores the survival value of repression and denial of mourning during the traumatic reality of the Holocaust and their impact on identity. In the case described in this chapter, mourning and guilt would have been a liability and could have interfered with survival. However, maintaining these defenses extracted a heavy emotional price—the destruction of integrity and self-identity.

The Holocaust was a cataclysmic event that changed the shape of human history forever. It was an unprecedented, systematic attempt to achieve racial purity through the extermination of innocent people. Reduced in the eyes of their persecutors to the lowest form of life, Jews, as well as homosexuals and those suffering from physical and mental abnormalities, were regarded as a threat to the Aryan race. As invaders of the Aryan body, they were to be totally and completely annihilated in order to purge the German genetic pool of their alleged taint. Even as late as the spring of 1944, when the tide had already turned against the German war effort, the official party line put forth by Joseph Goebbels and the German Ministry of Propaganda was still being broadcast: "In the case of the Jews, there are not merely a few criminals (as in other people), but all Jewry rose from criminal roots and in its very nature it is criminal. The Jews are no people like any other people, but a pseudo people welded together by hereditary criminality. . . . The annihilation of Jewry is no loss to humanity but just as useful as capital punishment or protective custody against other criminals" (Hilberg 1985, p.1021; quoted in Brenner 2004, p.117).

The Holocaust left its impact in endless ways. To illustrate my theme, I examine the remarkable life of Solomon ("Solly") Perel—the hero of the movie *Europa, Europa*—from a psychoanalytic perspective. Solly is a Jewish adolescent who, during World War II, found himself attending a Hitler Youth School, thereby saving his life. I will briefly summarize the movie for the readers who did not have a chance to see it.

Set between 1938 and 1945, the movie (directed by Agneshka Holland), which is based on the autobiography of Solomon Perel (1994), tells the story of Solly, the son of a Polish-Jewish shopkeeper living in Peine, Germany. Nazi persecution of Jews is already well under way when Solly's sister is killed in a pogrom. After this traumatic event, the Perels determine to save themselves and their two remaining children (Solly and his older brother, Isaac) by moving from Peine to Lodz, Poland. As the Nazi threat grows worse, Solly's parents insist that he and his brother, Isaac, save themselves by fleeing east. At the beginning of his journey east, Solly clings to his older brother, but the siblings are soon separated. This new, traumatic separation leaves Solly to fend for himself, alone in a world full of danger. Solly arrives at a Russian camp and is sent to a Soviet orphanage in Grodno, east Poland. From there, Solly corresponds with his parents, who inform him that they are being transferred to the local ghetto. The daily routine at the orphanage is devoted mostly to Communist instruction. Solly adapts easily to his new sociocultural environment and becomes an enthusiastic Komsomol youth. With the collapse of the nonaggression pact between Hitler and Stalin, the orphanage is bombed, and the teacher and children flee. The teacher stops a truck, the children climb aboard, and Solly, who turns his attention elsewhere for a moment, is suddenly left behind. Again, Solly finds himself on his own.

Adrift once more, this time Solly lands in the hands of Nazi soldiers. With his fluent German, he passes himself off as an Aryan; he is now Jupp, an East German. Strange providence intervenes again. Solly finds himself in the midst of a battle after which he is mistakenly celebrated as a hero and greatly honored by being sent to a Hitler Youth School. In this new environment, Solly is soon ready to shed both his Jewish identity as well as the Communist one. However, his Jewish identity is branded on his flesh by circumcision. Falling in love with Leni, a girl attending the same school, only adds to his plight, as he cannot give in to their desire for sex without endangering his life. Solly unsuccessfully attempts to erase the mark of his Jewish identity that is imprinted on his flesh. He tries to disguise his circumcision by pulling down the remaining foreskin and sewing it back in place. Leni, however, hurt by what she experiences as Solly's rejection, turns her attention to his best friend as a partner for giving the Fuhrer the gift of a child.

The movie shows Solly shifting identities under extreme life-threatening situations in the service of survival. Only at the end of the war does Solly decide to return to his roots and search for his early Jewish identity. He is saved by finding his brother among the concentration camp inmates who wish to kill him because they mistakenly consider him a German officer, and together they make their way to Israel. Solly has a family of his own, and states that he is prepared to circumcise his sons, thus bringing the story full circle.

To return to my theme—the survival value of defenses against pain and mourning during life-threatening situations and their impact on identity, I first briefly review some of the psychoanalytic views on identity. I will relate to the developmental aspects, focusing on the seeds of identity that exist before birth and in early childhood, and then proceed to the vicissitudes of identity that occur during adolescence. Each is discussed in light of the hero's life story.

## IDENTITY IN EARLY CHILDHOOD

The term *identity* was introduced into the psychoanalytic literature in 1919. Tausk described how the child discovers his or her self, and asserted that throughout life one must constantly find and experience one's self anew. Freud used the term *identity* only once (Guttman et al. 1980), in his address to B'nai Brith, where he spoke of his "inner identity" (Freud

1926a, p. 274) as a Jew. However, a number of his ideas are of great significance to the concept of identity. Freud coined the term *das ich* (the ego) and used it in two different ways: as an executive agency of the mind, and as a "person's self as a whole" (Strachey et al. 1923, p. 7). The latter conceptualization of the ego seems to correspond to what is today termed identity. With regard to this conceptualization, Freud states: "In the process of a child's development into a mature adult there is a more and more extensive integration of his personality" (1921, p. 18). This integration of personality may be damaged by traumatic separations from protective objects, such as by forced migration from one sociocultural environment to another, as we shall see in the movie under discussion.

As mentioned, a child's identity can be traced back not only to earliest infancy but even to before his or her birth. Two factors lay the ground for what will be the child's basic core (Weil 1970; Akhtar 1999): his genetic blueprint and the parental expectations of the yet unborn baby.

The story of Solly begins at the most logical, primal point—his circumcision. The circumcision ceremony is a physical manifestation of Jewish identity that has been passed on from generation to generation since the very beginning of Jewish history. Solly's circumcision is pregnant with meaning, reflecting his parents' wish that their child carry the Jewish identity. The ceremony is also a metaphorical event, a branding, and the blood from the wound of the circumcision reverberates throughout the film— the Nazi ideology of spilling Jewish blood.

Solly claims to remember his circumcision. This memory is an early introjection, or, in Kernberg's terms, "an organized cluster of memory traces" (1976, p. 26), which forms his Jewish identity. Other childhood memories, including the celebration of Jewish holidays such as Passover and the Feast of Tabernacles (Sukkot), reinforce this identity (Passover, in commemoration of the liberation of the Jewish people from Egypt, after which they wandered in the desert for forty years; Sukkot in commemoration of the booths in which the wandering Jews lived in the desert, after their delivery from Egypt). His memory of these two holidays exposes Solly's longing for the Jewish atmosphere of his parents' home. Solly may have remembered these two particular holidays, which recall the Jewish people's fate as migrants and wanderers, as they were symbols of his own forced migration from one ideological framework to another during his adolescence.

## DISRUPTION OF IDENTITY IN LATER CHILDHOOD

With the shifting of the scene from his circumcision, we now see Solly at age thirteen soaking in the bathtub on the eve of his bar mitzvah (an important ceremonial event in the life of a young Jewish boy, who at age thirteen becomes an adult and takes on the responsibilities that are part of belonging to the Jewish people). The Nazi persecution of the Jews is already well underway, and as Solly bathes, a brick flies through the window and soldiers swarm into the family's apartment. To escape, Solly jumps naked out the widow and hides in a barrel. After several hours, he plucks up enough courage to ask a waitress friend to bring him some clothes; all she can find is a black leather coat with a Nazi insignia on the sleeve. But eager to return home, he slips into it. This is Solly's first disguise, and it is also prophetic of his future disguise as a Nazi. Arriving back home, Solly discovers that his family has been the victim of a pogrom and that his sister has been killed. This traumatic event has a great impact on Solly's psychic life.

Greenacre (1967) maintains that in situations in which actual traumatic experiences are associated with an underlying fantasy stemming from difficult experiences, the impact of the actual trauma is more intense, and the tendency to fixation is greater than in instances where life experiences are bland and incidental. In the same vein, Anna Freud writes: "External traumas are turned into internal ones if they touch on, coincide with, or symbolize the fulfillment of either deep-seated anxieties or wish fantasies" (1967, p. 24). The horrific murder of Solly's sister, which occurred against a background of normal sibling rivalry, may have greatly intensified Solly's survival guilt.

Soon after their daughter's murder, the Perels decide to save themselves and their two remaining children by moving from Peine to Lodz, Poland. Here we observe Solly's adjustment to his new surroundings and the awakening of his libidinal urges. In the short interim before he begins his painful, lonely exile, we are shown Solly's penchant for the cinema and his dreaming of being an actor like Clark Gable. It was perhaps this theatrical urge, combined with his inner resourcefulness, which equipped him with a special ability to adapt to his surroundings.

At the movie house, Solly becomes friendly with the cashier, a Polish woman and hunchback. Solly's oedipal attraction to older women (also to his young teacher in the Communist school, later on in the movie) was part of his developing gender identity. From the metaphorical prism, the hunchback woman may be regarded as a symbol of Solly's new motherland, Poland, the country that he began to like but which was already carrying the Nazi war machine on its back.

With the Nazi threat intensifying, Solly's parents decide that he and his brother, Isaac, must save themselves by fleeing east. The boys refuse to go, but the father orders them to flee, thus conveying to them the message that they must survive at all costs. The movie shows the two boys making their way east. But let us pause for a moment and try to analyze the impact of this traumatic event on Solly's psychic life.

In spite of the fact that Solly's parents forced him to flee in order to save his life, Solly may have unconsciously experienced this as a rejection and expulsion from his family. Although this most likely caused him frustration and anger, he was not in touch with these feelings. Moreover, the image of a strong father who should have been able to protect the family from danger and destruction is shattered. Thus, Solly's feelings of abandonment, anger, and frustration caused by the traumatic separation from his parents at this early age may have contributed to his relatively easy disengagement from his Jewish identity later on in life. The massive trauma caused by this rupture from his family wrought havoc upon his identity, his sense of security, and all of his basic assumptions about the future (Elsass 1997; Kestenberg and Brenner 1996; Krystal 1968; Brenner 2004).

Freud has stated that "the character of the ego is a precipitate of abandoned object-cathexes and . . . it contains the history of those object choices" (1923, p. 29). When Solly encounters other sociocultural environments that provided him with a new "family" and idealized new parental figures, Solly is ready to shed his Jewish identity, his identification with primary objects and their/his own history, and become part of these new cultures.

Solly and his brother find themselves fleeing from destruction to a world full of danger and animosity. Solly has to deny his guilt feelings for leaving his parents behind to perish. Guilt feelings would have carried with them the potential for demoralization and would have distracted him from the task at hand—of surviving one more day (Lifton 1968; Hass 1996). Even though Solly experiences overwhelming loss and is under enormous stress, causing feelings of intolerable anger and fear, he has to block out painful feelings such as guilt and mourning, which would prevent him from adapting to a changing, hostile environment.

## THE ENCOUNTER WITH OTHER SOCIOCULTURAL ENVIRONMENTS AND THE ADOPTING OF NEW IDENTITIES

### The Communist Camp and Orphanage

At the beginning of his journey east, Solly clings to his older brother, his substitute father, but the siblings are soon separated. This new traumatic separation leaves Solly to fend for himself, alone in a world full of danger. Solly finds himself in a Russian camp and is transferred to a Soviet orphanage in Grodno, in eastern Poland. The daily routine at the orphanage is devoted mostly to Communist instruction. Partly out of his wish to find a new ego-ideal in the form of a powerful father figure (Stalin), partly out of a crush he has on a mother figure (a pretty young teacher who takes him under her wing), Solly adapts easily to the training and becomes an ideal student, a member of the Komsomol youth, renouncing his Jewish identity as easily as he slipped into the Nazi overcoat. Eagerly adopting the Communist ideology, the movie shows him avidly reading a strident pro-Stalinist article that denounces religion as the "opiate of the masses," with which he now identifies. In spite of the fact that his identity as a Jew is reasonably safe because of its irrelevance, his coexistence with his Christian classmates is not devoid of tension. A Polish boy attempts to bully him for belonging to those who killed Jesus, the father of all Christians. This theme recurs later on, when Solly's girlfriend Leni informs him that the Jews, the enemies of the Fuhrer, killed her father in battle.

After the nonaggression pact between Hitler and Stalin collapses, the orphanage is bombed and Solly is left behind. The new idealized father (the great Stalin) was unable to protect him, and his new beloved mother of whom he was enamored (the young teacher) was unable to save him. The new ego-ideals are broken and Solly is once again separated from his newly acquired "family."

### The Nazi Ideology

Solly is again adrift, and this time lands in the hands of Nazi soldiers. With his fluent German, he passes himself off as an Aryan; he is now Jupp, an Ost-Deutche. The soldiers treat him royally, partly because of his rosy, wide-eyed good looks, and partly because of his usefulness as a Russian translator.

Strange providence intervenes again. Solly finds himself involved in a battle between the Germans and the Russians and is afterwards mistakenly crowned a hero. The ultimate irony occurs when Solly (who shares the same birth date as Hitler) is sent in triumph to a Hitler Youth School. There he is presented with his personal copy of *Mein Kampf.* Regarded as a hero at the front and winning a swimming competition in a swastika-decorated pool while wearing his army helmet and carrying his rifle, Solly eventually becomes a respected member of the Hitler Youth. In classroom lectures on how to identify Jews on sight, Solly is selected as an example of a true East German Aryan.

In comparison with the earlier communities to which he belonged, which were unable to protect him and which had rejected and abandoned him, this new community appears strong and promising. His fellow students are qualified to become the elite and are meant to have a distinct self-awareness of their own elevated, elitist status. Solly experiences his fusion with this elite peer group as a source of strength. This fusion symbolizes a larger fusion with the German Volk (the mother figure) and the Führer (the father figure), which makes his identification with the group vitally important to him. Solly is soon ready to shed both his Jewish identity as well as his Communist identity. His Jewish identity, however, is branded on his flesh through circumcision. The physical evidence of his circumcised state, which is the only link to his Jewish heritage, gravely endangers his survival. The movie shows Solly's efforts to hide his true identity by avoiding being seen in the shower or in the bathroom; letting down his guard even slightly would result in certain death. Solly has to be forever on guard; even a casual pause to relieve himself in the woods is fraught with danger, for no matter how deeply he immerses himself in his new role, the evidence of his identity is always there to betray him.

Solly becomes confused over the meaning of being Jewish, as he is loved and admired by the officers who, he knows, would kill him were they to know his true identity. One officer falls in love with him; another, the company's commanding officer, wants to adopt him. He is constantly exposed to talk about the Jews, of how they are the "real enemy." The Führer has a solution to the Jewish problem, Solly is told, and he naively accepts the lie he is fed that the solution is to gather the Jews and ship them off somewhere, "to Madagascar or Siberia," where they would no longer pose a threat to the German way of life. Solly is thus in a situation of "knowing and not knowing psychic trauma" (Laub and Auerhahn 1993), a two-sided state in which conscious ignorance of the Holocaust forms one side of the coin, while unconscious knowledge of it forms the other. This "not knowing," which is actually a denial of reality, also serves as a survival mechanism.

Another aspect of Solly's identity that is worth exploring is his gender identity that, at this stage, includes both homosexual and heterosexual tendencies. The German officer who became enamored with Solly finds out the boy's secret, and, in spite of the danger that this love relationship poses for the officer, he keeps the secret and thus saves Solly's life. This man forgives Solly his biggest flaw—the fact that he is Jewish—which leads Solly to perceive this older member of the institution as a substitute father or substitute brother. His love for Solly brings him in touch with his humane aspects, and he even recalls that once, in a different world than the one they are living in, he had been an actor and part of a cultured society. This "good" German is killed in a Russian attack, and with him the love and protection bestowed on Solly vanish, along with the humane aspect of Germany that he possibly represents. The death of the only man in this environment who loved him for what he was and who had been the container of his secret is a grave loss for Solly; and superimposed upon his former traumatic separations from beloved objects, it intensifies his feelings of loss and abandonment.

In regard to Solly's bisexual gender identity during his adolescence, I wish to refer to Freud who states that "all human individuals, as a result of their bisexual disposition and of cross-inheritance, combine in them-selves both masculine and feminine characteristics" (1925, p. 258). Gen-der identity is a complex psychological process that has its roots in the experiences of early childhood and the identification with both parents (McDougall 1989). Although Solly's core gender identity is already formed when he joins the Hitler Youth School, the constraints on his heterosexual behavior (which would endanger his life), in addition to the well-known injunction that adolescents had to keep themselves "pure" until they were ready to give a child as a gift to the Führer, cause him to regress to the preadolescent phase in which the need for a father figure is greater (Kogan and Schneider 2002). This may explain Solly's homosexual leanings, which stem mainly from his need to acquire protection from an older member of the institution. The need for a father figure, which may have been intensified by his disappointment in his own father, is another factor in Solly's feelings toward the homosexual German officer who falls in love with him.

The need for a father is mentioned by Freud, who declares that he "cannot think of any need in childhood as strong as the need for a father's protection" (1930, p. 72). In a series of essays spanning two decades, Blos (1962, 1965, 1967, 1974, 1985) demonstrates that the early, pre-oedipal son-father relationship has a crucial effect on the son's self and world view for a lifetime. The little boy seeks the father's approval and praise, and if these are found, a deep and lasting bond is established between them. The father's approval instills in the son "a modicum of self-possession and self-assertion—distilled, as it were, out of mutual sameness or shared maleness—which renders the wider world not only manageable and conquerable, but infinitely alluring" (Blos 1985, p. 11). But what kind of maleness could the traumatized and broken Jewish father instill in his son? And could the world of the Nazi Holocaust be at all manageable and conquerable? To counter his inner representation of a weak father, Solly wishes to fuse with idealized, omnipotent figures. This wish is actually typical of adolescence, because of the normal process of devaluation of the parents that occurs during this phase of development. In the case of Solly, the fantasized protective figures are Stalin and Hitler, and in real life, the protective figure is the homosexual German officer, and, in his great confusion, he attempts to replace his father with them.

Solly's heterosexual tendency is expressed through his attraction to Leni, a fresh-faced German girl who attends the Hitler Youth School and who admires Solly as a German hero. Leni's father was killed in battle, and she strongly believes that Jews killed him. Leni regards the Jews as the enemies of the Führer, the idealized father figure, and therefore have to be destroyed. "If I ever catch a Jew, I'll cut his throat," she eventually tells Solly in an offhand manner that nonetheless offends and angers him, and he impulsively slaps her face.

Solly does not dare sleep with Leni in spite of his very intense desire for her. Unable to fulfill his sexual needs because they endanger his life, Solly attempts to erase the scar that his Jewish identity has branded upon his flesh. He tries to disguise his circumcision by pulling down the remaining foreskin and sewing it back in place.

An individual's existence is deeply anchored in the sense of his or her corporeal existence. Freud's (1923) declaration that "the ego is first and foremost a bodily ego" speaks to this very point. Twelve years after Freud's statement, Schilder (1935) defined the concept of body image as the psychic representation of the body. Solly's psychic representation of his body is that of a castrated, wounded body that bears the traces of belonging to an inferior race. Thus, thinking in a way typical of adolescence, Solly seeks a concrete solution for "repairing" his "damaged" body. This concrete style of thinking usually undergoes transformations and is mediated by changes in ego functions; these changes depend on the structural-cognitive development that takes place in this phase of development (Ehrlich 1978). In Solly's case, these changes most likely did not take place because of the traumatic circumstances under which he lived. Solly's solution is not only concrete, but also self-destructive. This is one of the few times in Solly's life that death forces take over: By trying to rid himself of his Jewish identity he develops a very serious infection that is life-endangering. It is only due to his tremendous resilience that he survives this self-affliction.

It is intriguing to explore the Joseph ("Jupp") Peters persona that Solly adopted among the German soldiers on the battlefront. This identity is reinforced in the Hitler Youth School. Perhaps this is an example of how humanity-as-civilized and humanity-as-beast are separated by a tissue-thin veil. In a sense, Solly does become Jupp the Nazi. He is thrilled when the radio announces that the Germans have won another victory, and is saddened when Stalingrad falls and is heartbroken along with his German schoolmates. The experience of living in close quarters with German soldiers on the Eastern Front, along with the Nazi indoctrination in school, with its music and military drill, consolidate his Hitler Youth identity; but even if his spirit allows it, his body does not. He cannot be one of them, nor can he be himself; he can only wander between the two, an actor trapped—and saved—by his role.

Wheelis (1958) defines identity as a coherent sense of self. In the case of Solly, trauma breaks this coherence and the alternation between his various identities implies such grossly contradictory ideologies and values that he cannot be regarded as a whole human being. There is a major difference, however, between adopting different identities in external life-threatening situations and the phenomenon of multiple personalities (DID), which is described by Brenner (2004) as being at the extreme end of character pathology, "a lower level dissociative character" (1996a, 1996b). In Solly's case, adopting different identities was purely a mechanism for survival, which did not have pathological roots.

The confusion and conflicts accompanying the various roles that Solly adopts cause him great psychic suffering. This suffering is illustrated in the episode in which Solly discloses his true identity to a German woman, Leni's mother. He attempts to find Leni, who has disappeared from his life, and is told by her mother that Leni is pregnant. Fed up with his refusal to have sex with her, she chose his close friend as a partner for giving the Führer the gift of a child. Leni preferred to surrender to the Führer, the idealized father figure, rather than continue her relationship with the ambivalent Solly.

At this point Solly breaks down. His narcissistic hurt over Leni's abandonment is stronger than his life-preserving instincts and compels him to explain to Leni's mother his real motive for abstaining from sex with Leni. Aware of his suffering, Leni's mother takes him in her arms. Apparently she belongs to a generation that did not grow up with Nazi ideology and did not succumb to the Führer's "charm." But her warmth towards him cannot change anything, because he is still living in a world fraught with peril and danger.

The issue of a consolidated identity has been amply explored in the psychoanalytic literature. Erikson claims that a consolidated identity provides individuals with the intrapsychic experience of self-sameness. In the diverse social situations existing in a normal reality, these individuals act and feel in a manner that is true to themselves. They experience themselves as essentially one personality and maintain similar preferences across various external circumstances (Erikson 1950a, 1950b, 1956, 1958, 1962; Lichtenstein 1963). When interacting with different age groups or with individuals with whom they are on various levels of intimacy, they can modulate their behavior without losing a core of inner sameness and demonstrate consistent attitudes and behaviors. They display a stable investment in personal values and ideologies, and possess a repertoire of behaviors that presume congruous and predictable parameters. The desire to act in ways that deviate too widely from the prevailing sense of self are repressed or consciously inhibited and discouraged, thus maintaining a sense of internal consistency (Akhtar 1999).

Under normal life circumstances, an essential characteristic of individuals with a consolidated identity is this capacity to maintain personal continuity amid change and with the passing of time. Stern's concept of "self-history," that is, a sense of enduring and of a continuation with one's own subjective past, refers to this specific capacity. Individuals who possess it retain genuine ties with their past, can comfortably locate themselves in their current realities, and can envision their future (Stern 1985).

But how could Solly establish a sense of identity and express consistent attitudes and behaviors while constantly living under life-threatening situations? How could he develop a sense of personal continuity and of self-history? Was it at all possible for him to develop a sense of generational continuity (Chasseguet-Smirgel 1984) in a situation where to continue to be Jewish meant death and destruction? How could he belong to a historical community (Volkan 1988) if the ethnic identity of the group to which he belonged was life-endangering?

The story of Solly illustrates how trauma broke the coherence of the self. In defining trauma, Freud (1920, 1926b) emphasizes how the mind, like the body, can be pierced and wounded by events. For Solly, the stress of living in a constant state of peril overcame the protective barriers of his mind and damaged the integrity of his personality. Even at the very end of the war, the identity that saved him also almost caused his death, as rocked on the stormy waves of fate, he is almost executed by the Russians who are convinced he is a Nazi in disguise.

Watching the movie, we are aware time and again of Solly's great resilience in the face of adversity. Solly's objective was survival and survive he did. His resilience was due to his good looks, his intelligence, and a special talent for adapting to his surroundings. His shape-shifting, his ability to change identities, which were the result of his immense resourcefulness, and his ability to block off pain and mourning, were also elements of this resilience.

Rutter (1987) maintains that resilience is not a fixed attribute, but rather hinges on a balance between the mechanisms and processes of protection and vulnerability. Solly had the ability to protect his vulnerability by denying and repressing the cluster of cognitions, emotions, and meanings inconsistent with his survival (Kogan 1995, 2004). Solly survived be-

cause he was endowed with the wish to live life, to create it, to live and
hope even in the face of adversity, as well as because his parents gave him
the message that he must survive, all of which were important elements of
his resilience. Love of life itself, stamina, courage, and inner resourcefulness when confronted with life-threatening situations contributed to his
resilience.

"Who am I?" or "Which group do I belong to?" were central and most
painful issues in Solly's psychic life. Towards the end of the war, Solly travels from his school to Poland to visit the Jewish ghetto near his childhood
home. From inside a closed tram he observes the dreadful suffering of the
ghetto's inhabitants and realizes that something terrible must have befallen his parents. This visit is his first attempt to rebuild his sense of continuity and broken identity.

I would like to quote what Perel writes about this visit in his autobiography, upon which the movie is based. Perel describes the guilt feelings
that this visit evoked in him at the time: "I did not know about the destruction, its forms and methods. . . . In the cocoon of my school I studied
theories, but my brain refused to acknowledge the fact that these theories
were being put into practice in the different death camps. A deep pain is
lodged inside me: How did I not understand when I traveled through the
Lodz Ghetto that these people would not be there long, that they would
be sent to the death camps? Looking back I remember that I saw only
grown-ups on the ghetto streets, and no children at all. How did I not ask
myself the meaning of this? I am greatly disturbed by the barrenness of
thinking that encompassed me. I failed to break through the fog that enve-
loped me, that prevented me from seeing the screaming writing on the
wall. The war I was caught up in sharpened my senses, but also blunted
them" (1994, p. 192).

At the end of the war, Solly becomes aware that he has paid a terrible
price for surviving and is overcome by depression. He feels lost, belongs
nowhere; he is neither Jewish nor German. "The faces of those who were
liberated radiate happiness. They know that in a few weeks they will return
to their country, their homes and families, renew their normal way of life.
For me there is no place to return to. . . . I fear that I am losing my sanity.
I do not know who I am and what I am" (p. 149).

Only after he becomes aware of his pain is Solly able to reflect and
begin the work of mourning. "I now wish to give some thought to my

emotional belonging. . . . It is strange and perhaps not understandable, but I can say for certain that at times I forgot my past. It was an amazing ability not to remember things, as if they never existed. Sometimes entire weeks passed, and even months, and nothing bothered me. I even erased the memory of father and mother. Except in times of extreme danger or attacks of anxiety about my future, my life went on as usual. I do not understand it, but that is how it was" (pp. 173–74).

Solly's partial erasing of history had definite survival value on a physical level. Although this defense was invaluable at the time and contributed to Solly's resilience, it led to the disintegration of his identity. As Laub and Lee (2003) maintain, erasing one's history also contains an element of destruction and death.

After the war, Solly underwent a long period of working through his mourning, as a result of which he decides to return to his roots and to his previous Jewish identity. He moves to Israel and raises a family. The movie, which began with Solly's circumcision and caused him endless survival problems, ends with Solly's readiness to nonetheless circumcise his own sons, thus openly affirming his Jewishness. This brings the movie full circle and demonstrates Solly's better-consolidated identity, which could only have been achieved by working through his mourning for his lost parents, and thus getting in touch with the lost parts of his own self.

# 9

# The Role of the Analyst in the Analytic Cure during Times of Chronic Crises

## INTRODUCTION

At a time when war and destruction are part of everyday life and our safety is increasingly threatened, one of the questions we Israeli analysts ask ourselves is, what is the place of psychoanalysis in such a world? Can we in good faith propose to practice psychoanalysis in situations of chronic crises,[1] and can we, in the face of the effect of terrorism, hold on to our identities as psychoanalysts?

My first attempt to deal with this issue is described in my book *The Cry of Mute Children* (Kogan 1995), in the chapter "In the Same Boat: Psychoanalysis during the Gulf War." There I examined the curative elements of psychoanalysis during a period of acute stress in which analyst and patient found themselves in a shared life-threatening situation. The relationship between external and internal realities in a situation of chronic life-threatening crisis provides a natural laboratory in which to reexamine fundamental questions regarding the practice, as well as the theory, of psychoanalysis.

In this chapter, situated at the boundary of external and internal reality, and at the boundary of the personal and the professional, I examine the role of the analyst in psychoanalytic treatment in such situations. For this purpose I use clinical material from two case studies.

## CASE ILLUSTRATION: SUSAN

Susan, a forty-one-year-old accountant, sought professional help for phobic symptoms and anxiety attacks that affected the quality of her life. Susan was married and the mother of three boys—a fifteen-year-old and twins age thirteen. Susan complained of feeling insecure, irritable, easily hurt, and isolated in her social environment. Although she felt her husband was loyal and a good provider, he was not a source of emotional support. When her twin boys were born, he became very depressed and underwent analytic treatment, which facilitated his recovery. The husband supported the idea that Susan also undergo analysis.

Susan grew up in Western Europe, the oldest of three children. Her mother was a child survivor who had lost both parents in the Holocaust and had spent the Holocaust years between her tenth and fourteenth birthdays in hiding. Her father had been drafted into the Russian army two years before the war and later disappeared in a concentration camp. Her mother hid for some time with her own mother (Susan's grandmother) until they were discovered; the grandmother was taken to Auschwitz, where she perished. Susan's mother ran away into the woods, where she almost died of hunger. More than once she came face to face with death when, disguised as a peasant girl, she encountered German soldiers.

Susan's mother was sent on a *Kindertransport* to England where she met Susan's father. He became a successful businessman, and the family was well off. Susan's mother was a psychotic person who suffered episodes of decompensation. She had seen psychiatrists at various stages during her life and had been treated with medication. Susan remembered that throughout her childhood her mother had often talked to herself and behaved strangely. Her mother often spoiled the family fun by stopping them from going on outings at the last moment, claiming she was not feeling well. She discouraged any connection with other family members or friends, thus isolating their family from everyone else.

Susan's relationship with her mother was complicated and painful. She felt that her mother was never satisfied with the way she looked or with her achievements. The mother especially disliked Susan's boyfriend, who eventually became her husband. She tried to convince Susan to break up with him, and when he came to visit, would totally ignore him.

Ten days before the wedding, the mother tried to commit suicide and was hospitalized in a mental institution. The wedding took place despite this, as in the Jewish religion weddings are not postponed under any circumstances. Susan's father always tried to camouflage the incident by saying that his wife had mistakenly overdosed on tranquilizers.

After the wedding, the couple immigrated to Israel, where their children were born. Susan's mother came to visit only once, after the birth of the twins. This was a difficult time for Susan, who had no help from her depressed husband and had to care for a two-year-old and two infants, her mother all the while complaining that Susan was not paying her enough attention.

Five years before Susan came to me, her mother stopped taking medication, and as a result, her situation deteriorated. She no longer left the house and would not allow visitors. When Susan last saw her, she was shocked by her mother's neglected appearance—her torn, dirty clothes, her unkempt hair, her missing teeth. Susan feared that this deterioration in her mother's psychic and physical condition would eventually lead to her death. Her father, preoccupied with his own affairs, continued to deny that his wife was mentally ill. The parents never allowed anyone to interfere in their lives. Susan believed that, in spite of her father's resistance, she should have sought psychiatric help to possibly save her mother. That she did not have the strength for this struggle with her parents put an even greater burden of guilt on her shoulders.

During the first two years of analysis, we attempted to work through Susan's complicated relationship with her primary objects. The elaboration on her feelings of anger and guilt led to a lessening of her depression, and her phobic symptoms subsided. She derived greater satisfaction from her work and became more self-assured in her role as wife and mother.

The terror of the current situation in Israel (a situation which we dealt with in the third year of analysis) evoked great fear in Susan, upsetting her emotional stability. In analysis it became clear that this fear was connected to Susan's greatest anxiety, which revolved around the possibility of loss of control and decompensation. Susan was afraid of becoming ill like her mother.

I will now illustrate Susan's reaction to the external reality, and my understanding of that reaction, with verbatim material followed by an enactment. The following two consecutive sessions are from the third year of analysis.

*Session 1.*

>   Susan: Do you remember the two little children from Tekoa (a place
>   in Israel) who had wandered off and were murdered? I felt I had to
>   go help their families. I take each day as it comes, and at the end of
>   the day I say, Thank God. It's like Russian roulette. It can happen to
>   anyone, anywhere. That's why I want my family to know where I
>   am.

She's so right, I thought to myself. We all feel the same, we're all afraid
of death and destruction. But another thought immediately crossed my
mind: Was it possible that, in addition to Susan's fear of external reality,
she was expressing her fear of psychic death and fragmentation? If so, did
she expect me, in the role of a family member, to know about it, so that I
could watch over her more closely?

>   S: Last week a mortar shell fell on my brother-in-law's house. It landed
>   on the couch in the living room, where we had all sat a few days
>   before. From the couch it fell to the floor. My sister-in-law came in
>   and touched it with her foot, and nothing happened. Soldiers came
>   and removed it, and then they called and told her that they should
>   be grateful for being alive. A week ago I was in Jerusalem. I was there
>   several days after a terrorist attack. I don't know what can happen
>   in the future. I live from day to day. I worry about the children and
>   hope we'll remain alive. My older son is fifteen, the twins are thir-
>   teen. They will be in the army at the same time. I don't like thinking
>   about it.

We remained silent for a while. My thoughts revolved around my own
feelings of impotence in this situation, and my fear for my own sons. This
is not projective identification, I thought to myself; this is our blood-
stained reality!

>   I: We are all vulnerable, we are all afraid of death and destruction.
>   S: I see people leaving Israel. I know somebody from Jerusalem whose
>   son was supposed to enter the army. They left. I don't know. On the
>   one hand, I'm proud of our children in the army, but on the other

hand, am I doing the right thing by living here and letting them serve in the army? It might be life-saving to leave. I told my husband that those who ran away during the Holocaust saved their lives. My husband, who is the more stable of the two of us, says that if there is no place for us here, there is no place for us anywhere in the world.

I: Maybe these are the two voices inside yourself. On the one hand you identify with your mother, who saved herself by running into the woods, but on the other hand you feel that you have to stay here and have a place of your own.

S: Right. I want my children to live a normal life. I don't want them to feel my fear.

I wondered silently to myself whether Susan was expressing her ambivalent attitude toward analysis: her wish to run away from it, and her simultaneous wish to continue her struggle with the dark forces inside herself.

*Session 2.*

Susan arrived crying and in between sobs stated that perhaps she should stop analysis. I asked her why she was so upset. She answered my question with the following story: Two days earlier she had taken her son to Jerusalem for a doctor's appointment. They first went to the "triangle" to do some shopping. (The "triangle" is an area where three main streets in the center of the city form a triangle; most people refer to it as "downtown.")

Susan and her son did not find what they needed in the store. The shopkeeper ordered it for them and they had to come back later to pick it up. They then took a bus and went to the doctor, after which Susan's son went to school. Just then Susan heard that a suicide bomber had blown himself up right next to the store they had shopped in. She immediately called the shopkeeper, asked if everyone was all right, and if she could come and pick up her order. The man said that the people working in the store were all alive, though the windows were broken and the police were everywhere, but she could come if she wanted to. Susan went back to the store. The place was deserted, with only policemen roaming around. She picked up her order and returned home.

The next day after work, she felt a terrible urge to go to the triangle again. She strolled the empty streets and bought some things. She told me between sobs that she did not know why she had acted in this way. She was very upset.

To understand Susan's behavior, which I felt contained unconscious symbolic meanings, I asked her to tell me more about her feelings regarding the episode. Bursting into tears, she told me that she felt guilty about not helping her depressed, mentally ill mother. She had purchased things in order to help the people in the store feel that life goes on.

My first thought was that throughout this episode Susan was attempting to enact the story of her mother in her own life (Kogan 2002). Like her mother running through the woods, who came face to face with death, Susan had to come close to death in order to overcome it. Viewed from this angle, her return to the site of the explosion was an attempt to achieve active mastery over the passive trauma.

I wondered though, what symbolic meaning the word *triangle* might have in this context. Was Susan returning to the oedipal triangle, and did the man in the store whom she had tried to help represent her father, whom she had often tried to help after her mother's psychotic outbreaks? Or was her need to see with her own eyes what had happened at the scene of the explosion an unconscious fantasy about the primal scene? Could the destruction in the triangle represent the pubic triangle of her mentally ill mother, who contained the life source but also destructive forces of psychic death and fragmentation?

Thinking about all of these possibilities, I said to Susan, "You asked me at the beginning of the session whether you should stop analysis. I think you might be afraid of an explosion within you, of being in touch with something that might destroy your sanity. But you are unable to run away from the dangerous triangle within yourself. You went back to it in order to make sure that you are alive and sane. I think that you want me to reassure you that I will not let you go there alone, but that I will accompany you on this journey." Susan sighed with relief and said, "I think you are right. I was unaware of it."

After this session, I left my office and met my cleaning lady, who had just come into the apartment. She appeared agitated, looked at me anxiously and said, "Did you hear what happened in Jerusalem? Another suicide bomber, in the same place as two days ago!"

I looked at her in surprise and shock. "What?" I said. "It can't be true!"

I had just been immersed during the last session in seeking the symbolic meanings of this terrible event, searching for the innermost personal meaning that my patient was attaching to it, and now reality struck me in the face. I had the uncanny feeling of reality and fantasy intermingling. True, my cleaning woman did not refer to the place as the triangle, and she was not flirting with death, as my patient was. But was it possible, I asked myself, that by thinking of the metaphorical meaning of the triangle—the oedipal constellation, the primal scene—I was actually trying to protect myself against our cruel shared reality? On the other hand, if I only took into account my patient's conscious attitude toward external reality, wouldn't I be missing the basic unconscious fear that made her want to stop analysis? What was my responsibility as an analyst in such times?

## CASE ILLUSTRATION: JACOB

Jacob is a forty-year-old scientist who works in a research institute. He is married for the second time, has two children, five and seven years old, and a six-month-old baby. Jacob sought analysis for what he perceived as his social inhibitions, and has been in analysis with me for the last five years.

Jacob is a Jew of Bulgarian origin, his family originally from Sophia. His father started from nothing as a car salesman and built up a successful business there.

Jacob, whose name was Jacko until he immigrated to Israel from Bulgaria, described himself as "wild" and unruly as a child. Hyperactive and suffering from problems of concentration, he did poorly in school and was considered stupid by family and friends. His behavior when playing with friends was often "wild"—he tore his clothes, caused damage, and sometimes injured himself and other children. He was very attached to his mother, who was dissatisfied with his poor scholastic achievement and irritated by his wild behavior.

Jacko, the "wild" child, turned into a stormy adolescent, rebelling against his family's materialistic values and those of the society in which he grew up. He developed an interest in antigovernment activities and became an active member of a dissident organization. His parents, worried about his safety, as well as their own, were greatly relieved when at the age of seventeen he emigrated to Israel. Upon his arrival, Jacko changed his name to Jacob and completely changed his lifestyle and behavior. Discovering his intellectual ability, he applied himself with great passion to the study of Slavic languages. He fell in love with a young woman, a fellow student, and married her. During this time, his mother developed cancer and died after terrible suffering. His father remarried shortly after her death.

Jacob and his wife worked hard at menial jobs in order to finance their studies. Jacob's father, meanwhile, was frittering away his wealth, and his health began to fail. During this time, Jacob became bored with his choice of profession, his marriage, and his life. Weary of being poor and feeling the urge to "make it big," he divorced his wife, left everything behind, and went to Europe to make a fresh start. There, Jacob changed his name, once again becoming Jacko. He began working as a car salesman (his father's occupation), and changed his lifestyle, once intellectual, restricted, and puritanical, to one dominated by appetites and drives. He discovered the joys of sex and enjoyed great sexual freedom; he looked for ways to make easy money on the stock market and drove "wildly." Although his father was ill, he never visited him, as he could not face the humiliation he felt over his father's poverty and ill health. Jacko was on his way to becoming a successful businessman when his father, after losing all of his property, including the house he lived in, died of a heart attack.

An important figure in Jacob's life was Shlomo, his father's best friend from Bulgaria. Jacob greatly admired Shlomo, whom he regarded as a successful businessman with a charismatic personality, a great deal of money, and power over the lives of others. As an adolescent, far from his parents and alone in Israel, he had often been invited to Shlomo's home, where he had been treated like a son. Having only daughters, Shlomo "adopted" him and spoiled him with expensive presents.

During a visit to his protégé in Europe, Shlomo introduced Jacob, now Jacko, to the world of financial speculation and gambling. Shlomo, who enjoyed an extravagant lifestyle, bedazzled Jacko with luxurious hotels and expensive restaurants. Little did Jacko know that his father's friend was a swindler who was now deeply in debt and on the run from creditors. Jacko put him in charge of all his money. It came as a shock when he discovered that Shlomo was in fact bankrupt. Jacko, learning he was just another "sucker" supporting his mentor's swindling and extravagant lifestyle, felt deeply betrayed by the man he had most loved and admired. As a result of this painful experience, Jacko gave up his newly acquired identity as a budding businessman, his dreams of easy money, and his new lifestyle. He returned to Israel, where he again reverted to Jacob, a science student working hard to make a living.

I will not describe our long and complex analytic journey. For our purposes here, suffice it to say that Jacob, the young man who sought analytic treatment, was a highly intelligent, serious, and hard-working scientist. He had remarried and was now the father of three small children. Jacob hoped to be granted tenure at the research institute where he worked. Lately, however, he had been troubled by the responsibility of another child and the burden of work he had taken on.

In analysis we understood that Jacob's attempt to become Jacko, a successful car salesman, stemmed from his inability to accept his father's downfall. His ego ideal was destroyed when the omnipotent, powerful father figure of his childhood deteriorated into a poor and miserable man. Unable to mourn his paternal representation, he himself tried to become the successful businessman his father had once been. He then modeled his ego ideal on his father's friend, his substitute father, with whom he wanted to identify. The discovery of this man's deceit destroyed his ego ideal once again and caused him deep narcissistic hurt. Much psychic work was needed to help Jacob work through his feelings of admiration, love, and hate toward the split paternal representation.

After working through the split father figure, we tried to elaborate the split in Jacob's self-representation. I helped Jacob realize that he envied Jacko, the young man who lived the easy life and loved soccer, money, and luxury. Jacko, with his lenient superego, with few aggressive and libidinal inhibitions, appeared to have vanished into thin air. He was replaced by Jacob, a shy, hard-working, periodically depressed young man who came to analysis because of his inhibitions, but who was terribly afraid of getting rid of them, lest Jacko take over again.

One of the objectives of analysis was to stitch together the conflicting aspects of Jacko and Jacob into a better-integrated self.

I will now present some verbatim material from a session that took place in the fourth year of analysis, during the *intifada*, that illustrates both my patient's perception of the reality of life here in Israel and my inability to stay with his fears, which were also my own.

> Jacob: What can I say about the current situation in our country! It's a
> catastrophe! The fact that I can be here with you is a great luxury.

In my lab I work alone. During my lunch break I sometimes listen to music or read. Yesterday I had quite an experience. I went back to work at four o'clock, and heard there had been another terrorist attack. As a scientist I work in another world, but when I leave that world, reality hits me. I feel that in therapy we are dealing with petty things. I know that this is the human condition, but analytic therapy deals with a world in which the notion of good exists. As a scientist I want to give people a better world to live in, but when such terrible things are occurring, it becomes irrelevant. (He reflected for a moment and then continued.) Am I using what is happening here now to avoid doing all the things I took upon myself, like work and a family? But actually I feel good doing what I'm now doing.

I wondered to myself whether I should be focusing on the defensive way Jacob was using external reality. Was he showing me that analysis was irrelevant to him during such frightening times?

J: (continuing) I usually come home at eight o'clock. I find my wife watching a stupid movie. She avoids watching the news. There is always tension when I want to watch the news. She's pregnant and bothered by the idea of raising children in this insane country. (This was before their third child was born.) The situation in the country is so hostile and unpleasant. My Israeli-born wife wants to leave the country and live a quiet, comfortable life someplace where she doesn't have to worry about her children's safety when they go to nursery school.

I: The situation is indeed difficult for all of us; we are all afraid. But in describing your wife's desire to leave the country, might you not actually be expressing your own desire to run away from your family, your profession, from analysis?

J: Yes, I am. I do have such a fantasy. But I am not acting upon it. And there are also great advantages to living here—it's our own country, we belong here. I'm slowly beginning to understand how complex the political situation is. A miracle would be needed to solve this conflict!

Jacob agreed with my interpretation of his wishes stemming from his internal world. From our work over the years I knew how compliant he was on the surface. But he immediately switched back to external reality. What should I do now? I thought. Isn't it my role as analyst to point out to him the unconscious meaning of the conflict he is referring to, which in my view represents the conflict between two polarized aspects of his personality, and not deal with the external reality?

> J: (continuing) I believe that the political conflict between Israel and the Palestinians cannot be solved. It won't destroy the country, but life will become such a nightmare that people will leave of their own free will.
>
> I: I think you're telling me something about the way you feel now about analysis, that perhaps you wish to leave it behind and not face your own conflicts and fantasies [again I bring the subject back to internal reality].
>
> J: Out there things are on fire, and we are sitting here discussing the fine nuances of feelings. It's such an indulgence! It's like placing myself inside a bubble, so that I can be left alone and have a decent life. It's sociopathic, egocentric! But first we have to stay alive. It's like Russian roulette. People are being murdered every day. Now, in my army reserve duty, I accompany soldiers to the front, to dangerous places. There's a new song by a famous singer, "Who will be next in line, who will be in the next line?" The way I understand politics, I feel that in the future, living in the shadow of fear, people will carry guns in the street, violence will increase, terrorism will increase, there will be economic problems, this country will become a Third World country.

Listening to Jacob, I was aware of being terrified by his grim prediction of the future. Unable to remain silent, I asked, "And where do you fit in all of this?"

> J: I wonder if everything I'm saying is showing that what I really want is to cop out of my present life. But I'm going to continue doing everything I'm doing. I'm confused. My wife recently changed from being a lefty to being an extreme right-winger. I think we need a sane voice in order to unite the people, so that they won't follow fanatics on either side.

I: I think that in describing our difficult external reality, you are actually also telling me something about the problems you are encountering in your inner reality. Perhaps you are telling me that, on the one hand, you took upon yourself the responsibility of a family, work, and the pressure of career advancement, but, on the other hand, you really want to run away from it all and leave everything behind, as you did in the past. And perhaps you are asking me here, in analysis, to be the sane voice that will help you unite the polarized aspects of your own personality, so that you can feel more whole.

As can be seen from this material, I finally became aware in this session that Jacob's perception of the frightening external reality was my perception of the situation as well, a realization that made me feel passive and helpless. And what about my analytic role? Could I give it up and "just" stay with my patient's fears, and my own? I was trying to hold on to my own identity as an analyst, and whenever he reverted to external reality, I found myself time and again striving to go back to internal reality. I found that I had to interpret the unconscious meaning behind his perception of external reality. His perception of external reality was not simply a reflection of conflicting wishes and fantasies that stemmed from his inner reality; he was using it also to repeat a defensive form of behavior that he had used several times previously. I could have considered his behavior to be an adaptation to real danger, but instead I clung to what made me feel safe—analyzing his defenses and working them through with him. And, indeed, following this lengthy process, Jacob became less ambivalent about his decision to stay with his family, in Israel, in his profession, and in analysis.

However, in my countertransference feelings, I suddenly found doubt sneaking up on me regarding Jacob's decision. If something were to happen to Jacob during his reserve army service, I would feel guilty, I thought to myself. I reminded myself that my duty was to point out to Jacob his unconscious wishes and fantasies, that he was a mature person, capable of making his own decisions, that he alone was responsible for his life. But what impact was the external reality having on me? I asked myself. Had the dangerous situation increased my omnipotence to such an extent that I thought I could save my patient's life by letting him run away from danger? Was I myself feeling threatened by the daily confrontation with my own and my family's possible destruction? Yet, how could I let this difficult situation destroy my analytic ability! Wasn't being able to continue functioning as an analyst a hope for the continuation of life?

## One Year Later

An episode one year later, which occurred during the threat of a possible biological or chemical attack on Israel from Iraq, put me more closely in touch with my own defenses when confronted with the possibility of death and destruction. During the past two years, faced with the *intifada*, Jacob mentioned several times that he wished to immigrate to another country. Lately he claimed that his wife was completely panicked; she wanted all of them to go to Bulgaria for a couple of months and stay with his brother until the threat of war passed. His wife loathed her sister-in-law and felt that life in Bulgaria was poor and miserable. But she was so anxious that she saw this as the only possible solution.

I told Jacob that his wife probably represented a voice inside himself, the voice of his own fear. I added that going away with his family now might diminish this fear, but would also give him the opportunity of fleeing from his conflicting wishes and the fantasies we were dealing with in analysis.

Jacob answered by trying to describe how difficult it was for him to leave the country, now that we might be faced with a terrible war. And what would happen to the people whose work he supervised, or his students? How would they feel if he, their boss, left in order to save himself and his children? But, he wondered immediately, what was more important, his own children or other people? During the Holocaust, those who fled from dangerous places were the ones who survived.

I was wondering to myself whether Jacob was afraid I might go away and take care of myself and my family, abandoning him here alone, in the midst of danger and destruction.

As if hearing my unspoken thoughts, Jacob said, "I fantasized that you would leave the country. I know how prominent you are in your field. You'd get the red-carpet treatment anywhere in the world; you would be very welcome, you have friends everywhere. Perhaps you would take a break and call it going on sabbatical."

Smiling to myself, I said, "I am often aware of the fact that you want to run away from me, from analysis. But now you are sending me away;

you are arranging for me to have friends abroad and to get the red-carpet treatment. All you have to do is to bring me the tickets next session."

Jacob did not find this funny. He said, "Maybe this is only my fear that you are going to leave me? If you had to choose between a quiet, peaceful life or a life full of terror, maybe it wouldn't be so difficult to disappoint a few patients!"

My thoughts revolved around the transference reflected in his remarks about my going way. Jacob was indeed frightened that I would leave him. But I also felt that in the transference Jacob was now placing me in the role of Shlomo, his father's friend, the man he had once greatly admired and loved. I had become the charismatic con man who had power over people's lives, and who always saved his own skin by disappointing those close to him. Jacob bestowed those qualities on me, while at the same time identifying with me and thus attributing them to himself. Apparently, the red carpet was Jacob's own wish, which he projected onto me.

## A Turning Point

I will now present an important event from my personal life that increased my awareness of the extent to which I had been denying external reality. I mention this event only because it constituted a turning point for me in the analysis and caused me to work through my own fears of death and destruction, as well as the threat to my identity as an analyst. This event, during this tense period in which a chemical or biological attack was looming high on the horizon, was the birth of my first grandchild.

Babies were now being discharged from the hospital with a little plastic tent, for use in the eventuality of war, which would completely insulate them and keep them safe in the case of a chemical or biological attack. I envisaged what could happen during such an attack: the young parents (my son and his wife, in particular) wearing gas masks, and frantically attempting to put the screaming baby into this device, and then being unable to touch and calm her. This image made me aware that I was not coping with the situation. What I really wished was that the parents and the baby would stay abroad through this threatening period, with its uncertain outcome. They could stay with my daughter-in-law's family in France, just for a few weeks. Only now did the possibility occur to me that my interpretation of fleeing from analysis, though connected to Jacob's way of dealing with life, may also have been a projection of a fantasy of mine that was intruding on the analysis.

When Jacob came for his next session and again talked about going away with his family to Bulgaria, I was very quiet. The only thing I could say was, "It is indeed very frightening to be here with little children during such times." Now, at last, I was acknowledging external reality. Jacob was silent. Then he said, "Thank you for being with me during these difficult times." Jacob must have sensed that my attitude had changed. As I accepted his fears of external reality, instead of just focusing on his internal reality, Jacob felt supported. This gave him the courage, as the analysis progressed, to deal with his internal and external conflicts in a different way. Until now, Jacob had perceived me as representing a persecutory internal reality that seemed to him irrelevant in a period of danger. He therefore kept focusing the analysis on external reality only. Now he could relate to me more as an ally in his struggle with his own self in our shared life-threatening situation.

## DISCUSSION

My work as a psychoanalyst during a period of chronic crises, and especially the change in my patient's fears that I experienced during the war with Iraq, led me to explore the following issues: (1) the impact of the person of the analyst on the analytic cure in a shared life-threatening situation; (2) the relation between external and internal reality in a situation of terror; and (3) the goal of psychoanalysis in an age of terror.

### The Impact of the Person of the Analyst on the Analytic Cure in a Shared Life-Threatening Situation

This issue preoccupied me for some time and made me ask myself several questions. Is it possible that for a while I was unable to contain my patient's fear because I was denying my own? What made me adhere so blindly to the ordinary rules of psychoanalysis during such frightening times? Was my fear of losing my analytic function so great that I lost sight of reality?

On the issue of containing the patient, I wish to quote Bion, who so eloquently stated: "When the patient strove to rid himself of fears of death which were felt to be too powerful for his personality to contain he split off his fears and put them into me, the idea apparently being that if they were allowed to repose there long enough they would undergo modification by my psyche and could then be safely reintrojected" (1959, p. 103).

Are we able to contain and modify the fears of our patients while we find ourselves confronted with death and destruction? Isn't our psyche, the inner space in which these fears are to repose, constricted by such a situation? Regarding this issue Abend has remarked that "the impact of daily events, inner as well as outer, plays upon our psychic integration and produces those fluctuations of mood, thought, and behavior which are part of our so-called normal personalities. Since our receptivity and reactivity to our analysands depends upon our psychic balance, how can we imagine that this 'analyzing instrument,' as Isakower liked to call it, is unaffected by its constantly shifting dynamism?" (1986, p. 565).

In the shared life-threatening situation we are living under in Israel, I have found that our "analyzing instrument" is indeed affected by current events. The turning point for me in the treatment of Jacob was when I realized that my countertransference feelings were not induced only by the typical patient's transference and actions toward me (Boyer 1983, 1999; Giovacchini 2000; Kernberg 1984; Volkan 1987; Volkan and Ast 1992, 1994); they were also the result of my own defense mechanisms in confrontation with death and destruction. These defenses had a deep impact on the analytic encounter and therefore deserve to be scrutinized just as closely as reactions normally regarded as countertransferential.

Perhaps I was denying my own wishes of fleeing with my family to safety, since these wishes ran directly counter to my ideological reasons for living in Israel. I found it easier to struggle with Jacob's wishes to run away (which could come under the "normal" heading of resistance) than to accept his fears as well as my own. Thus, "denial in the service of normality" was most likely my way of living in a life-threatening situation. In this case, denial of external reality made me, to a certain extent, unempathic toward my patient's fears and restricted my ability to contain and modify them so that he would feel supported. This hindered the analytic work, and the patient rightly felt that analysis had become irrelevant to his most pressing needs ("Out there things are on fire, and we are sitting here discussing the fine nuances of feelings. It's such an indulgence! . . . It's sociopathic, egocentric!").

I have found Carpy's words about the normal development of the infant very useful. "The normal infant needs . . . an experience of being fed by a mother in whom he can sense the panic, but who is nevertheless able to give him milk. This is what makes pain tolerable" (1989, p. 293). Patients who fear external reality need this experience—of a "holding environment" (Modell 1976) or "mutative support" (De Jonghe, Rijnierse, and Janssen 1992) no less than when they are afraid of projections coming from their internal world. It was only when I could be in touch with my own panic that I was able to give my patient the containment that he needed.

A great difficulty for me in the case of Jacob was that fleeing from a dangerous reality could be considered a realistic solution to real danger, as well as a "manic defense" (Klein et al. 1952; Winnicott 1935) that he had employed several times previously in order to flee from his internal conflicting wishes. My feelings of omnipotence and guilt, which were greatly increased by the fact that I was experiencing external reality as a threat, made it difficult for me to take both of these perspectives into consideration.

Regarding Susan, it was easier to feel empathy with her plight. I was aware of the possibility that external reality facilitated the omnipotent enactment of traumatic fantasized past events connected to her mother's Holocaust history, in order to lessen or undo their impact. From another angle, we explored the current traumatic reality that enhanced Susan's feelings of guilt in relation to her ill mother. This helped Susan understand that she tried to mitigate her self-blame by helping others who found themselves in a difficult situation. Finally, because I was better able to contain our shared fears evoked by external reality, I succeeded in helping her realize that her enactment had an unconscious meaning related to her fears and anxieties over losing her sanity (which arose from her inner reality).

The threat to my identity as an analyst symbolized for me the possible destruction of my own and my patient's psychic life. The current situation reminded me of the Holocaust history of our parents and grandparents and of the damage to metaphorical thinking that has been demonstrated in studies of Holocaust survivors (Grubrich-Simitis 1984; Herzog 1982; Krystal 1985; Oliner 1983). This fear of a return of the past made me experience the current situation as no less a threat to our psychic life than it is to our physical existence. The damage to metaphorization has been attributed to the deadening of inner life as the result of an overwhelming reality.

I felt that the current reality was threatening to erase inner reality by diminishing the place of symbolism in analysis. To counteract this, I purposely focused on inner reality. I did this in order to create a sense of safety, to confirm the continuity of normal life, and to ensure the survival of both psychic and physical reality. But by doing so, I sometimes paid a high price, as I have discussed.

### The Relation between External and Internal Reality in a Situation of Terror

In the current wave of violence that is overwhelming us, we can observe the disintegration of the normal fabric of life and the destruction of a sense of safety.

The sense of safety is described by Sandler (1960) as a feeling that is so much a part of us that we take it for granted as a background to our everyday experiences. It is a feeling that bears the same relation to anxiety as the positive bodily states of satiation and contentment bear to instinctual tension. It is a feeling of well-being. The need to maintain a sense of safety is of greatest importance in learning and development, and is therefore one of the fundamental components of the therapeutic situation. In treatment we often deal with the internal anxieties and conflicting wishes that underlie our patients' reactions to external reality. As analysts we try to provide an environment that is safe and protected, that will enable the therapeutic regression to unfold,[2] and that will facilitate the search into the internal world of the individual.

But what happens to this "safe haven" when external conditions are filled with terror and violence? Should we, as analysts, try to preserve the safety of the setting? Can this be done by clinging to the ordinary notions of "classical analysis," by encouraging the exploration of inner conflicts and anxieties and denying the dangers outside?

There is an ongoing controversy over the impact of external reality on our inner life. This controversy has been reviewed in depth by Oliner (1996). I will bring only a few illustrations of the polarized attitude of psychoanalysts toward the place of traumatic external reality in our inner world.

A classic example is Melanie Klein's famous analysis (1961) of Richard, a ten-year-old boy brought to London for her to treat during World War II. The analysis focused solely on the psychic reality of the boy, while the outside reality of the Blitz under which he lived was totally ignored. At the other pole we find the work of Melitta Schmideberg (1942), Melanie Klein's daughter, who, in conducting analysis during wartime acknowledged the traumatic external reality, as well as the common fears of patient and analyst sharing a life-threatening situation.

A most important figure with regard to traumatic reality in psychoanalytic history is Winnicott. In a meeting of the British Psychoanalytical Society that took place during World War II, he pointed out the existence of external reality to a group that preferred to ignore it. In his bibliography of Winnicott, Phillips describes the incident: "Margaret Little, one of Winnicott's analysands, recalls that in the first Scientific Meetings of the British Society that she attended, there were bombs dropping every few minutes and people ducking as each crash came. In the middle of the discussion, someone I later came to know as D.W. stood up and said 'I should like to point out that there is an air-raid going on', and sat down. No-one paid any notice, and the meeting continued!" (1988, p. 61).

The controversy over the impact of traumatic external reality on psychic reality continues to this day. Therapists treating victims of known abuse claim that classical psychoanalysis pays too little attention to real events in a person's life to be of use to traumatized patients. Shevrin disagrees with this assumption. In his contribution to an issue of *JAPA* devoted to trauma, he noted that "psychoanalysis came in at the fault line between presumed sexual seduction at an early age as a cause of neurosis, and the role of fantasy" (1994, pp. 991–92). His conclusion is that classical psychoanalysis considers external traumatic reality and its effect on psychic life to be a most important element in neurotic conflict.

Normally there is a mutual influence of elements from the external and the internal worlds, each modifying the other. According to Arlow, "There is a constant mutual interaction between the individual's mental set, as dictated by his persistent unconscious fantasies, and the events of his daily conscious experience" (1991, p. 60).

The reciprocal relation between external reality and unconscious fantasy in normal life situations has been studied in depth by Winnicott. He felt that reality is useful for setting limits to fantasy, thus having a reassuring effect. Referring to Freud (1923), who views reality as that which frustrates the individual, Winnicott writes, "The point is that in fantasy things work by magic: there are no brakes on fantasy, and love and hate cause alarming effects. External reality has brakes on it, and can be studied and known and, in fact, fantasy is only tolerable at full blast when objective reality is appreciated well" (1964, p. 153).

I wish to raise the hypothesis that external reality of a traumatic nature differs from reality under normal life conditions in that the former cannot modify fantasy and thus contribute to the internal world by serving as a reassuring entity.[3] Unable to establish factual limits to aggressive and destructive wishes, it cannot mitigate omnipotence and feelings of guilt. This hypothesis, which I will discuss in greater depth in the epilogue, is relevant to the effect of the traumatic external reality on the entire population in Israel.

### The Goal of Psychoanalysis in an Age of Terror

It would seem that in an age of terror, we cannot claim that the aim of psychoanalysis is to continue to "verbalise the nascent conscious in terms of the transference" (Winnicott 1962, p. 169); instead we must think about the death anxieties of the patient evoked by the life-threatening situation.

Modell (1996) has referred to the problem of the analyst's perception of the patient's mind by stating that interpretation not only reestablishes the frame of the psychoanalysis, but also introduces the analyst's construction of reality. This leads to the question, Is the content of the interpretation entirely the analyst's construction or does it also reflect the patient's mind?

As analysts, our subjective experience of a shared life-threatening situation may facilitate interpretations that reflect our patients' construction of reality, as well as our own. This subjective experience is the only alley through which we may become the repository of our patients' need to contain the intense death anxiety occasioned by the traumatic reality; this paradoxically provides a hopeful investment in the future. It thus becomes part of our function as analysts to recognize our own reactions to external reality and to acknowledge them. In the cases I have described, this occurred when I came in touch with my own fears in reaction to the threatening reality I experienced along with my patients.

As a result of the long and painful working through of my own defenses and conflicts in reaction to psychoanalytic work in a shared life-threatening situation, I have become aware of the need to respect external reality even as I try, together with my patient, to explore the inner universe that processes and handles this reality in unique and idiosyncratic ways. As Eissler has so pointedly stated, "No individual can divorce himself from the historical period in which he is living, any more than he can put himself beyond time and space" (1953, p. 107). We should respect the historical period in which we are living and adjust the analytic tool accordingly.

## NOTES

1. The recurrence of crisis in Israel during the last three-and-a-half years of the *intifada*, the guerrilla war, and the threat of a U.S. war with Iraq and its possible repercussions for Israel, induced me to use the paradoxical term *chronic crises* to describe the current situation.

2. As Treurniet has noted, "Regression may be therapeutic in analysis, because it gives the subject an opportunity to become acquainted with himself through experiences. This is conditioned upon the setting and the analyst's attitude in providing sufficient security" (1993, p. 879).

3. Wallerstein draws attention to the problem of reality and its place in our psychological scheme of things. "[B]eyond what I have stated of the contemporary breakdown in consensus about reality, and of our having to self-consciously face and discriminate amongst a profusion of competing views of reality, there is the frightfully real question, in this day of nuclear power and environmental despoliation, of what kind of future does our or any reality have" (1973, p. 7).

# Working with Sons and Daughters of Holocaust Survivors in the Shadow of Terror

## INTRODUCTION

As I have shown in earlier chapters, the trauma of the Holocaust is often transmitted to and absorbed by the children of survivors. The psychoanalytic literature on the offspring of Holocaust survivors states that the Holocaust is transmitted to them through early, unconscious identifications that carry in their wake the parents' perception of an everlasting, life-threatening inner and outer reality (Axelrod et al. 1978; Barocas and Barocas 1973; Kestenberg 1972; Klein 1971; Laufer 1973; Lipkowitz 1973; Rakoff 1966; Sonnenberg 1974). These children, whose minds have been impregnated with mental representations of the atrocities of the Holocaust deposited by their parents, carry within themselves powerful feelings of loss and humiliation, guilt and aggression.

Volkan coined the concept of "deposited representations" (1987, p. 73), emphasizing the role of the parent, who unconsciously, and sometimes even consciously, forces aspects of himself onto the child. By doing so, the parent affects the child's sense of identity and gives the child certain specific tasks to perform. In these cases, the children become the reservoirs for deposited images connected to the trauma, which often initiate unconscious fantasies linked to it. The children are compelled to deal with the shame, rage, helplessness, and guilt that the parents have been unable to work through for themselves (Volkan et al. 2002).

The question I wish to address here is what happens when children whose Holocaust-survivor parents have undergone victimization, actual abuse and humiliation, encounter traumatic reality in the present? What is the impact of this external reality on their inner life, their perception of reality, and their defenses?

I show that life-threatening reality does not reactivate only a simple recollection of traumatic events, but it also reactivates in the children the mental representation of the Holocaust that they share with their parents. These include real events of a traumatic nature, conscious and unconscious fantasies regarding these events, intense feelings of mourning and guilt, and defenses against unacceptable feelings such as shame, guilt, or aggression (Roth 1993; Moses 1993; Kogan and Schneider 2003). For this purpose I will use clinical vignettes from two cases in which the life-threatening situation of the *intifada* in Israel reactivated mental representations of the Holocaust and had an impact on their perception of reality, reinforcing their manic defenses.

## THE CASE OF DAPHNA

Daphna, a forty-six-year-old high-school teacher, married and mother of a sixteen-year-old boy, was a member of a small group of extreme leftists who strongly advocated the pro-Palestinian position. Not only did she participate in the big peace demonstrations organized by Israel's left-wing parties, but she also stood at crossroads together with several other women, holding up signs that promoted their pro-Palestinian views. These signs often evoked furious reactions from passersby, many of whom responded by shouting angrily at the demonstrators. These angry reactions never deterred Daphna from what she was doing. On the contrary, they increased her emotional excitement and the importance of these demonstrations for her.

Daphna was the daughter of a Holocaust survivor father and a mother who arrived in Israel with her parents before World War II. Her father's parents and siblings were taken to Auschwitz where they were gassed and their bodies cremated in the ovens. Daphna's mother had suffered from depression throughout her life, which worsened with age. Her psychic situation deteriorated after the birth of Daphna, the younger of two children.

Daphna remembered her mother as a sad, passive, very silent woman, who could not cope with the simple chores of life. "I grew up with a shadow," was how Daphna described the mother of her childhood.

Daphna's parents lived in a little village. From the time she was a baby, Daphna lived in a children's home, together with the other children. She was told that after her birth her mother had become so depressed that she would sometimes forget to feed her. When this was discovered, she was put in a children's home, and there they took charge of her.

When Daphna was nine years old, the family moved to the United States for a period of three years. Her mother had a very bad reaction to leaving Israel, where she had led a sheltered life and where her children had been cared for. Daphna remembered that during this period her mother would lie in bed for days on end, unable to buy food or cook for her family, never responding to teachers' requests to discuss the problems the child was having in school. Father took care of these matters, and Daphna learned to live with a depressed, psychically dead mother.

Upon their return to Israel, Daphna was placed in a boarding school where she began to thrive. She was a good student, had many friends, and led the life of a normal adolescent.

When Daphna was twelve, her mother committed suicide. Father was the one who found her burnt corpse near the oven, and an empty bottle of pills which she had apparently swallowed before putting her head inside the oven (it was an old-fashioned gas oven with an open flame). It was never clear whether the mother had died from gas inhalation or from the flames that consumed her body after she had poured gasoline over herself. Daphna was shocked and horrified by this terrible event. Nobody talked with Daphna about what happened; the father never mourned his wife. Daphna knew that the shocking death of her mother must have reminded him of his lost relatives who died in the gas chambers. After about two years, he was hospitalized because of a psychotic depression. Daphna visited him regularly in the hospital and was terribly ashamed of the way he looked and behaved.

After the initial shock, Daphna made a conscious decision to get on with her life. She studied and worked, and married a man she did not love, out of fear that she would remain an old maid. She gave birth to her first child, a boy. Throughout her life, Daphna was plagued by pseuriasis and periodic depressions. She encountered great difficulties in raising her son, and in spite of giving him love and care, she sometimes lost her temper and became violent, a fact which tormented her deeply and aroused feelings of guilt. Daphna was in therapy for a period of ten years, at the end of which her therapist developed a terminal illness.

Daphna sought analysis two years ago, when her older brother, at the age of fifty-one, became ill and was hospitalized in a mental institution because of a mental breakdown. Concerned that she, like her older brother, might suffer a psychotic breakdown at the fatal age of fifty-one (the age at which her mother had committed suicide), Daphna decided to seek analytic treatment.

I will not describe our painful analytic journey over the last three years. Instead, I will examine Daphna's reaction to the life-threatening situation in Israel over the last few years as revealed in analysis. I will illustrate this with a vignette from one of our sessions.

> D: There are so many terrorist attacks. I am so angry about it. I feel like another Holocaust is descending on us.

We were silent for some moments.

> D: (continuing): There is a story about a frog. A frog is insensitive to differences in temperature. So, if you slowly warm up water to boil the frog, it will not jump out of it, because it does not feel the danger. This happened to the Jewish people in the past. Those who did not run away from the Holocaust, look what happened to them, they all got cooked in the oven. It's the same with us now. We don't pay attention to what's going on until the situation gets really bad.

I was frightened by Daphna's words. Perhaps she is right, I thought to myself. Nobody knows what the future will bring upon us. Then, my thoughts turned to Daphna's tragic mother who had put her head in an oven, possibly choosing to concretely follow the fate of her relatives who had been gassed and cremated in Auschwitz. Was the mother the "frog who was insensitive to pain," I asked myself, or was her psychic pain so overwhelming that she destroyed herself in order to get rid of it?

Further on we delved into Daphna's fantasies regarding the political demonstrations that she participated in at crossroads. We discovered that

Daphna was not reacting to external reality only out of political conviction and striving for peace, but she was also reacting to an internal world full of fear and feelings of guilt.

> D: You know, yesterday I was demonstrating together with other women against the occupation of the territories. When I took part in these demonstrations in the past, people threw tomatoes at us or cursed us. I heard that women who demonstrated were beaten and needed hospitalization. I thought, with the level of violence being so high, there are people who might shoot us. I feel like the Jews at the beginning of the Nazi era, when they were persecuted in the streets.

What a mixture of past and present, I thought to myself. Apparently, Daphna felt that she lived back at the beginning of the Nazi era and that her persecutors were after her.

> D: (after some moments of silence) I feel I do not have the right to live a life of my own, that I have to be punished. Like religious people, I also say to God: "I am paying my dues, I demonstrate against the war every Friday at noon, every Saturday night, you should have mercy on me."
>
> I: What do you feel you should be punished for?
>
> D: I don't know. It has to do with my mother. How could I never have noticed what was going to happen to her? I was so preoccupied with the stupid things of adolescence. I wasn't really concerned with her well-being. You know, when I came home for visits from the boarding school before she killed herself, she always wanted to hug me and kiss me. I didn't want her to do that, I rejected her. I wasn't a baby anymore, and she never did that when I was a child. Suddenly she wanted to hug me all the time; is it possible that she needed my embrace and I wasn't aware of it? And what about my father? I knew that all his relatives perished in the ovens, and now [my] mother perished in the same way. He could not survive that. I knew it, but I could not save him. How can I allow myself to live a normal life in Israel when life is so crazy!

From this short vignette we can see that by participating in demonstrations, Daphna on a conscious level was fighting for pacifist ideas, while unconsciously she was trying to mitigate the tremendous burden of guilt she felt toward her parents.

Daphna transferred the guilt-ridden relationship with her mother and father to her son, and this relationship became another source of torment for her. Daphna perceived herself as a hungry, needy person who destroyed all those who became close to her—her parents, her son, her former therapist, as well as myself in analysis. I illustrate this with the following excerpt from a session:

> D: Sometimes I think I don't want Benny to go to the army. I am forty-eight and he is eighteen; it is the end of my life. Sometimes I think about my ambivalence toward him, maybe I want him to die. When he was little, I was sometimes so aggressive toward him, almost violent. I went to work once a week, and then my husband gave him a bottle. Benny hated it. I felt I was forcing him to do something he didn't want to do, that I was traumatizing him. I know that my mother was very depressed after my birth and that she sometimes forgot to feed me. When this was discovered, neighbors came in and fed me the bottle.
>
> I: Perhaps you are afraid that in the relationship with your son you were unconsciously repeating some of your own experiences with your mother.
>
> D: Yes, definitely. I feel terribly destructive, especially toward people who are close to me. I have very powerful needs.
>
> I: Are you perhaps afraid that you will destroy me with your powerful needs and that I will break down like your mother, or become ill like your former therapist, and will not be able to give you the caring and support you need from me in analysis?
>
> D: Exactly so. I'm afraid that nobody can really withstand my own needy self, nobody can survive my needs and my destructiveness. And I am also afraid that Israel is a short episode in the history of the Jewish people, this *intifada* can become our next Holocaust.

This material illustrates how the shadow of the Holocaust affected Daphna's life. Daphna identified with her mother's victim/aggressor aspects. In the role of victim, she was the baby of a persecutory mother who could have murdered her by starving her to death. In the role of aggressor, not only did she feel guilty for not saving her mother (and indirectly also her father) from death and destruction, but she also accused herself of destroying her mother because of her needy, ravenous self. This polarized attitude, in which love and hatred were split apart, was projected onto her son, and she felt that she was simultaneously his potential savior and his murderer.

## THE CASE OF ISAAC

Isaac, a thirty-year-old scientist, married and father of a three-year-old child, sought analysis because of uncontrolled outbursts of anger toward his family and his subsequent feelings of guilt and unhappiness.

Isaac came to analysis during a time of crisis in his life: his father, aged seventy-two, had committed suicide several weeks previously. The father had suffered from pain in his testicles for over a year before being diagnosed with prostate cancer. He underwent an operation and radiation therapy, after which tests showed that the cancerous cells had completely disappeared. Only the pain persisted, increasingly affecting his psychic state.

Isaac's father was a simple man who had worked as a technician his entire life, devoting most of his free time to sports and athletics. Recently, these activities were greatly hindered by the constant pain that had begun tormenting him, and which gradually led to overwhelming depression. Despite his recovery and the good prognosis, despite all the love and support he received from his family, Father decided to end his life. It was Isaac's mother who found his body dangling from a rope in the shower. Father left a note for his family: "My dear family, please forgive me, I cannot stand it anymore."

Isaac came to me during the first month after his father's death. His appearance was striking: he had delicate features and long hair, which gave him a feminine appearance. He observed the Jewish custom of not shaving during the period of mourning, and the beard adorning his face lent him a most bizarre look. He had great difficulty talking and stuttered terribly during the first session. His strange appearance and fragmented speech made me regard him as more emotionally ill than he really was, a fact that I realized later on in analysis.

During this stage of treatment we reconstructed his parents' story. Isaac was the son of a Holocaust survivor father and a mother whose family had been living in Israel for several generations. His father had been in a concentration camp between the ages of fourteen and nineteen. Isaac knew very little of his father's life during that period, except for the fact that only his father and his father's brother had survived.

Isaac's own history revealed a very intelligent and talented young man. During high school he was already taking courses at university, and at the age of twenty he had completed a first degree in science. He was then drafted into the army, working there in his field of expertise, and at the same time was sent by the army to study for a Ph.D. Now, at the age of thirty, he had a family whom he loved, he had close friends, and was conducting research at a prominent scientific institute.

Isaac complained that in spite of all this, he would sometimes feel depressed. During these periods, he had little energy for work. Nowadays, he was especially upset by his angry outbursts toward his wife and child.

Isaac described the atmosphere in his parents' home as coercive. He was the only son of a couple who had been childless for many years, and was very much loved and overprotected by his mother. The relationship with his father was more complex and ambivalent. Though proud of the boy's intellectual achievements, the father was never ever satisfied with him. In contrast to his mother, who spoiled him, his father wanted him to be totally independent, physically and emotionally. The sensitive young boy learned that he had to "become a man." He was urged to look out for himself and to engage in sports in order to develop his body. He was expected to learn a profession that would earn him a great deal of money, with no regard for his real interests.

The boy found himself under great pressure to fulfill his father's ego-ideal, but also felt very antagonistic about it. He felt a great deal of anger toward his father, but afraid to hurt him, he learned to keep his feelings in check and behaved in a passive-aggressive manner. In my view, he adopted the mechanism of turning his aggressive feelings against himself, which caused him to become periodically depressed.

Certain changes occurred in Isaac's appearance and behavior during therapy. He stopped stuttering, and his speech became clearer. At the end of the first month after his father's death, he shaved off his beard. His long hair still adorned his feminine features, but without the beard, he no longer looked so bizarre.

Inquiring about his hair, I discovered that Isaac had not always worn his hair long. (Hair length has symbolic value. The unconscious meaning of hair length in children of Nazi persecutors has been the subject of research [Kogan and Schneider 2002a].) There was a period in school and during his army service when he said that he had looked like a "normal" guy. In the attempt to understand how he defined "normal" or "abnormal," Isaac mentioned a homosexual encounter that almost occurred at the age of nineteen, during his army service. Immediately after breaking up with a girlfriend, he became very close to a young man several years older. He and this man were supposed to meet and spend the night together, but at the last moment Isaac got cold feet and didn't turn up. The man was very offended and the relationship ended.

In analysis, we tried to understand this episode in light of information about his father's life that was revealed to Isaac during the first month after his father's death. A cousin told Isaac about some of the dreadful events in his father's life during the Holocaust. One terrible episode was about his father and the uncle who had survived peeping through a fence and seeing their mother and sister being marched off to the gas chambers. Another terrifying story was that Father, who was a handsome boy at the time, had been sexually exploited by men in the concentration camps. The cousin remembered one of the things Father had said: "Men were always after me, the younger ones during the day, the older ones at night." Isaac remembered his father warning him in this regard: "You are such a handsome boy, you are the type for men, they will be after you!"

We tried to understand Isaac's behavior in light of his father's powerful message to "behave like a man." Isaac now realized that having long hair and looking feminine was the most rebellious action he could have taken against his father. Consciously, Isaac was rebelling against the masculinity that he felt was expected of him. Unconsciously, Isaac almost repeated his father's fate when he came close to a homosexual encounter, but fled from it at the last moment.

After elaborating this episode in analysis, Isaac cut his hair. Having to a certain extent worked through his love and anger toward his father, this rebellion was no longer necessary.

Describing his feelings about the life-threatening situation in Israel, Isaac revealed that he had years ago acquired a revolver, which he kept in a locked drawer. He said, "I have to have a revolver; it can be very useful in case we are attacked by terrorists; in case they break into my house, I will not be completely impotent." After further inquiry, Isaac connected his feelings of impotence to the past sexual exploitation of his father by the Nazis.

Working through his father's suicide, we connected the father's traumatic history to his illness and its outcome. Apparently the illness, the surgery and the radiation therapy had left his father impotent. The unbearable pain he complained of might have been an unbearable combination of physical as well as psychic pain. This trauma, superimposed upon his father's earlier trauma, possibly led to his final act of self-destruction.

The life-threatening situation in Israel reactivated in Isaac traces of his father's concern over his masculinity, which he had transmitted to Isaac in ways that went beyond words. In acquiring the revolver, Isaac was attempting to defend not only himself and his family from Palestinian terrorists, but he was also trying to ensure that his manhood would not be damaged, living his father's past in his own present life.

## DISCUSSION

I will now discuss the impact of traumatic external reality on the perception of reality and on the defenses of Holocaust survivors' offspring, as shown by the previous cases.

In the two cases described earlier, the patients' psychic realities were in large part structured by unconscious fantasies and guilt feelings related to their parents' traumatic past. Life-threatening external reality and terror reinforced their internal fears and made it more difficult for them to differentiate between internal and external reality, and this had an impact on their defenses. It caused them to react to their external world with behavior dominated by fantasies and unconscious fears evoked by their parents' Holocaust past. The reality of the Holocaust often penetrated the current reality through real or imagined enactments (Bergmann 1982; Kogan and Schneider 2002b).

In the case of Daphna, the threatening external situation increased her feelings of omnipotence, leading her to recreate, through her pro-Palestinian demonstrations, a past world in which she was exposed to death and destruction. She experienced these demonstrations as life-threatening situations that "transposed" (Kestenberg 1972) her into the Holocaust past of her father. The tragic repetition of the Holocaust trauma by her mother reinforced the mental representations of the Holocaust. This brought a distortion of reality and she regarded the angry Jews as her Nazi persecutors. In addition, by demonstrating for peace and exposing herself to an imagined danger, she fulfilled her conscious wish of acting as a savior to Jews (by omnipotently trying to prevent another Holocaust) as well as to Palestinians (by helping the underdog). On an unconscious level, Daphna was attempting to alleviate the guilt stemming from the trauma of her mother's suicide, followed by her father's illness and death, while at the same time coming close to death in order to overcome it.

In the case of Isaac, external reality was experienced not only as an existential threat, but also as a potential threat to his manhood. Fearing his father's fate, Isaac acquired a revolver to defend himself against a possible attack on his manhood, which had been his father's misfortune. Perhaps in his unconscious fantasies, Isaac perceived the Palestinian terrorists who might break into his house as Nazi aggressors raping his body. The threatening external reality reactivated the lack of differentiation between Isaac and his father, causing him to relive his father's traumatic past in his own present. In this mixed reality, the revolver represented the phallus (thus fulfilling his father's message to become a man) as well as the weapon that enabled Isaac to defend his manhood against those who wished to destroy it.

Both cases are marked by great confusion between past and present, fantasy and reality, internal and external. External life-threatening situations reinforced the patients' manic defenses, leading to a distorted perception of reality in each case.

I wish to conclude by saying that we can conceive of Daphna's and Isaac's parents as typical of many Jewish mothers and fathers who were damaged by the Holocaust. Therefore these patients represent a large group of individuals for whom the encounter with a life-threatening situation reinforced their manic defenses, leading to a distorted perception of reality.

# Epilogue

Mourning was first defined as a process that occurs in reaction to the loss of an object. The work of mourning thus included a massive psychic effort to recover a link with reality and to detach oneself from the persecutory aspects of the lost object by assimilating its positive and kindly aspects. Viewing it from this perspective, Burch regarded mourning as "a kind of final act of love" (Burch 1989, p. 622).

After examining the mourning process for nearly two decades, Pollock (1978) arrived at a different conclusion, namely that the mourning process is not linked absolutely to object loss. Instead, it is "a universal adaptational series of intrapsychic operations occurring in sequential successive stages involved in the reestablishment of a new level of internal and related external equilibrium" (p. 262). These series of operations are caused by different stages of change that occur throughout a person's development and that can be interpreted as threats to one's integrity and self-identity, forcing the individual to suffer deep, painful affects.

Similarly to Pollock, Grinberg (1992) maintained that mourning is not linked exclusively to object loss, but also to growth and to the passage from one stage of life to another. This process involves the loss of certain attitudes, ways of life, and relationships, which, even though replaced by other, more developed ones, nonetheless evoke pain and mourning. Living therefore necessarily requires that an individual go through a succession of mourning processes that are not always successfully completed.

When we pass from one stage of life to another, as well as when we are confronted with loss and bereavement, trauma, and stress, reality is often distorted or denied. In some cases, neither time nor therapy, perhaps nothing, may completely change this. What is required for recovery is not

retribution and triumph, not just the relief of rage, not even simply forgiveness, but an emotional awareness of the loss, genuinely experienced,
however painful[1] it is. This means acceptance of one's perpetual vulnerability to loss and betrayal, as well as the vulnerability caused by one's own
limitations and by the finality of life.

In the various chapters of this book we have found detailed descriptions
of the journey from the absence of conscious grieving—a form of pathological mourning (Bowlby 1980)—to emotional awareness of the pain
evoked by loss and its elaboration. The work of mourning includes the
painful toll on the individual, whether in everyday life or in analysis, as he
confronts his losses. By means of the mourning process, the individual
strives to accept loss, overcome pathological defenses, and readapt the ego
to reality in situations of object loss and in a variety of other situations
which cause the individual to suffer painful feelings.

The work of mourning may be impeded by depressive anxiety, pain,
and "persecutory guilt" (Grinberg 1992).[2] These feelings can flood the
ego, which attempts to counteract them by reverting to primitive defenses
(e.g., denial and manic defenses). The struggle of the ego may result in
nonreceptivity to loss and, in varying degrees, a splitting and denial of
reality. The struggle against pain and mourning may have adaptive and/
or pathological aspects, as demonstrated in the various chapters of this
book. The individual's strategies against mourning prevent the despair
that often accompanies emotional awareness, thus helping him survive
physically as well as psychically, but leaving him emotionally depleted.

The book deals with the individual's and society's use of defenses
against emotional awareness of pain and mourning in situations of internal and external stress. On the individual level, it deals with manic defenses against pain and loss in cases of individuals who are threatened by
fragmentation and psychic death. On the societal level, it explores enactment as a substitute-for-mourning mechanism among Holocaust survivors' offspring, a specific population group scattered to the four corners
of the earth, who carry the burden of pain and guilt transmitted to them
by their traumatized parents. The book also examines the impact of life-
threatening situations in Israel on the perception of reality and on the defenses of Holocaust survivors' offspring and on Israeli society as a whole.

In the first section of the book I described individuals who, threatened
by fragmentation, mobilized manic defenses against emotional awareness

of loss. These patients suffered psychic wounds that could not be completely healed by therapy. Nonetheless, their emotional experience in analysis enabled them to discover their original attachment and its betrayal, and helped them bear the torment of mourning, guilt, and persecution without fear of being flooded by it. Consequently, their internal world was less denied and the compulsive need to erase it by various types of defenses diminished. The patients' growing ability to mourn increased their capacity to love and to mitigate hate, in spite of the manic mechanisms that still persisted for the most part.

In the second and third sections of the book I examined the impact of unresolved mourning on the individual and society. The struggle against mourning shapes one's perception of reality, fantasy world, relationships, decision making, and actions, thus leaving an impact both on the individual and on society.

The second section deals primarily with the way in which Holocaust survivors' offspring contend with the unresolved mourning transmitted to them by their parents. Holocaust survivors' offspring suffer from a longing and nostalgia that is akin to a depressive state (Shoshan 1989). In spite of significant achievements in their professional lives, wealth, substantial personal acclaim, or social status, they have no full sense of living in the present and are left with a void and mourning for a past they do not know (Auerhahn and Prelinger 1983; Fresco 1984; Auerhahn and Laub 1998). These individuals employ various defenses, such as enactment, obsessive-compulsive symptoms, splitting, denial, and so on to avoid the pain and grief transmitted to them by their parents. In this section, I focused primarily on the mechanism of enactment, which includes split off, fragmented behaviors, cognition, and affect. Holocaust survivors' offspring have no cognitive understanding of the trauma that is enacted, no emotional awareness of the painful feelings connected to the enactment. The mourning of the second generation is often decontextualized and therefore no longer meaningful. It is only by understanding that it belongs to their parents' past, by putting it into the context of the Holocaust, that it acquires meaning and ceases to be irrational, thus strengthening their lifeforces. As Victor Frankl (1963) stated: "The search for meaning is the primary source of life."

The chapters that dealt with Holocaust survivors' offspring illustrate their discovery of the "unknown" story of their parents and the lifting of the repression. It is followed by the process of working through, which transforms the phenomenon of enactment into an "affective understanding" (Freud 1915). This understanding links thoughts and feelings, which have often been severed by the parents' repression of the trauma and by traces of the repression in the child. The resulting integration of cognition and emotions greatly diminishes the offspring's need to repeatedly enact the parents' stories in his or her current life, a need that is often reactivated by a current life-threatening reality.

In this section I examined the difficult experience of the survivors' offspring in learning details about the parents' traumatic past. Here I would add that the missing pieces of the parents' history may often be connected to the offspring's own feelings of shame and guilt. The realization that the traumatic past is persecuting him up to the present and has an impact on the way he perceives reality may be experienced as a narcissistic hurt for the offspring, thus mobilizing his manic defenses. Much psychic work is needed for working through feelings of guilt and shame connected to the parents' Holocaust past. As demonstrated by the various clinical illustrations, the overcoming of defenses against pain, and the subsequent work of mourning in the further stages of analysis, enables these offspring to proceed with their lives in the face of the overwhelming evil that was part of their parents' experiences and therefore part of the offspring themselves.

In the last section of the book, I explored the impact of external traumatic reality in Israel on Israeli society as a whole. In writing about the reaction to the Gulf War among second-generation Holocaust survivors living in Israel, I observed that "a large segment of the Israeli population linked the threat of the Gulf War to the Holocaust history of the Jewish people. It is therefore possible that the collective memory of past traumas, in a certain sense, turned us all into the second generation" (Kogan 1995, p. 145). Thus, I would dare say that the current ongoing threatening and terrifying situation in Israel has reactivated the traumatic Holocaust past, with all its devastating affects and implications, not only among those who were directly affected by it (Moses 1993; Volkan et al. 2002; Brenner 2002) and their offspring, but among an entire population.

Living in a life-threatening situation presents us with the question of how present trauma affects the memory of the past. According to Freud (1915), there is no time in the unconscious. Past and present merge there, so that meanings that *were* still *are*, and the meanings that are affect and change those that were (Schaeffer 1980; Loftus and Loftus 1980). There is an unconscious component in fearing the repetition of the past, which is found particularly among Holocaust survivors (Moses 1993), even though it is not based on reality. This fear does not belong only to the large group of Holocaust survivors and their offspring. For all of us in Israel who share the collective memory of the Holocaust, the possibility of a destructive attack reactivates the trauma of our parents' past.

We can understand this reactivation by means of the psychoanalytic model of trauma, which posits two events: a later event that revivifies an original event, which only then becomes traumatic (Laplanche and Pontalis 1967). As it is linked to past horrors, the present terror takes on the quality of childhood fears and nightmares. This threatens to destroy the boundary between inside and outside, between reality and fantasy (Auerhahn and Prelinger 1983). These "unfortunate encounters" (Green 1973) between fantasy and traumatic events in reality can be terrifying because the communication from inside to outside is damaged to the point that inner spaces are no longer able to contain the inner world (Janin 1996). The subject can no longer tell whether excitation is of internal or external origin, and so is overwhelmed by feelings of helplessness and fear—the famous *hilflosigkeit* described by Freud (1917). Traumatic external reality becomes the embodiment of the worst fantasies of inner reality, overwhelming the subject with the realization of his or her own potential destructiveness. The life-threatening external reality in Israel may lead to a perception of reality based on past scripts and may reinforce the imprints of the past, which insidiously spill into and permeate the present.

To be free of the burden of the past, we must learn from history, both on the individual level and on the societal level. Learning from history means becoming acquainted with elements of the present by understanding what entered the present from the past. The memory of past events, both as ideas and feelings, should ideally constitute a means for avoiding the repetition of past errors or perseverating unsuccessful patterns of performance. Or, more informally, learning from the past means "learning from experience" (Novey 1968).

As I illustrated in various chapters of the book, history is never properly over. That is, the past is never dead; it lives in the mind, never to perish. The intermeshed nature of past and present has been eloquently expressed by Turner (1938): "For the present is simply the undeveloped past, the past is the undeveloped present."

This connection between past and present derives from the difference between the "facts" of history, and the meaning and significance that we attribute to these facts. The initial fact has many ramifications and is not a thing unto itself with sharp and clear outlines. Becker (1955) posed three questions about historical fact: the what, the where, and the when of it. Regarding the *what*, Becker states that historical fact is not the past event, but a symbol that enables us to recreate it imaginatively. As to the *where*, Becker places it in the mind and insists that a historical fact *is*—not *was*. While the actual past event is gone forever, it is remembered and it is the persistence of records and memories, rather than the ephemeral event, that makes a difference to us now. He then addresses himself to the *when* of historical fact as follows: "If the historical fact is present, imaginatively, in someone's mind, then it is now a part of the present."

This mutual impact of present terror on past terror and vice versa raises some crucial questions: Is there a way to break the unending cycle of hatred and violence that is passed on from one generation to another? Can psychoanalysis help us uncover traumatizations that wars and catastrophes have left within us or our parents? Can it help us work through the mourning connected to them? Can the elaboration of mourning reinforce life forces on the societal level and replace destructiveness with creativity?

I do not presume to have answers to these questions. In an exchange with Albert Einstein, Freud (1933) stated clearly that mankind is capable of destroying itself, a fact that leads to a race for time between civilization and our potential for destruction (p. 214). Freud regarded the experience of World War I as a witness to the breakdown of the ideals of our civilization and the hopes linked to them. It was evident that people were ready to kill each other, to destroy lives and property in the name of exalted ideas such as "fatherland," "brotherhood," and so on. In this context, Freud also regarded Christianity as a failure. He scrutinized man's destructive forces and raised fundamental questions about civilization in his great works of the late 1920s: "The future of an illusion" (1927) and "Civilization and its discontents" (1930). For Freud, the only hope was the voice of reason: "Die Stimme des Intellekts ist leise . . ." ("The voice of the intellect is a soft one . . ." (Freud 1927, p. 53).

Various disciplines have claimed primacy in understanding the "voice of reason" as an effective tool against human destructiveness. Kant and other Enlightenment philosophers claimed that reason, a mental faculty with which every individual is endowed, has an impact on history. For Kant, only reason can indicate how to reshape the present into a better future.

In contrast to Kant, Hegel stated that reason—the ability to think—is indelibly shaped by time and culture. Reason, for Hegel, is not an abstract human faculty that all human beings come equipped with and can affirm on autonomous grounds; rather, it grows out of the way in which the individual understands himself as part of a community. Reason, thus, is history-dependent, and, in his view, history is the only science that is able to reveal human nature and its place in the world.

In our modern world, various sciences claim to be the most effective tool against global terrorism, the opening trauma of the new millennium. The specter of global terrorism wounds our present and haunts our sense of the future. In all its horror, September 11, 2001, has left us waiting for the worst. The violence of the attacks against the Twin Towers in New York City and the Pentagon in Virginia has revealed an abyss of terror that is going to haunt our existence and thinking for years and perhaps decades to come.

In the realm of modern philosophy, Borradori conducted dialogues with Habermas and Derrida, two representatives of modern philosophy, in an attempt to understand the complexity underlying terrorism and terror. Claiming the supremacy of philosophy in this realm, she states: "Philosophy knows better than any science how to reorient itself, even as the familiar points of reference seem to have been pulverized, as it is in the case with both the elusive concept of terrorism and the experience of terror that radiates from it" (Borradori 2003, p. 2).

In the same vein, Bollas, in an interview with Vincenzo Bonaminio at the EPF Conference in Athens, regards psychoanalysis as the only effective tool for dealing with social violence: "I think that the Freudian moment arrived just after the discovery of mass armaments that could kill thousands of people. The twentieth century is a precursive warning. Either we understand ourselves and others, either we find a way to think about our conflicts with one another, to analyze destructive processes, or we shall cease to exist. I think that psychoanalysis is the arrival of the only means to think about destructive processes" (Bollas 2006, pp. 134–35).

And indeed, as we and psychoanalysis face the emergence of new forms of mass destruction, we must strive to learn about, comprehend, and analyze the states of mind that are conducive to such acts. The recent psychoanalytic literature reflects some of the important attempts that have been made to understand the terrorist's mind (Stein 2002; Akhtar 2003; Awad 2003; Bohleber 2003; Erlich 2003; Berke 2006). Yet much remains to be learned about the psychodynamic issues involved in terror attacks such as those of September 11, 2001, and the bombings in Madrid and London, which caused horrible suffering and grief to masses of people. But, since war and social violence are "a matter of life and death for civilization" (Einstein 1932), I believe, in contrast to the various approaches mentioned earlier, that a multidisciplinary effort must be made to confront this issue.

Psychoanalysis has made important strides over the years, and such concepts as working through mourning and reconciliation, which were not part of the psychoanalytic discourse, now play a prominent role in dealing with trauma on the individual as well as on the societal level (Wangh 1993; Bohleber 1997, 1998; Parens 2004). Though a painful one, the journey from absence of mourning to an emotional awareness of pain and loss, and the process involved in working them through, is essential so that loss may be converted into gain for society as a whole.

## NOTES

1. Puzzled by the pain of mourning, Freud (1917) stated: "Why this process of carrying out the behest of reality bit by bit, which is in the nature of a compromise, should be so extraordinarily painful is not at all easy to explain in terms of mental economics" (p.154).

2. This type of guilt includes anxiety and persecution caused by loss and frustration and it appears in the most regressive states. Grinberg links "persecutory guilt" to the mechanism of the schizoid-paranoid phase, as described by Melanie Klein.

# References

**INTRODUCTION (Part I)**

Bowlby, J. (1960). Grief and mourning in infancy. *The Psychoanalytic Study of the Child* 15: 9–52.

Brenner, I. (2002a). Foreword. In *The Third Reich in the Unconscious— Transgenerational Transmission and Its Consequences*, ed. Vamik D. Volkan, Gabrielle Ast, and William F. Greer, Jr. New York and London: Brunner-Routledge, pp. xi–xvii.

———. (2002b). Reflections on the aftermath of September 11. The Philadelphia Interpreter—The Newsletter of the Psychoanalytic Center of Philadelphia, February 2002, p. 4.

Grinberg, L. (1992). *Guilt and Depression.* London and New York: Karnac Books.

Freud, A. (1960). Discussion of Dr. John Bowlby's paper. In *Psychoanalytic Study of the Child*, 15: 52–62.

Freud, S. (1913 [1912–1913]). Totem and Taboo. *Standard Edition* 13: 1–162.

Kogan, I. (1995). *The Cry of Mute Children—A Psychoanalytic Perspective of the Second Generation of the Holocaust.* London and New York: Free Association Books.

Moses, R., ed. (1993). *Persistent Shadows of the Holocaust: The Meaning to Those Not Directly Affected.* Madison, CT: International Universities Press.

Parens, H. (2001). We all mourn: C'est la condition humaine. In *Three Faces of Mourning—Melancholia, Manic Defense and Moving On*, ed. Salman Akhtar. Northvale, NJ: Jason Aronson, pp. 1–13.

Poland, W. (2006). Remarks for awards meeting. Washington, DC, 2006.

Schafer, R. (1973). Termination. *International Journal of Psychoanalytic Psychotherapy* 2: 135–48.

Volkan, V. D. (1998). Chosen trauma: Unresolved mourning. In *Blood Lines.* Boulder, CO: Westview Press, pp. 36–50.

Volkan, V. D., Gabrielle Ast, and William Greer Jr. (2002). *The Third Reich in the Unconscious—Transgenerational Transmission and Its Consequences*. New York and London: Brunner-Routledge.

## CHAPTER 1

Abend, S. M., and M. S. Porder. (1986). Identification in the neurosis. *International Journal of Psychoanalysis* 67: 201–8.

Abraham, K. (1924). A short study of the development of the libido viewed in the light of mental disorders. In *Selected Papers on Psychoanalysis*. London: Hogarth Press, 1948; reprinted London: Karnac Books, 1979.

Akhtar, S. (2000). From mental pain through manic defense to mourning. In *Three Faces of Mourning—Melancholy, Manic Defense and Moving On*, ed. Salman Akhtar. Northvale, NJ: Jason Aronson.

———. (2001). Mental pain and the cultural ointment of poetry. *International Journal of Psychoanalysis* 81: 229–45.

Auerhahn, N. C., and E. Prelinger. (1983). Repetition in the concentration camp survivor and her child. *International Review of Psychoanalysis* 10: 31–45.

Bergmann, M. V. (1982). Thoughts on super-ego pathology of survivors and their children. In *Generations of the Holocaust*, ed. M. S. Bergmann and M. E. Jucovy. New York: Basic Books, pp. 287–311.

Bowlby, J. (1961). Processes of mourning. *International Journal of Psychoanalysis* 42: 317–40.

Burch, B. (1989). Mourning and failure to mourn—An object-relations view. *Contemporary Psychoanalysis* 25: 608–23.

Chasseguet-Smirgel, J. (1984). Thoughts on the concept of reparation and the hierarchy of creative arts. *International Review of Psychoanalysis* 11: 399–406.

Cooper, A. (1988). The narcissistic-masochistic character. In *Masochism: Current Psychoanalytic Perspectives*, ed. R. A. Glick and D. I. Meyers. Hillsdale, NJ: Analytic Press, pp. 117–38.

Dorpat, T. L. (1977). Depressive Affect. *Psychoanalytic Study of the Child* 32: 3–27.

———. (1979). Is splitting a defense? *International Review of Psychoanalysis* 6: 105–13.

———. (1987). A new look at denial and defense. *Annual of Psychoanalysis* 15: 23–47.

Fingarette, H. (1969). *Self-Deception*. New York: Routledge and Kegan Paul.

Freeman-Sharpe, E. (1935). Similar and divergent unconscious determinants underlying the sublimations of pure art and pure science. *International Journal of Psychoanalysis* 16: 186–202.

Freud, A. (1936). *The Ego and the Mechanisms of Defense*. New York: International University Press, 1966.

Freud, S. (1908). "Civilized" sexual morality and modern nervous illness. *Standard Edition* 9.

———. (1916). Some character-types met with in analytic work: III. Criminals from a sense of guilt. *Standard Edition* 14.

———. (1917). Mourning and melancholia. *Standard Edition* 14.

———. (1923). The infantile genital organization. *Standard Edition* 19.

———. (1926). Inhibitions, symptoms and anxiety. *Standard Edition* 20.

———. (1940). Splitting of the ego in the processes of defense. *Standard Edition* 23.

———. (1950 [1985]). Project for a scientific psychology. *Standard Edition* 1: 281–388.

Freyberg, S. (1980). Difficulties in separation-individuation, as experienced by offspring of Nazi-Holocaust survivors. *American Journal of Orthopsychiatry* 5: 87–95.

Grinberg, L. (1964). Two kinds of guilt—their relations with normal and pathological aspects of mourning. *International Journal of Psychoanalysis* 45: 366–71.

———. (1992). *Guilt and Depression*. London and New York: Karnac Books.

Grubrich-Simitis, I. (1984). From concretism to metaphor. *Psychoanalytic Study of the Child* 39: 301–19.

Hamilton, J. (1969). Object loss, dreaming and creativity: The poetry of John Keats. *Psychoanalytic Study of the Child* 24: 488–31.

———. (1976). Early trauma, dreaming and creativity. Works of Eugene O'Neil. *International Review of Psychoanalysis* 3: 341–64.

———. (1979). Transitional phenomena and the early writings of Eugene O'Neil. *International Review of Psychoanalysis* 6: 49–60.

Hartmann, H. (1964). *Essays on Ego Psychology*. New York: International University Press.

Hilgard, E. R. (1949). Human motives and the concept of the self. *American Psychologist* 4: 374–82.

Hinshelwood, R. D. (1991). *A Dictionary of Kleinian Thought*. London: Free Association Books.

Jacobson, E. (1959). Denial and repression. *Journal of American Psychoanalytic Association* 7: 581–609.

Joffee, W. G., and J. Sandler. (1965). Pain, depression and individuation. In *From Safety to Superego*, ed. J. Sandler. New York: Guilford, pp. 154–79.

Joseph, B. (1981). Towards the experiencing of psychic pain. In *Psychic Equilibrium and Psychic Change*, ed. M. Feldman and E. B. Spillius. London: Routledge, 1989, pp. 88–97.

Kahn, M. M. (1979). From masochism to psychic pain. In *Alienation in Perversions*. New York: International University Press, pp. 210–18.

Klein, M. (1920). Inhibitions and difficulties at puberty. *Works of Melanie Klein* 1, pp. 54–58.

———. (1927). Criminal tendencies in normal children. *British Journal of Medical Psychology* 7: 177–92.

———. (1929). Infantile anxiety-situations reflected in a work of art and in the creative impulse. *Works of Melanie Klein* 1, pp. 210–18.

———. (1935). A contribution to the psychogenesis of manic-depressive states. *International Journal of Psychoanalysis* 16: 145–74.

———. (1946). Notes on some schizoid mechanisms. *International Journal of Psychoanalysis* 27: 99–110. Republished (1952) in *Developments in Psychoanalysis*, ed. Melanie Klein, Paula Heimann, Susan Isaacs, and Joan Riviere. London: Hogarth Press, pp. 292–320.

Klein, H., and I. Kogan. (1989). Some observations on denial and avoidance in Jewish Holocaust and post-Holocaust experience. In *Denial—A Clarification of Concepts and Research*, ed. E. L. Edelstein, Donald L. Nathanson, and Andrew M. Stone. New York and London: Plenum Press, pp. 299–309.

Kogan, I. (1990). A journey to pain. *International Journal of Psychoanalysis* 71: 629–40. Reprinted in *Libro Annual de Psicoanalisis*, 1991. Also in *Zeitschrift fur Psychoanalytische Theorie und Praxis*, Jahrgang VI (1), 1991, pp. 62–79.

———. (1995). *The Cry of Mute Children—A Psychoanalytic Perspective of the Second Generation of the Holocaust*. London and New York: Free Association Books. In German: (1998). *Der Stumme Schrei der Kinder—Die Zweite Generation der Holocaust—Opfer*. Frankfurt/Main: S. Fischer Verlag. In French: (2001). *Le Cri des Enfants sans Voix—L'Holocauste et la Deuxieme Generation: Une Perspective Analytique*. Paris and Suisse: Delachaux et Niestle. In Romanian: (2001). *Strigatul Copiilor Muti. Psihanaliza si Holocaust: O Perspectiva Asupra Celei de-a Doua Generatii a Holocaustului*. Bucharest: Editura Trei. In Croatian: (2004). *Nijemi Krik—Druga generacija zrtava Holokausta*. Zagreb: O. B. izdanja antiBarbarus.

———. (1998). The black hole of dread: The psychic reality of children of Holocaust survivors. In *Even Paranoids Have Enemies—A New Perspective on Persecution and Paranoia*, ed. Joseph H. Berke, Stella Pierides, Andrea Sabbadini, and Stanley Schneider. London and New York: Routledge, pp. 47–59.

Laub, D., and N. C. Auerhahn. (1993). Knowing and not knowing psychic trauma. Forms of traumatic memory. *International Journal of Psychoanalysis* 74: 287–302.

Lewin, B. (1950). *The Psychoanalysis of Elation*. New York: Norton.

Metcalf, A. (1977). Childhood: from process to structure. In *Hysterical Personality*, ed. M. J. Horowitz. New York: Jason Aronson, pp. 273–81.

Ogden, T. (1986). *The Matrix of the Mind*. New York: Jason Aronson.

Person, E. S. (1988). Review of *Creativy and Perversion* by Janine Chasseguet-Smirgel. New York: Norton, 1984.

Pollock, G. (1975). On mourning, immortality and utopia. *Journal of American Psychoanalytic Association* 23: 334–62.

———. (1977). The mourning process and creative organizational change. *Journal of American Psychoanalytic Association* 25: 3–34.

Pontalis, J. B. (1981). *Frontiers in Psychoanalysis: Between the Dream and Psychic Reality*. New York: International University Press.

Renik, O. (1990). Comments on the clinical analysis of anxiety and depressive affect. *Psychoanalytic Quarterly* 59: 226–48.

Rosenfeld, H. (1983). Primitive object relations and mechanisms. *International Journal of Psychoanalysis* 64: 261–67.

———. (1987). *Impasse and Interpretation*. London and New York: Tavistock.

Schafer, R. (1968). The mechanisms of defense. *International Journal of Psychoanalysis* 49: 49–62.

———. (1976). *A New Language for Psychoanalysis*. New Haven and London: Yale University Press.

Segal, H. (1983). Some clinical implications of Melanie Klein's work. *International Journal of Psychoanalysis* 64: 269–76.

Volkan, V. D. (1981). *Linking Objects and Linking Phenomena: Study of the Forms, Symptoms, Metapsychology and Therapy of Complicated Mourning*. New York: International University Press.

Waelder, R. (1951). The structure of paranoid ideas. *International Journal of Psychoanalysis* 32: 167–77.

Weisman, A. D. (1972). *On denying and denying. A psychiatric study of terminality*. New York: Behavioral Publications, Inc.

Weiss, E. (1934). Bodily pain and mental pain. *International Journal of Psychoanalysis* 15: 1–13.

Winnicott, D. W. (1935). The manic defense. In *Through Pediatrics to Psychoanalysis: Collected Papers*. New York: Brunner/Mazel, 1992, pp. 129.

## CHAPTER 2

Akhtar, S. (2001). From mental pain through manic defense to mourning. In *Three Faces of Mourning—Melancholia, Manic Defense and Moving On*, ed. S. Akhtar. Northvale, NJ: Jason Aronson, pp. 95–115.

Arlow, J. A. (1970). Some problems in current psychoanalytic thought. In *The World Biennial of Psychiatry & Psychotherapy*, vol. 1, ed. S. Arieti. New York: Basic Books, pp. 34–54.

Balkoura, A. (Reporter) (1974). Panel: The fate of the transference neurosis after analysis. *Journal of the American Psychoanalytic Association* 22: 875–903.

de Berenstein, S. P., and S. S. de Fondevila. (1989). Termination in analysis in the light of the evolution of a link. *International Review of Psychoanalysis* 16: 385–89.

Blum, H. P. (1989). The concept of termination and the evolution of psychoanalytic thought. *Journal of the American Psychoanalytic Association* 37: 275–95.

Cooper, A. M. (1985). The termination of the training analysis: process, expectations, achievement. *International Psychoanalytic Association Monograph Series* 5: 1–17.

Deutsch, H. (1933). Motherhood and sexuality. *Psychoanalytic Quarterly* 2: 476–88.

Dewald, P. (1982). The clinical importance of the termination phase. *Psychoanalytic Inquiry* 2: 441–61.

Fast, I. (1979). Developments in gender identity: gender differentiation in girls. *International Journal of Psychoanalysis* 60: 443–53.

Firestein, S. K. (Reporter) (1969). Panel. Problems of termination in the analysis of adults. *Journal of the American Psychoanalytic Association* 17: 222–37.

———. (1982). Termination of psychoanalysis: theoretical, clinical and pedagogic considerations. *Psychoanalytic Inquiry* 2: 473–97.

Freud, S. (1915). Thoughts on war and death. *Standard Edition* 14: 273–303.

———. (1937). Analysis terminable and interminable. *Standard Edition* 23: 209–55.

Greenson, R. R. (1967). *The Technique and Practice of Psychoanalysis*. New York: International University Press, 1971.

Grinberg, L. (1980). The closing phase of the psychoanalytic treatment of adults and the goals of psychoanalysis: "The search for truth about one's self." *International Journal of Psychoanalysis* 61: 25–37.

Hoffer, W. (1950). Three psychological criteria for the termination of treatment. *International Journal of Psychoanalysis* 31: 194–95.

Hurn, H. (Reporter) (1973). Panel: On the fate of transference after the termination of analysis. *Journal of the American Psychoanalytic Association* 21: 182–92.

Jaques, E. (1965). Death and the middle life crisis. *International Journal of Psychoanalysis* 46: 458–72.

Kantrowitz, J. L. et al. (1990). Follow-up of psychoanalysis five to ten years after termination. II. Development of the self-analytic function. *Journal of the American Psychoanalytic Association* 38: 637–54.

Klein, M. (1935). A contribution to the psychogenesis of manic-depressive states. In *Love, Guilt and Reparation and Other Works 1921–1945*. New York: Free Press, 1992, pp. 262–89.

Kramer, M. K. (1959). On the continuation of the analytic process after psychoanalysis (a self-observation). *International Journal of Psychoanalysis* 40: 17–25.

Novick, J. (1982). Termination: themes and issues. *Psychoanalytic Inquiry* 2: 329–65.

Pfeffer, A. (1963). The meaning of the analyst after analysis—a contribution to the theory of therapeutic results. *Journal of the American Psychoanalytic Association* 11: 229–44.

Pines, D. (1993). The relevance of early psychic development to pregnancy and abortion. In *A Woman's Unconscious Use of Her Body*. London: Virago Press, pp. 97–116.

Rangell, L. (1982). Some thoughts on termination. *Psychoanalytic Inquiry* 2: 367–92.

Robbins, W. (Reporter) (1975). Panel: Termination: problems and techniques. *Journal of the American Psychoanalytic Association* 23: 166–76.

Schachter, J. (1992). Concepts of termination and post-termination. Patient-analyst contact. *International Journal of Psychoanalysis* 73: 137–54.

Schafer, R. (1973). Termination. *International Journal of Psychoanalytic Psychotherapy* 2: 135–48.

Schlessinger, N., and F. P. Robbins. (1983). *A Developmental View of the Psychoanalytic Process: Follow-up Studies and their Consequences*. Madison, CT: International Universities Press.

Siegel, B. L. (1982). Some thoughts on "Some thoughts on termination" by Leo Rangell. *Psychoanalytic Inquiry* 2: 393–98.

Symposium. (1937). The theory of the therapeutic results of psychoanalysis. *International Journal of Psychoanalysis* 18:125–88.

———. (1948). On the evaluation of therapeutic results. *International Journal of Psychoanalysis* 29: 7–33.

———. (1950). On the criteria for the termination of an analysis. *International Journal of Psychoanalysis* 31: 78–80, 179–205.

Ticho, E. E. (1972). Termination of psychoanalysis: treatment goals, life goals. *Psychoanalytic Quarterly* 41: 315–33.

Weigert, E. (1952). Contribution to the problem of terminating psychoanalysis. *Psychoanalytic Quarterly* 21: 465–80.

Winnicott, D.W. (1935). The manic defense. In *Through Pediatrics to Psycho-Analysis: Collected Papers*, pp. 129–44. New York: Brunner/Mazel, 1992.

## CHAPTER 3

Anzieu, D. (1986). *Un Peau Pour Les Pensees. Entretiens avec Gilbert Tarab*. Paris: Clancier-Guenod.

Bacal, H. (1985). Optimal responsiveness and the therapeutic process. In *Progress in Self-Psychology*, vol. 1, ed. A. Goldberg. New York: Guilford Press, pp. 202–27.

Balint, M. (1952). *Primary Love and Psychoanalytic Technique*. London: Tavistock.

———. (1968). *The Basic Fault*. London and New York: Tavistock.

Bion, W. R. (1989). *Learning from Experience*. London: Karnac Books; original work published 1962.

Bollas, C. (1992). Cruising in the homosexual arena. In *Being a Character— Psychoanalysis and Self-Experience*. London: Routledge, p. 147.

Breckenridge, K. (2000). Physical touch in psychoanalysis: A closet phenomenon? *Psychoanalytic Inquiry* 20: 2–21.

Casement, P. (1982). Some pressures on the analyst for physical contact during the reliving of an early trauma. *International Review of Psychoanalysis* 9: 279–86.

Chasseguet-Smirgel, J. (1984). *Creativity and Perversion*. New York: Norton.

Chused, S. F. (1990). Neutrality in the analysis of action-prone adolescents. *Journal of American Psychoanalytic Association* 38: 679–704.

Ferenczi, S. (1953). *The Theory and Technique of Psychoanalysis*. New York: Basic Books.

Fosshage, J. L. (2000). The meaning of touch in psychoanalysis: A time for reassessment. *Psychoanalytic Inquiry* 20: 21–44.

Freud, S. (1915). The unconscious. *Standard Edition* 15: 205–18.

———. (1927). Fetishism. *Standard Edition* 21: 147–57.

Fromm-Reichmann, F. (1950). *Principles of Intensive Psychotherapy*. Chicago: University of Chicago Press.

Gedo, J. E. (1944). Analytic interventions: The question of form. In *The Spectrum of Psychoanalysis—Essays in Honor of Martin S. Bergmann*, eds. A. Kramer Richards and A. D. Richards. Madison, CT: International Universities Press, pp. 111–29.

Goethe, J. W. (1984). Faust I and II. In *Goethe: The Collected Works* (vol. 2), ed. and trans. S. Atkins. Princeton, NJ: Princeton University Press. (Original work published 1808.)

Green, A. (1986). The dead mother. In *On Private Madness*. London: Hogarth Press, pp. 142–73.

Greenberg, J. (1991). Countertransference and reality. *Psychoanalytic Dialogues* 1: 52–73.

Grunes, M. (1984). The therapeutic object relationship. *Psychoanalytic Review* 71: 123–43.

Jones, E. (1955). *The Life and Work of Sigmund Freud*, vol. 2. New York: Basic Books.

Kahn, M. M. R. (1979). *Alienation in Perversion.* New York: International University Press.

Kernberg, O. (1975). *Borderline Conditions and Pathological Narcissism.* New York: Jason Aronson.

Kernberg, O. F. (1992). Psychoanalytic psychotherapy with borderline patients. Paper presented at University College, London, Psychoanalysis Unit.

Klein, M. (1935). A contribution to the psychogenesis of manic-depressive states. *International Journal of Psychoanalysis* 16: 145–74.

Klein, M., P. Heimann, S. Isaacs, and J. Riviere. (1952). *Developments in Psychoanalysis.* London: Hogarth Press.

Kohut, H. (1971). A clinical contribution to the analysis of a perversion. *International Journal of Psychoanalysis* 52: 441–49.

———. (1977). *The Restoration of the Self.* New York: International University Press.

———. (1981). Lecture presented at the annual conference on self-psychology, Berkeley, CA, October.

Lecourt, E. (1990). The musical envelope. In *Psychic Envelopes*, ed. D. Anzieu. London: Karnac Books, pp. 211–37.

Little, M. (1966). Transference in borderline states. *International Journal of Psychoanalysis* 47: 135–54.

———. (1990). *Psychotic Anxieties and Containment.* Northvale, NJ: Jason Aronson.

Loewald, H. W. (1960). On the therapeutic action of psychoanalysis. *International Journal of Psychoanalysis* 41: 16–33.

Maroda, K. J. (1999). Therapeutic necessity or malpractice? Physical contact reconsidered. In *Seduction, Surrender and Transformation: Emotional Engagement in the Analytic Process.* Hillsdale, NJ: Analytic Press, pp. 141–59.

McDougall, J. (1978). The primal scene and the perverse scenario. In *Plea for a Measure of Abnormality.* New York: International University Press, 1980, pp. 53–86.

———. (1986). Identifications, neoneeds and neosexualities. *International Journal of Psychoanalysis* 67: 19–31.

McLaughlin, J. (1995). Touching limits in the analytic dyad. *Psychoanalytic Quarterly* 64: 433–65.

Meltzer, D. (1973). *Sexual States of Mind.* Pertshire, Scotland: Clunie Press.

Mintz, E. (1969). Touch and the psychoanalytic tradition. *Psychoanalytic Review* 56: 365–76.

Modell, A. (1990). *Other Times, Other Realities.* Cambridge, MA: Harvard University Press.

Ogden, T. (1994). The concept of interpretive action. In *Subjects of Analysis*. Northvale, NJ: Jason Aronson, pp. 107–37.

———. (1996). The perverse subject of analysis. *Journal of American Psychoanalytic Association* 44: 1121–46.

———. (1999). *Reverie and Interpretation—Sensing Something Human*. London: Karnac Books.

Pedder, J. R. (1986). Attachment and new beginning: Some links between the work of Michael Balint and John Bowlby. In *The British School of Psychoanalysis—The Independent Tradition*, ed. G. Kohon. London: Free Association Books, pp. 295–309.

Rechy, J. (1967). *Numbers*. New York: Grove, 1981.

Renik, O. (1995). The ideal of the anonymous analyst and the problem of self-disclosure. *Psychoanalytic Quarterly* 64: 466–95.

Reppen, J. (1999). Discussion of I. Kogan's paper, Physical contact and affect in the analytic situation. Presented at the IPA Congress, Santiago de Chile, August.

Rilke, R. M. (1904). Letters. In *Rilke* on *Love and Other Difficulties*, trans. J. J. L. Mood. New York: Norton, 1975, p. 27.

Riviere, J. (1929). Womanliness as a masquerade. *International Journal of Psychoanalysis* 10: 303–13.

Rycroft, C. (1986). An enquiry into the function of words in the psychoanalytical situation. In *The British School of Psychoanalysis—The Independent Tradition*, ed. G. Kohon. London: Free Association Books, pp. 237–53.

Schlesinger, H. J., and A. H. Appelbaum. (2000). When words are not enough. *Psychoanalytic Inquiry* 20: 124–44.

Searles, H. (1965). *Collected Papers on Schizophrenia*. New York: International University Press.

Shapiro, S. (1992). The discrediting of Ferenczi and the taboo on touch. Presented at the APA Division 39 spring meeting, Philadelphia, PA, April.

Singer, E. (1977). The fiction of analytic anonymity. In *The Human Dimension in Psychoanalysis*, ed. K. A. Frank. New York: Grune & Stratton, pp. 181–92.

Stern, D. N. et al. (1998). Non-interpretive mechanisms in psychoanalytic psychotherapy. *International Journal of Psychoanalysis* 79: 903–23.

Stoller, R. (1975). *Perversion*. New York: Pantheon.

Winnicott, D. W. (1965). *The Maturational process and the facilitating environment. Studies in the Theory of Emotional Development*. New York: International University Press.

———. (1992). The manic defence. In *Through pediatrics to psychoanalysis: Collected papers*. New York: Brunner/Mazel, pp. 129–44; original work published in 1935.

Zetzel, E. (1968). The so-called good hysteric. In *The Capacity for Emotional Growth*. New York: International University Press; reprinted 1972, London: Hogarth.

## INTRODUCTION (PART II)

Barocas, H. A., and Barocas, C. B. (1979). Wounds of the fathers': The next generation of Holocaust victims. *International Review of Psychoanalysis* 6: 331–40.

Bion, W. R. (1959). *Experiences in Groups*. New York: Basic Books.

Brenner, I. (2002). Foreword. In *The Third Reich in the Unconscious*, ed. V. D. Volkan. New York and London: Bruner-Routledge, pp. xi–xvii.

Freud, S. (1921). Group psychology and the analysis of the ego. *Standard Edition* 18: 16–143.

Moses, R., ed. (1993). *Persistent Shadows of the Holocaust: The Meaning to Those Not Directly Affected*. Madison, CT: International Universities Press.

Volkan, V. D. (1991). On chosen trauma. *Mind and Human Interaction* 4: 3–19.

———. (1992). Ethnonationalistic rituals. An introduction. *Mind and Human Interaction* 4: 3–19.

———. (1997). *Bloodlines: From ethnic pride to ethnic terrorism*. New York: Farrar, Straus and Giroux.

———. (1999). Psychoanalysis and diplomacy. Part 1 Individual and large group identity. *Journal of Applied Psychoanalytic Studies* 1: 29–55.

———. (2002). *The Third Reich in the Unconscious*. New York and London: Bruner-Routledge.

Volkan, V. D., and N. Itzkowitz. (1994). *Turks and Greeks: Neighbors in Conflict*. Cambridgeshire, England: Eothen Press.

## CHAPTER 4

Akhtar, S. (1999). *Immigration and Identity—Turmoil, Treatment and Transformation*. Northvale, NJ: Jason Aronson.

Akhtar, S., and A. Smolar. (1998). Visiting the father's grave. *Psychoanalytic Quarterly* 3: 474–83.

Amati-Mehler, J., S. Argentieri, and J. Canestri. (1993). *The Babel of the Unconscious: Mother Tongue and Foreign Languages in the Psychoanalytic Dimension*, trans. J. Whitelaw-Cucco. Madison, CT: International Universities Press.

Anzieu, D. (1976). L'envelope sonore du Soi. *Nouvelle Revue de Psychanalyse* 13: 161–79.

Cioran, E. M. (1982). *Storia e Utopia*. Milan: Adelphi.

Erikson, E. H. (1950). Growth and crises of the healthy personality. In *Identity and the Life Cycle*. New York: International University Press, 1959, pp. 50–100.

————. (1956). The problem of ego identity. *Journal of American Psychoanalytic Association* 4: 56–121.

Freud, S. (1913). Totem and Taboo. *Standard Edition* 13: 1–162.

————. (1917). Mourning and melancholia. *Standard Edition* 14: 237–59.

————. (1926). Inhibitions, symptoms and anxiety. *Standard Edition* 20: 77–174.

Garza-Guerrero, A. C. (1974). Culture shock: Its mourning and the vicissitudes of identity. *Journal of American Psychoanalytic Association* 22: 408–29.

Grinberg, L. (1964). Two kinds of guilt—their relations with normal and pathological aspects of mourning. *International Journal of Psychoanalysis* 45: 366–71.

Grinberg, L. and R. Grinberg. (1989). *Psychoanalytic Perspectives on Migration and Exile*. Translated by Nancy Festinger. New Haven, CT, and London: Yale University Press. Originally published as *Psicoanalisis de la migración y del exilio*, 1984, Alianza Editorial.

Joffe, W. G., and J. Sandler. (1965). Pain, depression and individuation. In *From Safety to Superego*, ed. Joseph Sandler. London: Karnac (1987).

Kahn, C. (1997). Emigration without leaving home. In *Immigrant Experiences—Personal Narrative and Psychological Analysis*, ed. Paul H. Elovitz and Charlotte Kahn. Madison: Teaneck.

Kogan, I. (1995). *The Cry of Mute Children—A Psychoanalytic Perspective of the Second Generation of the Holocaust*. London and New York: Free Association Books.

————. (1996). Die Suche nach Geschichte in den Analysen der Nachkommen von Holocaust-Uberlebenden: Rekonstruktion des "seelischen Lochs." In *Psychoanalyse Heute Und Vor 70 Jahren*, eds. Heinz Weiss and Hermann Lang. Tubingen: edition diskord, pp. 201–308. Also in: *Traumatisierung in Kindheit und Jugend*, eds. Manfred Endres and Gerd Biermann. Munchen and Basel: Ernst Reinhardt Verlag (1998b) p. 83–98.

————. (1998). The black hole of dread: the psychic reality of children of Holocaust survivors. In *Even Paranoids Have Enemies—New Perspectives on Paranoia and Persecution*, ed. Joseph H. Berke, Stella Pierides, Andrea Sabbadini, and Stanley Schneider. London and New York: Routledge, pp. 36–47.

————. (2000). Breaking the cycle of trauma—from the individual to society. In *Mind & Human Interaction* 11: 2–10.

————. (2002). "Enactment" in lives and treatment of Holocaust survivors' offspring. *Psychoanalytic Quarterly* 71: 251–73.

Pfeiffer, E. (1974). Borderline states. *Disorders of the Nervous System*. 35: 212–19.

Sandler, J., A. Holder, and D. Meers. (1987). Ego-ideal and ideal self. In *From Safety to Superego*, ed. Joseph Sandler. London: Karnac, pp. 73–90.

Stern, D. (1985). *The Interpersonal World of the Infant*. New York: Basic Books.

Urdang, L., ed. (1968). *The Random House Dictionary of the English Language.* New York: Random.

Volkan, V. (1998). Totem and Taboo in Romania: The internalization of a "dead" leader and re-stabilization of an ethnic tent. In *Blood Lines.* Boulder, CO: Westview Press, pp. 181–202.

Zac de Filc. (1992). Psychic change in the analyst. *International Journal of Psychoanalysis* 73: 323–29.


## CHAPTER 5

Auerhahn, N. C., and D. Laub. (1998). Intergenerational memory of the Holo caust. In *International Handbook of Multigenerational Legacies of Trauma,* ed. Yael Danieli. New York and London: Plenum, pp. 21–43.

Auerhahn, N. C., and E. Prelinger. (1983). Repetition in the concentration camp survivor and her child. *International Review of Psychoanalysis* 10: 31–46.

Axelrod, S., O. L. Schnipper, and J. H. Rau. (1978). Hospitalized offspring of Holocaust survivors: problems and dynamics. *Bulletin: Menninger Clinic* 44 (1980): 1–14.

Barocas, H. A., and C. B. Barocas. (1973). Manifestations of concentration camp effects on the second generation. *American Journal of Psychiatry* 30: 820–21.

Bergmann, M. V. (1982). Thoughts on super-ego pathology of survivors and their children. In *Generations of the Holocaust,* ed. M. S. Bergmann and M. E. Jucovy. New York: Basic Books, pp. 287–311.

Bion, W. R. (1962). *Learning from Experience.* London: Heinemann.

———. (1970). *Attention and Interpretation.* London: Tavistock.

Boesky, D. (1982). Acting out: a reconsideration of the concept. *International Journal of Psychoanalysis* 63: 39–55.

Brenner, I. (2000). Transmission of trauma in children of survivors: a review of cases. Paper presented at the American Psychoanalytic Association Holocaust Discussion Group, New York, December.

———. (2002). Foreword. In *The Third Reich in the Unconscious,* by V. D. Volkan. New York: Brunner-Routledge, pp. xi–xvii.

Chused, J. (1991). The evocative power of enactments. *Journal of American Psychoanalytic Association* 39: 615–38.

Eshel, O. (1998a). Meeting acting out, acting in and enacting or going into the eye of the storm. *Sihot-Dialogue, Israel Journal of Psychotherapy* 13: 4–16.

———. (1998b). "Black holes," deadness and existing analytically. *International Journal of Psychoanalysis* 79: 1115–31.

Etchegoyen, R. H. (1991). *The Fundamentals of Psychoanalytic Technique.* London: Karnac.

Fenichel, O. (1945). Neurotic acting out. In *Collected Papers*, ed. Hanna Fenichel and David Rapaport. New York: Davis Lewis, 1953.

Fresco, N. O. (1984). Remembering the unknown. *International Review of Psychoanalysis* 11: 417–27.

Freud, S. (1905). Fragment of an analysis of a case of Hysteria. *Standard Edition* 7: 3–125.

———. (1914). Remembering, repeating and working through. *Standard Edition* 12: 145–57.

———. (1915). The unconscious. *Standard Edition* 14: 159–215.

———. (1917). Mourning and melancholia. *Standard Edition* 14: 239–58.

———. (1920). Beyond the pleasure principle. *Standard Edition* 18:7–64.

———. (1940). An outline of psycho-analysis. *Standard Edition* 23: 141–95.

Freyberg, S. (1980). Difficulties in separation-individuation, as experienced by offspring of Nazi Holocaust survivors. *American Journal of Orthopsychiatry* 5: 87–95.

Gampel, Y. (1982). A daughter of silence. In *Generations of the Holocaust*, ed. M. S. Bergmann and M. E. Jucovy. New York: Basic Books, pp. 120–36.

Garland, C. (1991). External disasters and the internal world: an approach to psychotherapeutic understanding of survivors. In *Textbook of Psychotherapy in Psychiatric Practice*, ed. J. Holmes. London: Churchill Livingstone, (chapter 22).

———. (2002). Thinking about trauma. In *Understanding Trauma—A Psychoanalytical Approach*, ed. J. Holmes. London and New York: Karnac, pp. 9–31.

Green, A. (1986). The dead mother. In *On Private Madness*. London: Hogarth, pp. 142–73.

Greenacre, P. (1950). General problems of acting out. *Psychoanalytic Quarterly* 19: 445–67. Also in *Trauma, Growth and Personality*. London: Maresfield Library, 1953, pp. 208–19.

———. (1963). Problems of acting out in the transference relationship. In *A Developmental Approach to the Problem of Acting Out*, ed. E. W. Rexford. New York: International University Press, pp. 215–34.

Gribbin, J. (1992). *In Search of the Edge of Time: Black Holes, White Holes, Worm Holes*. London: Penguin.

Grinberg, L., and R. Grinberg. (1974). The problem of identity and the psychoanalytical process. *International Journal of Psychoanalysis* 1: 499–507.

Grotstein, J. S. (1986). The psychology of powerlessness; disorders of self-regulation as a newer paradigm for psychopathology. *Psychoanalytic Inquiry* 6: 93–118.

———. (1989). A revised psychoanalytic conception of schizophrenia: an interdisciplinary update. *Psychoanalytic Psychology* 6: 253–75.

———. (1990a). "Black hole" as the basic psychotic experience: Some newer psychoanalytic and neuroscience perspectives on psychosis. *Journal of American Academic Psychoanalysis* 18: 29–46.

———. (1990b). Nothingness, meaninglessness, chaos and "black hole." I: The importance of nothingness, meaninglessness and chaos in psychoanalysis. *Contemporary Psychoanalysis* 26: 257–91.

———. (1990c). Nothingness, meaninglessness, chaos and "black hole." II: The black hole. *Contemporary Psychoanalysis* 26: 377–407.

———. (1993). Boundary difficulties in borderline patients. In *Master Clinicians on Treating the Regressed Patient*, vol. 2, ed. L. B. Boyer and P. L. Giovacchini. Northvale, NJ: Jason Aronson, pp. 107–42.

Grubrich-Simitis, I. (1984). From concretism to metaphor. *Psychoanalytic Study of the Child* 39: 301–19.

Hinshelwood, R. D. (1989). Acting in. In *A Dictionary of Kleinian Thought*. London: Free Association Books, pp. 213–14.

Jacobs, T. J. (1986). On countertransference enactments. *Journal of American Psychoanalytic Association* 34: 289–307.

———. (1991). On countertransference enactments. In *The Use of the Self: Countertransference and Communication in the Analytic Situation*. Madison, CT: International Universities Press, pp. 139–56.

———. (2000). Unbewusste Kommunikation und verdeckte Enactments in analytischen Setting. In *Errinern, Agieren und Inszenieren*, ed. Ulrich Streeck. Gottingen: Vanderhoeck & Ruprecht, pp. 97–27.

Kestenberg, J. S. (1972). How children remember and parents forget. *International Journal of Psychoanalytic Psychotherapy* 1–2: 103–23.

———. (1982). A metapsychological assessment based on an analysis of a survivor's child. In *Generations of the Holocaust*, eds. M. S. Bergmann and M. E. Jucovy. New York: Basic Books, pp. 137–58.

Kinston, W., and J. Cohen. (1986). Primal repression: clinical and theoretical aspects. *International Journal of Psychoanalysis* 67: 337–55.

Klein, H. (1971). Families of Holocaust survivors in the kibbutz: Psychological studies. In *Psychic Traumatization: After-effects in Individuals and Communities*, ed. H. Krystal and W. G. Niederland. Boston: Little & Brown.

Klein, H., and I. Kogan. (1986). Identification and denial in the shadow of Nazism. *International Journal of Psychoanalysis* 67: 45–52. Also in *Psychoanalyse im Exil—Texte Verfolgter Analytiker*, ed. Stephen Brose and Gerda Pagel. Wurzburg: Konigshausen & Neumann (1987), pp. 128–37.

Kogan, I. (1987). The second skin. *International Review of Psychoanalysis* 15: 251–61. Also in *The Cry of Mute Children*. London and New York: Free Association Books (1995), pp. 46–69.

————. (1989). The search for self. *International Journal of Psychoanalysis* 70: 661–71. Also in *The Cry of Mute Children*. London and New York: Free Association Books (1995), pp. 29–46.

————. (1993). Curative factors in the psychoanalyses of Holocaust survivors' offspring before and during the Gulf War. *International Journal of Psychoanalysis* 74: 803–815. Also in *The Cry of Mute Children*. London and New York: Free Association Books (1995), pp. 133–48.

————. (1995). *The Cry of Mute Children—A Psychoanalytic Perspective of the Second Generation of the Holocaust*. London and New York: Free Association Books.

————. (1996). Die Suche nach Geschichte in den Analysen der Nachkommen von Holocaust Uberlebenden; Rekonstruktion des 'seelischen Lochs.' In *Psychoanalyse Heute Und Vor 70 Jahren*, ed. Heinz Weiss and Hermann Lang, Tubingen: edition diskord, pp. 291–308. Also in *Traumatisierung in Kindheit und Jugend.*, ed. Manfred Endres and Gerd Biermann, Basel: E. Reinhardt (1998), pp. 83–98. Also in *Das Ende der Sprachlosigkeit?* Ed. Liliane Opher-Cohn, Johannes Pfafflin, Bernd Sonntag, Bernd Klose, Peter Pogany-Wnendt. Giessen: Psychosozial-Verlag (2000), pp. 163–83.

————. (1998). The black hole of dread: the psychic reality of children of Holocaust survivors. In *Even Paranoids Have Enemies—New Perspectives on Paranoia and Persecution*, ed. Joseph H. Berke, Stella Pierides, Andrea Sabbadini, and Stanley Schneider. London and New York: Routledge, pp. 47–59.

————. (2000). Die Suche nach Gevissheit: Enactments traumatischer Vegangenheit. In *Errinem, Agieren und Inszenieren: Enactments und szenische Darstellungen im therapeutishen Prozess*, ed. Ulrich Streeck, Gottingen: Vandehoeck & Rupricht, pp. 127–43.

————. (2002). "Enactment" in lives and treatment of Holocaust survivors' offspring. *Psychoanalytic Quarterly* 71: 251–73.

Krell, R. (1979). Holocaust families: The survivors and their children. *Comprehensive Psychiatry* 20(6): 560–67.

Laplanche, J., and J. B. Pontalis. (1973). *The Language of Psychoanalysis*. London: Hogarth, pp. 4–6.

Laub, D., and N. C. Auerhahn. (1984). Reverberations of genocide: Its expression in the conscious and unconscious of post-Holocaust generations. In *Psychoanalytic Reflections of the Holocaust: Selected Essays*, ed. S. A. Luel and P. Marcus. Denver: Ktav Publishing House, pp. 151–67.

————. (1993). Knowing and not knowing psychic trauma: Forms of traumatic memory. *International Journal of Psychoanalysis* 74: 287–302.

Laub, D., and D. Podell. (1995). Art and trauma. *International Journal of Psychoanalysis* 76: 871–1081.

Laufer, M. (1973). The analysis of a child of survivors. In *The Child in His Family: The Impact of Disease and Death*, ed. E. J. Anthony and C. Koupernik. New York: John Wiley, vol. 2: 363–73.

Lipkowitz, M. H. (1973). The child of two survivors: the report of an unsuccessful therapy. *Israeli Annals of Psychiatry and Related Disciplines* 11: 2.

Marty, P., and M. de M'Uzan. (1963). La pensee operatoire. *Revue Francaise de Psychanalyse* 27: 345–56.

McLaughlin, J. (1992). Nonverbal behavior in the analytic situation: The search for meaning in nonverbal cues. In *When the Body Speaks: Psychological Meanings in Kinetic Cues*, ed. S. Kramer and S. Akhtar. Northvale, NJ: Jason Aronson, pp. 131–61.

Meltzer, D. (1967). *The Psychoanalytic Process*. London: Heinemann.

Micheels, L. J. (1985). Bearer of the secret. *Psychoanalytic Inquiry* 5: 21–30.

Ogden, T. (1994). The concept of interpretive action. *Psychoanalytic Quarterly* 63: 219–45.

Phillips, R. (1978). Impact of Nazi Holocaust on children of survivors. *American Journal of Psychotherapy* 32: 370–77.

Quinodoz, D. (1996). An adopted analysand transference of a "hole-object." *International Journal of Psychoanalysis* 77: 323–36.

Rakoff, V. (1966). Long-term effects of the concentration camp experience, *Viewpoints* 1: 17–21.

Renik, O. (1993). Analytic interactions. Conceptualizing technique in light of the analyst's irreducible subjectivity. *Psychoanalytic Quarterly* 562: 553–71.

Rosenfeld, H. A. (1965). An investigation into need of neurotic and psychotic patients to act out during analysis. In *Psychotic States*. London: Hogarth, pp. 200–17.

Sandler, J., and A. M. Sandler. (1978). On the development of object-relations and affects. *International Journal of Psychoanalysis* 59: 285–93.

Schafer, R. (1982). *Retelling a Life*. New York: Basic Books.

Sonnenberg, S. M. (1974). Children of survivors: workshop report. *Journal of American Psychoanalytic Association* 22: 200–4.

Tustin, F. (1972). *Autism and Childhood Psychosis*. London: Hogarth.

———. (1986). *Autistic Barriers in Neurotic Patients*. London: Tavistock.

———. (1990). *The Protective Shell in Children and Adults*. London: Karnac.

———. (1992). *Autistic States in Children*. London: Routledge.

**CHAPTER 6**

Anthony, E. J. (1974). The syndrome of the psychologically invulnerable child. In *The Child in His Family: Children at Psychiatric Risk*, ed. E. J. Anthony and C. Koupernik. New York: Wiley.

Auerhahn, N. C., and D. Laub. (1998). Intergenerational memory of the Holocaust. In *International Handbook of Multigenerational Legacies of Trauma*, ed. Yael Danieli. New York and London: Plenum Press.

Barocas, H., and H. Barocas. (1973). Manifestations of concentration camp effects on the second generation. *American Journal of Psychiatry* 130: 820–21.

Bergmann, M. V. (1982). Thoughts on super-ego pathology of survivors and their children. In *Generations of the Holocaust*, ed. M. S. Bergmann and M. E. Jucovy. New York: Basic Books, pp. 287–311.

Bion, W. (1959). *Experience in Groups*. London: Routledge, 1989.

———. (1962). A theory of thinking. *International Journal of Psychoanalysis*, 43: 306: 10; republished (1967) in W. R. Bion, *Second Thoughts*, pp. 110–19.

Brenner, I. (1988). Multisensory bridges in response to object loss during the Holocaust. *Psychoanalytic Review* 75: 573–78.

———. (2002). Foreword. In *The Third Reich in the Unconscious— Transgenerational Transmission and its Consequences*, ed. Vamik D. Volkan, Gabrielle Ast, and William F. Greer Jr. New York & London: Brunner-Routledge, pp. xi–xvii.

Cyrulnik, B. (1993). *Les Nourritures Affectives*. Paris: Editions Odile Jacob, 2000.

———. (1997). *L'Ensorcellement du Monde*. Paris: Editions Odile Jacob, 2001.

———. (1999). *Un Merveilleux Malheur*. Paris: Editions Odile Jacob, 2002.

———. (2001). *Les Vilains Petits Canards*. Paris: Editions Odile Jacob, 2004.

———. (2003). *Le Murmure des Fantômes*. Paris: Editions Odile Jacob, 2003.

———. (2004). *Parler D'amour au Bord du Gouffre*. Paris: Editions Odile Jacob.

Danieli, Yael, ed. (1998). Introduction. In *Intergenerational Handbook of Multigenerational Legacies of Trauma*. New York and London: Plenum Press, pp. 1–21.

Eitinger, L. (1964). *Concentration Camp Survivors in Norway and Israel*. London: Allen & Unwin.

Flach, F. (1988). *Resilience—Discovering a New Strength at Times of Stress*. New York: Fawcett Columbine.

Frankl, V. E. (1963). *Man's Search for Meaning: An Introduction to Logotherapy*. New York: Washington Square (121).

Freud, A. (1936). *The Ego and the Mechanisms of Defense*. New York: International University Press (1960).

Freud, A., and S. Dann. (1951). An Experiment in Group Upbringing. *Psychoanalytic Study of the Child* 6: 127–68.

Freud, S. (1897). Draft N. *Standard Edition* 1: 254–57.

———. (1908). Creative writers and daydreaming. *Standard Edition* 9: 143–53.

———. (1913 [1912–1913]). Totem and Taboo. *Standard Edition* 13: 1–162.

———. (1916). Introductory lectures in Psychoanalysis. *Standard Edition* 15–16: 9–463.

Freyberg, S. (1980). Difficulties in separation-individuation as experienced by off-spring of Nazi Holocaust survivors. *American Journal of Orthopsychiatry* 5: 87–95.

Grinberg, L. (1992). Analysis of guilt feelings and mourning in artistic creation. In *Guilt and Depression*. London and New York: Karnac Books, pp. 231–45.

Grubrich-Simitis, I. (1984). From concretism to metaphor. *Psychoanalytic Study of the Child* 39: 301–19.

Hass, A. (1996). *The Aftermath—Living With The Holocaust*. Cambridge: Cambridge University Press.

Hogman, F. (1983). Displaced Jewish children during World War II: How they coped. *Journal of Humanistic Psychology* 23: 51–66.

Kestenberg, J. S. (1972). Psychoanalytic contributions to the problem of survivors from Nazi persecution. *Israel Annals of Psychiatry and Related Disciplines* 10: 311–25.

Kestenberg, J. S., and Brenner, I. (1986) Children who survived the Holocaust—The role of rules and routines in the development of the superego. *International Journal of Psycho-Analysis* 67: 309–16.

Klein, H. (1981). Yale Symposium of the Holocaust. Proceedings, September 1981. New Haven.

Klein, H., and I. Kogan. (1986). Identification and denial in the shadow of Nazism. *International Journal of Psychoanalysis* 67: 45–52.

Klein, M. (1930). The importance of symbol formation in the development of the ego. In *Love, Guilt And Reparation and Other Works 1921–1945*. London: Virago Press (1988), pp. 219–32.

Kogan, I. (1995). *The Cry of Mute Children—A Psychoanalytic Perspective of the Second Generation of the Holocaust*. London and New York: Free Association Books.

———. (1998). The black hole of dread: the psychic reality of children of Holocaust survivors. In *Even Paranoids Have Enemies—New Perspectives on Paranoia and Persecution*, ed. Joseph H. Berke, Stella Pierides, Andrea Sabbadini, and Stanley Schneider. London and New York: Routledge, pp. 47–59.

———. (2002). "Enactment" in the lives and treatment of Holocaust survivors' offspring. *Psychoanalytic Quarterly* 71: 251–73.

Kris, E. (1952). *Psychoanalytic Exploration in Art*. New York: International University Press.

Krystal, H. (1968). Patterns of psychological damage. In *Massive Psychic Trauma*, ed. Henry Krystal. New York: International University Press, pp.1–8.

Laub, D., and N. C. Auerhahn. (1993). Knowing and not knowing massive psychic trauma: Forms of traumatic memory. *International Journal of Psychoanalysis* 74: 287–302.

Laub, D., and S. Lee. (2003). Thanatos and massive psychic trauma: The impact of the death instinct on remembering and forgetting. *Journal of American Psychoanalytic Association* 51(2): 433–64.

Laub, D., and D. Podell. (1995). Art and trauma. *International Journal of Psycho-Analysis* 76: 995–1005.

Lee, B. S. (1988). Holocaust survivors and internal strengths. *Journal of Humanistic Psychology* 28: 67–96.

Lifton, R. J. (1968). Survivors of Hiroshima and Nazi persecution. In *Massive Psychic Trauma*, ed. Henry Krystal. New York: International University Press, pp. 168–89.

———. (1978). Witnessing Survival. *Transactions* (March 1978): 40–44.

McLaughlin, J. (1995). Touching limits in the analytic dyad. *Psychoanalytic Quarterly* 64: 433–65.

Moskovitz, S. (1983). *Love Despite Hate*. New York: Schocken Books.

Niederland, W. C. (1964). Psychiatric disorders among persecution victims: A contribution to the understanding of the concentration camp pathology and its after effects. *Journal of Nervous and Mental Diseases* 139: 458–74.

Parsons, M. (2000). Creativity, psychoanalytic and artistic. In *The Dove that Returns, The Dove that Vanishes*. London and Philadelphia: Routledge, pp. 146–71.

Rutter, M. (1987). Psychosocial resilience and protective mechanisms. *American Journal Orthopsychiatry* 57: 316–31.

———. (1993). Resilience: Some conceptual considerations. *Journal of Adolescent Health* 14: 626–31.

Segal, H. (1952). A psychoanalytic approach to aesthetics. In *The Work of Hanna Segal*. New York: Jason Aronson (1981), pp. 101–9.

———. (1991). Imagination, play and art. In *Dream, Fantasy and Art*. London and New York: Tavistock/Routledge.

Trossman, B. (1968). Adolescent children of concentration camp survivors. *Canadian Psychiatric Association Journal* 12: 121–23.

Valent, P. (1988). Resilience in child survivors of the Holocaust. *The Psychoanalytic Review* 85: 517–35.

Winnicott, D. W. (1964). Correspondence: Love or skill? In *The Spontaneous Gesture: Selected Letters of D. W. Winnicott*, ed. F. Robert Rodman. London: Karnac Books, 1999, pp. 140–42.

———. (1971a). Transitional objects and transitional phenomena. In *Playing and Reality*. London: Tavistock, pp. 1–31.

———. (1971b). Creativity and its origins. In *Playing and Reality*. London: Tavistock, pp. 76–100.

## CHAPTER 7

Auerhahn, N. C., and E. Prelinger, E. (1983). Repetition in the concentration camp survivor and her child. *International Review of Psychoanalysis* 10: 31–45.

Bergmann, M. V. (1982). Thoughts on super-ego pathology of survivors and their children. In *Generations of the Holocaust*, ed. M. S. Bergmann and M. E. Jucovy. New York: Basic Books, pp. 287–311.

Bion, W. (1959). *Experience in Groups*. London: Routledge, 1989.

Blum, H. (1983). Adoptive parents: generative conflict and generational continuity. *Psychoanalytic Study of the Child* 38: 141–63.

———. (1985). Superego formation, adolescent transformation and the adult neurosis. *Journal of American Psychoanalytic Association* 4: 887–909.

Brenner, I. (2001). Personal communication.

Chasseguet-Smirgel, J. (1971). *Pour une Psychanalyse de l'Art et de la Creativite*. Paris: Payot.

Fairbairn, W. R. D. (1943). The repression and the return of bad objects. In *Psychoanalytic Studies of the Personality*. London: Tavistock, 1952, pp. 59–81.

Freud, S. (1915). The unconscious. *Standard Edition* 14: 159–209.

Freyberg, S. (1980). Difficulties in separation-individuation as experienced by offspring of Nazi Holocaust survivors. *American Journal of Orthopsychiatry* 5: 87–95.

Green, A. (1974). L'analyste, la symbolisation et l'absence. *Nouvelle Revue de Psychanalyse* 10: 225–52.

Grubrich-Simitis, I. (1984). From concretism to metaphor. *Psychoanalytic Study of the Child* 39: 301–19.

Guntrip, H. (1968). *Schizoid Phenomena, Object Relations and the Self*. London: Hogarth.

Kestenberg, J. S. (1982). The experience of survivor-parents. In *Generations of the Holocaust*, ed. M. S. Bergmann and M. E. Jucovy. New York: Basic Books, pp. 46–62.

Kierkegaard, S. (1941). *Repetition: An Essay in Experimental Psychology*. New York: Harper & Row, 1964.

Klein, M. (1929). Infantile anxiety situations reflected in a work of art and the creative impulse. In *The Writings of Melanie Klein*. London: Hogarth, 1975. Also in *Love, Guilt And Reparation*. London: Virago Press, pp. 210–19.

———. (1935). A contribution to the psychogenesis of manic-depressive states. *International Journal of Psychoanalysis* 16: 145–74.

Kogan, I. (1995). *The Cry of Mute Children—A Psychoanalytic Perspective of the Second Generation of the Holocaust*. London and New York: Free Association Books.

————. (1996). Die Suche nach Geschichte in den Analysen der Nachkommen von Holocaust-Uberlebenden: Rekonstruktion des "seelischen Lochs." In *Psychoanalyse Heute Und Vor 70 Jahren*, ed. H. Weiss and H. Lang. Tübingen, Germany: Edition Diskord.

————. (1998b). The black hole of dread: the psychic reality of children of Holocaust survivors. In *Even Paranoids Have Enemies—New Perspectives on Paranoia and Persecution*, ed. J. H. Berke, S. Pierides, A. Sabbadini, and S. Schneider. London/New York: Routledge, pp. 47–58.

————. (2000). Breaking the cycle of trauma—from the individual to society. In *Mind & Human Interaction* 11: 2–10.

————. (2002). "Enactment" in the lives and treatment of Holocaust survivors' offspring. *Psychoanalytic Quarterly* 71: 251–73.

Lorenzer, A. (1968). Some observations on the latency of symptoms in patients suffering from persecution sequelae. *International Journal of Psychoanalysis* 49: 316–18.

McLaughlin, J. (1995). Touching limits in the analytic dyad. *Psychoanalytic Quarterly* 64: 433–65.

Moses, R., ed. (1993). *Persistent Shadows of the Holocaust: The Meaning to Those Not Directly Affected*. Madison, CT: International Universities Press.

Olagner, P. (1975). *La Violence de L'Interpretation*. Paris: Presse Universitere de France.

Oliner, M. M. (1996). External reality: the elusive dimension of psychoanalysis. *Psychoanalytic Quarterly* 65: 267–300.

Olinick, S. (1969). On empathy and regression in the service of the other. *British Journal of Medical Psychology* 42: 41–49.

Renik, O. (1998). Getting real in analysis. *Psychoanalytic Quarterly* 67: 566–93.

Roth, S. (1993). The shadow of the Holocaust. In *Persistent Shadows of the Holocaust: The Meaning to Those Not Directly Affected*, ed. R. Moses. Madison, CT: International Universities Press, pp. 37–79.

Volkan, V. D. (1987). *Six Steps in the Treatment of Borderline Personality Organization*. Northvale, NJ: Jason Aronson.

Volkan, V. D., G. Ast, and W. F. Greer. (2002). *The Third Reich in the Unconscious*. New York and London: Bruner-Routledge.

Winnicott, D. W. (1935). The manic defence. In *Through Paediatrics to Psycho-Analysis: Collected Papers*. New York: Bruner/Mazel, 1992, pp. 129–44.

————. (1965). *The Maturational Processes and the Facilitating Environment*. London: Hogarth.

————. (1971). The use of an object and relating through identification. In *Playing and Reality*. London: Tavistock, pp. 101–12.

## INTRODUCTION (PART III)

Klein, M. (1935). A contribution to the psychogenesis of manic-depressive states. *International Journal of Psychoanalysis* 16: 145–74. Also in *Love, Guilt and Reparation and Other Works 1921–1945*. New York: Free Press, 1992, pp. 262–89.

Winnicott, D. W. (1935). The manic defence. In *Through Paediatrics to Psycho-Analysis: Collected Papers*. New York: Bruner/Mazel, 1992, pp. 129–44.

## CHAPTER 8

Akhtar, S. (1999). *Immigration and Identity—Turmoil, Treatment and Transformation*. Northvale, NJ: Jason Aronson.

Blos, P. (1962). *On Adolescence*. New York: Free Press.

———. (1965). The initial stage of male adolescence. *Psychoanalytic Study of the Child* 20: 145–64. New York: International University Press.

———. (1967). The second individuation process of adolescence. *Psychoanalytic Study of the Child* 22: 162–86. New York: International University Press.

———. (1974). The genealogy of the ego ideal. *Psychoanalytic Study of the Child* 29: 43–88. New Haven, CT: Yale University Press.

———. (1984). Father and son. *Journal of American Psychoanalytic Association* 32: 301–24.

———. (1985). *Son and fathers: Before and beyond the Oedipus Complex*. New York: Free Press.

Brenner, I. (1996a). On trauma, perversion, and multiple personality. *Journal of American Psychoanalytic Association* 44: 785–814.

———. (1996b). The characterological basis of "multiple personality." *American Journal of Psychotherapy* 50:154–66.

———. (2004). *Psychic Trauma—Dynamics, Symptoms and Treatment*. Oxford, UK: Jason Aronson.

Chasseguet-Smirgel, J. (1984). *Creativity and Perversion*. New York: Norton.

Ehrlich, S. (1978). Adolescent suicide-maternal longing and cognitive development. *Psychoanalytic Study of the Child* 33: 261–77.

Elsass, P. (1997). *Treating Victims of Torture and Violence*. New York: New York University Press.

Erikson, E. H. (1950a). Growth and crises of the healthy personality. In *Identity and the Life Cycle*, pp. 50–100. New York: International University Press, 1959.

———. (1950b). *Childhood and Society*. New York: Norton.

———. (1956). The problem of ego identity. In *Identity and the Life Cycle*, pp. 104–64. New York: International University Press, 1959.

———. (1958). *Young Man Luther: A Study in Psychoanalysis and History*. New York: Norton.

———. (1962). *Identity: Youth and Crisis.* New York: Norton.

Freud, A. (1967). Comments on trauma. In S. Furst, ed., *Psychic Trauma.* New York: Basic Books.

Freud, S. (1920). Beyond the pleasure principle. *Standard Edition*, 18: 7–68.

———. (1921). Group psychology and the analysis of the ego. *Standard Edition*, 18: 67–144.

———. (1923). The ego and the id. *Standard Edition*, 19: 12–68.

———. (1925). Some psychical consequences of anatomical distinction between the sexes. *Standard Edition*, 19: 243–58.

———. (1926a). Address to the society of B'nai Brith. *Standard Edition*, 20: 271–74.

———. (1926b). Inhibitions, symptoms and anxiety. *Standard Edition*, 20: 1–260.

———. (1930). Civilization and its discontents. *Standard Edition*, 21: 64–145.

Greenacre, P. (1967). The influence of infantile traume on genetic patterns. In *Psychic Trauma* ed. S. S. Furst, pp. 260–99. New York and London: Basic Books.

Guttman, S. A., R. L. Jones, and S. M. Parrish. (1980). *The Concordance to the Standard Edition of the Complete Psychological Works of Sigmund Freud*, vol. 1. Boston: G. K. Hall.

Hass, A. (1996). *The Aftermath—Living With The Holocaust.* Cambridge: Cambridge University Press.

Hilberg, R. (1985). *The Destruction of the European Jews*, revised edition, vol. 3. New York: Holmes & Meier.

Kernberg, O. F. (1976). *Object Relations Theory and Clinical Psychoanalysis.* New York: Jason Aronson.

Kestenberg, J., and I. Brenner. (1996). *The Last Witness.* Washington, DC: American Psychiatric Press.

Kogan, I. (1995). *The Cry of Mute Children—A Psychoanalytic Perspective of the Second Generation of the Holocaust.* London and New York: Free Association Books.

———. (2004). Trauma, Resistenz und Kreativität—Beobachtungen aus Analysen von Kindern Holocaustüberlebenden. In Margrit Fröhlich, Yariv Lapid, and Christian Schneider, eds., *Representationen des Holocaust im Gedächtnis der Generationen.* Frankfurt: Brandes & Apsel, pp. 90–112.

Kogan, I. and C. Schneider. (2002). The Nazi heritage and gender identity. *Journal of Applied Psychoanalytic Studies* 4 (1): 49–63.

Krystal, H. (1968). Patterns of psychological damage. In Henry Krystal, ed. *Massive Psychic Trauma.* New York: International University Press.

Laub, D., and N. C. Auerhahn. (1993). Knowing and not knowing massive psychic trauma: Forms of traumatic memory. *International Journal of Psychoanalysis* 74: 287–302.

Laub, D., N. C. Auerhahn, and S. Lee. (2003). Thanatos and massive psychic trauma: The impact of the death instinct on remembering and forgetting. *Journal of American Psychoanalytic Association* 51 (2): 433–64.

Lichtenstein, H. (1963). The dilemma of human identity: Notes on self transformation, self-objectivation and metamorphosis. *Journal of the American Psycho analytic Association* 11: 173–223.

Lifton, R. J. (1968). Survivors of Hiroshima and Nazi persecution. In Henry Krystal, ed., *Massive Psychic Trauma*. New York: International University Press.

McDougall, J. (1989). The dead father. *International Journal of Psychoanalysis* 2: 205–21.

Perel, S. (2004). *Europa, Europa*. Tel-Aviv: Miskal. First published 1994, Yediot Achronot Vesifrei Hemed.

Rutter, M. (1987). Psychosocial resilience and protective mechanisms. *American Journal of Orthopsychiatry* 57: 316–31.

Schilder, P. (1935). *The Image and Appearance of the Human Body*. New York: International University Press.

Stern, D. N. (1985). *The Interpersonal World of the Infant*. New York: Basic Books.

Strachey J., A. Freud, A. Strachey, and A. Tyson. (1923). Editor's introduction, pp. 3–11. In *The Ego and the Id*, S. Freud. *Standard Edition* 19: 1–66.

Tausk, V. (1919). Uber die enstehung des beeinflussungapparates in der schizophrenie. *International Journal of Psychoanalysis*, 5: 1–33.

Volkan, V. D. (1988). *The Need to Have Enemies and Allies*. Northvale, NJ: Jason Aronson.

Weil, A. (1970). The basic core. *Psychoanalytic Study of the Child* 25: 442–60. New York: International University Press.

Wheelis, A. (1958). *The Quest for Identity*. New York: Norton.

Wiesel, Elie. (1972). *One Generation After*. New York: Avon Books.

## CHAPTER 9

Abend, S. (1986). Countertransference, empathy, and the analytic ideal: the impact of life stresses on analytic capability. *Psychoanalytic Quarterly* 55: 563–75.

Arlow, J. A. (1991). Derivative manifestations of perversions. In *Perversions and Near-Perversions in Clinical Practice: New Psychoanalytic Perspectives*, ed. G. I. Fogel and W. A. Mye. New Haven and London: Yale University Press, pp. 59–74.

Bion, W. (1959). Attacks on linking. In *Second Thoughts—Selected Papers on Psychoanalysis*. London: Heinemann, 1967. Reprinted London: Karnac Books, 1984, pp. 93–109.

Boyer, C. B. (1983). *The Regressed Patient*. New York: Jason Aronson.

———. (1999). *Countertransference and Regression*. Northvale, NJ: Jason Aronson.

Carpy, D. V. (1989). Tolerating the countertransference: a mutative process. *International Journal of Psychoanalysis* 70: 287–94.

De Jonghe, F., P. Rijnierse, and R. Janssen, R. (1992). The role of support in Psychoanalysis. *Journal of the American Psychoanalytic Association* 40: 475–99.

Eissler, K. R. (1953). The effect of the structure of the ego on psychoanalytic technique. *Journal of the American Psychoanalytic Association* 1: 104–43.

Freud, S. (1923). The ego and the id. *Standard Edition* 13: 1–60.

Giovacchini, P. I. (2000). *Impact of Narcissism: The Errant Therapist as a Chaotic Quest*. Northvale, NJ: Jason Aronson.

Grubrich-Simitis, I. (1984) From concretism to metaphor. *Psychoanalytic Study of the Child* 39: 301–19.

Herzog, J. (1982). World beyond metaphor: Thoughts on the transmission of trauma. In *Generations of the Holocaust*, ed. M. S. Bergmann and M. E. Jucovy. New York: Basic Books, pp. 103–19.

Kernberg, O. F. (1984). *Severe Personality Disorders: Psychotherapeutic Strategies*. New Haven: Yale University Press.

Klein, M. (1961). *Narrative of a Child Analysis—The Conduct of the Psychoanalysis of Children as seen in the Treatment of a Ten-Year-Old Boy*. London: Hogarth Press (1975).

———. (1935). A contribution to the psychogenesis of manic depressive states. In *Love, Guilt and Reparation and Other Works 1921–1945*, pp. 262–89. New York: Free Press, 1992.

Klein, M., P. Heimann, S. Isaacs, and J. Riviere. (1952). *Developments in Psychoanalysis*. London: Hogarth Press.

Kogan, I. (1995). *The Cry of Mute Children—A Psychoanalytic Perspective of the Second Generation of the Holocaust*. London and New York: Free Association Books.

———. (2002). "Enactment" in the lives and treatment of Holocaust survivors offspring. *Psychoanalytic Quarterly* 71: 251–72.

Krystal, H. (1985). Trauma and stimulus barrier. *Psychoanalytic Inquiry* 5: 131–61.

Loftus, E. F., and G. R. Loftus. (1980). On the permanence of stored information on the human brain. *American Psychologist* 5: 405–20.

Modell, A. H. (1976). "The holding environment" and the therapeutic action of psychoanalysis. *Journal of the American Psychoanalytic Association* 24: 285–307.

———. (1996). *Other times, other realities*. Cambridge, MA: Harvard University Press.

Moses, R. (1993). *Persistent Shadows of the Holocaust—The Meaning to Those Not Directly Affected*. New York: International University Press.

Oliner, N. M. (1983). *Cultivating Freud's Garden in France*. Northvale, NJ, and London: Jason Aronson.

———. (1996). External reality: The elusive dimension of psychoanalysis. *Psychoanalytic Quarterly* 65: 267–300.

Phillips, A. (1988). *Winnicott*. Cambridge, MA: Harvard University Press.

Sandler, J. (1960). The background of safety. In *From Safety to Superego*. London: Karnac Books, 1987, pp. 1–9.

Schaeffer, S. F. (1980). The unreality of realism. *Critical Inquiry* 6: 727–38.

Schmideberg, M. (1942). Some observations on individual reactions to air raids. *International Journal of Psychoanalysis* 23: 146–76.

Shevrin, H. (1994). The uses and abuses of memory. *Journal of the American Psychoanalytic Association* 42: 991–96.

Treurniet, N. (1993). What is psychoanalysis now? *International Journal of Psychoanalysis* 74: 873–93.

Volkan, V. D. (1987). *Six Steps in the Treatment of Borderline Personality Organisation*. Northvale, NJ: Jason Aronson.

Volkan, V. D. and G. Ast. (1992). *Ein Borderline Therapie: Strukturelle und Objektbeziehungskonflikte in der Psychoanalyse der Borderline-Personlichkeitsorganisation*. Gottingen: Vanderhoeck & Ruprecht.

———. (1994). *Spektrum des Narzismuss: Ein klinishce studie des gesunden Narzismus, des narzisstische-masochistischen charakters, der narzisstischen Personlichkeits-organisation, des malign Narzissmus und des erfolgreichen Narzissmus*. Gottingen: Vanderhoeck & Ruprecht.

Wallerstein, R. S. (1973). Psychoanalytic Perspectives on the Problem of Reality. *Journal of the American Psychoanalytic Association* 21: 5–33.

Winnicott, D. W. (1935). The manic defense. In *Collected Papers*. New York: Basic Books, 1958, pp. 129–44.

———. (1962). Ego integration and child development. In *The Maturational Process and the Facilitating Environment*. London: Hogarth, 1965, pp. 56–64.

———. (1964). Group influences and the maladjusted child. In *The Family and Individual Development*. London: Tavistock, pp. 146–54.

## CHAPTER 10

Axelrod, S., O. L. Schnipper, and J. H. Rau. (1978). Hospitalized offspring of Holocaust survivors: problems and dynamics. *Bulletin: Menninger Clinic* 44 (1980): 1–14.

Barocas, H. A., and C. B. Barocas. (1973). Manifestations of concentration camp effects on the second generation. *American Journal of Psychiatry* 30: 820–21.

Bergmann, M. V. (1982). Thoughts on superego pathology of survivors and their children. In *Generations of the Holocaust*, ed. M. S. Bergmann and M. E. Jucovy. New York: Basic Books, pp. 287–311.

Kestenberg, J. S. (1972). How children remember and parents forget. *International Journal of Psychoanalytic Psychotherapy* 1–2: 103–23.

Klein, H. (1971). Families of Holocaust survivors in the kibbutz: Psychological studies. In *Psychic Traumatization: After-effects in Individuals and Communities*, Boston: Little & Brown.

Kogan, I. (1995). *The Cry of Mute Children—A Psychoanalytic Perspective of the Second Generation of the Holocaust*. London and New York: Free Association Books.

———. (2002). "Enactment" in the lives and treatment of Holocaust survivors' offspring. *Psychoanalytic Quarterly* 71: 251–73.

———. (2003). On being a dead, beloved child. Psychoanalytic Quarterly 72: 727–67.

Kogan, I. and C. Schneider. (2002a). The Nazi heritage and gender identity. *Journal of Applied Psychoanalytic Studies* 4: 49–63.

Laufer, M. (1973). The analysis of a child of survivors. In *The Child in His Family: The Impact of Disease and Death*, ed. E. J. Anthony and C. Koupernik. New York: John Wiley, 2: 363–73.

Lipkowitz, M. H. (1973). The child of two survivors: the report of an unsuccessful therapy. *Israeli Annals of Psychiatry and Related Disciplines* 11: 2.

Moses, R. (1993). *Persistent Shadows of the Holocaust—The Meaning to Those Not Directly Affected*. Madison, CT: International Universities Press.

Rakoff, V. (1966). Long-term effects of the concentration camp experience. *Viewpoints* 1: 17–21.

Roth, S. (1993). The shadow of the Holocaust. In *Persistent Shadows of the Holocaust: The Meaning to Those Not Directly Affected*, ed. R. Moses. Madison, CT: International Universities Press, pp. 37–79.

Sonnenberg, S. M. (1974). Children of survivors: workshop report. *Journal of American Psychoanalytic Association* 22: 200–4.

Volkan, V. D. (1987). *Six Steps in the Treatment of Borderline Personality Organisation*. Northvale, NJ: Jason Aronson.

Volkan, V. D., G. Ast, and W. F. Greer. (2002). *The Third Reich in the Unconscious*. New York & London: Bruner-Routledge.

## EPILOGUE

Akhtar, S. (2003). Dehumanization, origins, manifestations, and remedies. In *Violence or Dialogue? Psychoanalytic Insights on Terror and Terrorism*, ed. Sverre

Varvin and Vamik Volkan. London: International Psychoanalytical Association, pp. 131–46.

Auerhahn, N. C., and D. Laub. (1998). Intergenerational memory of the Holocaust. In *International Handbook of Multigenerational Legacies of Trauma*, ed. Yael Danieli. New York and London: Plenum Press.

Auerhahn, N. C., and E. Prelinger. (1983). Repetition in the concentration camp survivor and her child. *International Review of Psychoanalysis* 10: 31–45.

Awad, G. A. (2003). The minds and perception of "the others." In *Violence or Dialogue? Psychoanalytic Insights on Terror and Terrorism*, ed. Sverre Varvin and Vamik Volkan. London: International Psychoanalytical Association, pp. 153–79.

Becker, C. L. (1955). What are historical facts? *Western Political Quarterly* 8 (3). pp. 327–40.

Berke, J. H. (2006). The psychology of Muslim terrorism. In *Malice Through the Looking Glass*. London: Teva Publications, pp. 333–55.

Bohleber, W. (1997). Trauma, Identifizierung und historischer Kontext. In *Psyche* 51: 958–95.

———. (1998). Traumata und deren Bearbeitung in der Psychoanalyse. *BIOS Jg.* (1998). Heft 2, Verlag Leske & Budrich GmBH.

———. (2003). Collective Phantasms, destructiveness, and terrorism. In *Violence or Dialogue? Psychoanalytic Insights on Terror and Terrorism*, ed. Sverre Varvin and Vamik Volkan. London: International Psychoanalytical Association, pp. 111–31.

Bollas, C. (2006). Transformations wrought by the unconscious. Creativities of the unconscious. Vincenzo Bonaminio interviewing Christopher Bollas. *Psychoanalysis in Europe*, Bulletin 60, pp. 133–61.

Borradori, G. (2003). *Philosophy in a Time of Terror—Dialogues with Jurgen Habermas and Jacques Derrida*. Chicago and London: The University of Chicago Press.

Bowlby, J. (1980). *Attachment and Loss. Volume 3: Loss.* New York: Basic Books.

Brenner, I. (2002). Foreword. *The Third Reich in the Unconscious.* New York and London: Bruner-Routledge, pp. xi–xvii.

Burch, B. (1989). Mourning and failure to mourn—An object relations view. *Contemporary Psychoanalysis* 25: 608–23.

Einstein, A. (1932). Why war? In *Standard Edition*, 22: 199–203.

Erlich, H. S. (2003). Reflections on the terrorist's mind. In *Violence or Dialogue? Psychoanalytic Insights on Terror and Terrorism*, ed. Sverre Varvin and Vamik Volkan. London: International Psychoanalytical Association, pp. 146–53.

Frankl, V. E. (1963). *Man's Search for Meaning: An Introduction to Logotherapy.* New York: Washington Square, 121.

Fresco, N. O. (1984). Remembering the unknown. *International Review of Psychoanalysis* 11: 417–27.

Freud, S. (1915). The unconscious. *Standard Edition* 14: 159–215.

———. (1917). A metapsychological supplement to the theory of dreams. *Standard Edition* 14: 222–35.

———. (1927). The future of an illusion. *Standard Edition* 21: 1–56.

———. (1930). Civilisation and its discontents. *Standard Edition* 21: 57–145.

———. (1933). Why war? *Standard Edition* 22: 203–19.

Green, A. (1973). *Le Discours Vivant. La Conception Psychanalytique de L'affect.* Paris: P.U.F.

Grinberg, L. (1978). The "Razor's Edge" in depression and mourning. *International Journal of Psychoanalysis* 59: 245–54.

———. (1992). *Guilt and Depression.* London and New York: Karnac Books.

Janin, C. (1996). *Figures et Destins du Traumatisme.* Paris: P.U.F.

Klein, M. (1935). A contribution to the psychogenesis of manic-depressive states. *International Journal of Psychoanalysis* 16: 145–74.

Kogan, I. (1995). The Cry of Mute Children—A Psychoanalytic Perspective of the Second Generation of the Holocaust. London and New York: Free Association Books.

———. (1996). Die suche nach Geschichte in den Analysen der Nachkommen von Holocaust Uberlebenden: Rekonstruktion des seelischen Lochs. In Heinz Weiss and Hermann Lang (Hg.), *Psychoanalyse Heute Und Vor 70 Jahren.* Tubingen: edition diskord.

———. (1998). The black hole of dread: the psychic reality of children of Holocaust survivors. In *Even Paranoids have Enemies—New Perspectives on Paranoia and Persecution,* ed. Joseph H. Berke, Stella Pierides, Andrea Sabbadini, and Stanley Schneider. London and New York: Routledge.

Laplanche, J., and J. P. Pontalis. (1967). *The Language of Psychoanalysis,* trans. D. Nicholson-Smith. New York: Norton, 1973.

Loftus, E. F., and G. R. Loftus. (1980). On the permanence of stored information on the human brain. *American Psychologist* 5: 405–20.

Moses, R., ed. (1993). *Persistent Shadows of the Holocaust: The Meaning to Those Not Directly Affected.* Madison, CT: International Universities Press.

Novey, S. (1968). *The Second Look—The Reconstruction of Personal History in Psychiatry and Psychoanalysis.* Baltimore: The Johns Hopkins Press.

Parens, H. (2004). *Renewal of Life—Healing from the Holocaust.* Rockville, MD: Schreiber Publishing.

Pollock, G. H. (1978). Process and affect: Mourning and grief. *International Journal of Psychoanalysis* 59: 255–76.

Schaeffer, S. F. (1980). The unreality of realism. *Critical Inquiry* 6: 727–38.

Shoshan, T. (1989). Mourning and longing from generation to generation. *American Journal of Psychotherapy* 43 (2): 193–207.

Stein, R. (2002). Evil as love and liberation. *Psychoanalytic Dialogues* 12: 393–420.

Turner, F. J. (1891). The significance of history. In *The Early Writings of Frederick Jackson Turner*, ed. Everett E. Edwards. Madison: University of Wisconsin Press, 1938, pp. xi, 316.

Volkan, V. D., G. Ast, and W. F. Greer. (2002). *The Third Reich in the Unconscious.* New York and London: Bruner-Routledge.

Wangh, M. (1993). The working through of the Nazi experience in the German Psychoanalytical Community. In *The Trauma of the Past—Remembering and Working Through*, ed. Hella Ehlers and Joyce Crick. London: Goethe Institut.

Winnicott, D. W. (1935). The manic defence. In *Collected Papers*. New York: Basic Books, 1958.

# Index

abortion, 153

Abraham, K., 9

abstinence, rule of, 48

acting in, 89, 91; negative connotations of, 91; problems with, 91

acting out, 89; Boesky on, 90; Cohen on, 91; Etchegoyen on, 90; as expression of resistance, 90; Fenichel on, 91; Freud, Sigmund, on, 90; Kinston on, 91; primary repression and, 91; trauma and, 91; as way of remembering, 90

actualization, 91, 93; wish-fulfilling aspects of, 93

"addiction to treatment," 35

"affective understanding," 60, 98, 102–3, 214

age, limitations of, 33, 34, 40

"Airplanes that take you away from me," 114

Akhtar, S.: on identity, 84; on psychic pain, 11

alter ego, 130

analysis: classical, 194; of deviant sexuality, 67; Dewald on limitations of, 44; fleeing from, 189, 190; in foreign languages, 75; "getting real in," 154; lovemaking and, 31; symbolism in,

diminishing place of, 194; threat to, 193; during wartime, 195

analysis, termination of, 5, 42; Arlow on, 45; criterion for, 42; fantasies/conflicts involved in, 45; Freud, Sigmund, on, 43; Greenson on, 42; Grinberg on, 42–43; Novick on, 42; Rangell on, 42; satisfactory aspects of, 43; Schachter on, 44; Siegel on, 42, 44; Ticho on, 44; Weigert on, 42

analyst: anonymity of, 63; perception of patient's mind by, 198; responsibility of, 2

analyzing instrument, 192

anger, defensive, 143

annihilation anxiety, 107

anorexia, 96

Anzieu, D., 64

Arlow, J. A., 195; on termination of analysis, 45

art. See creative activity

artificial insemination, 30, 34, 36

Auerhahn, N. C., 149

Auschwitz, 129–30

Barocas, H., 72, 111

Becker, C. L., 216

bereavement, 9

# About the Author

Ilany Kogan serves as training analyst of the Israel Psychoanalytic Society and chief supervisor of the Psychotherapy Center for the Treatment of the Child and Adolescent, Bucharest, Romania. She is a member of the scientific advisory board of the Fritz Bauer Institute for Holocaust Studies in Frankfurt, Germany.

For many years, she worked extensively with Holocaust survivors' offspring and was awarded the Elise M. Hayman Award for the Study of the Holocaust and Genocide at the IPA Congress, Rio de Janeiro (2005) for the work in the realm of the second generation of the Holocaust.

She has published many papers and her books include *The Cry of Mute Children—A Psychoanalytic Perspective of the Second Generation of the Holocaust* (1995), which has been published in German, Romanian, French, and Croatian in addition to English, and *Escape from Selfhood—Breaking Boundaries and Craving for Oneness* (2007).